The Peg Leg Politician

The Peg Leg Politician
ADAM HUNTSMAN OF TENNESSEE

KEVIN D. McCANN

BRAYBREE
Publishing

Copyright © 2013 Kevin D. McCann
All rights reserved

Published by BrayBree Publishing Company LLC
FIRST EDITION

No part of this book may be reproduced, stored in or introduced into a retrieval system or transmitted in any form or by any means (electronic, mechanical, photocopying, recording, or otherwise) without the prior written permission of the copyright owner.

The scanning, uploading, and distribution of this book on the Internet or through any other means is not permitted without permission from the copyright owner.

Frontispiece: Adam Huntsman
Courtesy of the East Tennessee Historical Society

ISBN-13: 978-0-9671251-4-5

Printed in the United States of America

BrayBree Publishing Company LLC
P.O. Box 1587
Dickson, Tennessee 37056-1587
Visit our website at www.braybreepublishing.com

For
Patricia Grames Pollock

and to
Cindy, Braden, and Brianna

Contents

Abbreviations in Notes	ix
Foreword	xi
Preface	xiii
1. Beginnings (1786-1813)	3
2. Law and Politics (1813-1821)	19
3. Return to the Senate (1821-1831)	44
4. Davy of the River Country (1831-1833)	67
5. A Good Constitution (1834-1835)	89
6. Campaign for Congress (1835)	111
7. Spice of the West (1835-1836)	129
8. A White Man (1836-1837)	151
9. Log Cabins and Flummery (1837-1840)	171
10. Stay at Home (1841-1849)	189
APPENDIX A—Huntsman Genealogy	213
APPENDIX B—The Huntsman Farm	227
APPENDIX C—Selected Letters	241
APPENDIX D—The Book of Chronicles	267
Bibliography	279
Index	293

Abbreviations in Notes

The following abbreviations are used throughout the footnotes to identify frequently cited persons, books, and institutions.

AH	Adam Huntsman
AJ	Andrew Jackson
CJKP	Correspondence of James K. Polk, Vols. 5-13
DC	David Crockett
JKP	James K. Polk
JMCPL	Jackson-Madison County Public Library, Jackson TN
PAJ	Papers of Andrew Jackson
TSLA	Tennessee State Library and Archives, Nashville

Foreword

Very little has been written about Adam Huntsman, the colorful peg-legged politician who worked indefatigably for Jacksonian Democracy. This may be due in part to the death of his political opponent David Crockett at the Alamo, which brought him fame that has endured into the 21st century. Conversely, Huntsman—who knew so many prominent politicians in Tennessee as well as in the nation's capital in his lifetime—has become a mere footnote in history.

As his great-great granddaughter, I am grateful for all the time and diligent research Kevin McCann has devoted to this book, and that he has retained his fascination for Adam that he acquired as a schoolboy in Jackson, Tennessee, where my ancestor is buried.

Adam has many direct descendants, most of whom currently live in Texas. I am descended through my paternal grandmother, Edith Huntsman Grames. My father Charles M. Grames—who talked so much about the man with the wooden leg—aroused my deep interest in him. But it wasn't until I moved from New Jersey to East Tennessee and read Kevin's first book, *The Peg-Legged Politician*, that I discovered I could lay claim to more Huntsman ancestors than I realized. My hope is that this book will stir even more interest, and that our family can get in touch with one another and compare notes. My cousin E. Alvin Schay of Little Rock, Arkansas is the only descendant I know personally who practices law as Adam did.

From this book, the reader will be able to travel back to a very young America and learn some of the ins and outs of politicians back in the day when Washington was not yet known as D.C., but rather Washington City. I also became familiar with Adam's feelings about slavery and other issues no longer spoken of much, if at all. Many answers to questions I once believed to be unanswerable are contained in this book. The one question that persistently runs through my mind is: What would Adam Huntsman think if he could revisit his earthly stomping ground today?

Patricia Grames Pollock
Red Wolf Lodge
Maryville, Tennessee

Preface

Tennessee state historian Walter T. Durham wrote that the study of "selected lives of the near great" is as worthy a pursuit in historical research as studying those who achieved far greater distinction in their public careers.[1] The life of frontier lawyer and politician Adam Huntsman (1786-1849)—though not ranked among the most remarkable or even the "near great" in antebellum Tennessee history—nonetheless merits such consideration. Wearing a wooden peg leg, he was certainly among its most colorful personalities. A politician known for his intelligence, wit, and sarcasm both in speech and print, he served ten years in the Tennessee state senate and was a member of the 1834 state constitutional convention, helping craft the amended document that endured until the end of Reconstruction. He served one term in the U.S. House of Representatives before retiring from elected office and devoting himself to the campaign efforts of the Democratic party in West Tennessee.

Although Huntsman's passion undoubtedly was politics, it was the law that earned his living. A respected lawyer in Middle and West Tennessee, Huntsman's legal skills were compared by one writer to those of Felix Grundy, one of the state's premier attorneys in the early nineteenth century. He was also a slaveholder who held many of the same beliefs about the institution as men of his class in Southern society. At the

---

1. Walter T. Durham, *Balie Peyton of Tennessee* (Franklin, TN: Hillsboro Press, 2004): ix

constitutional convention he opposed petitions to emancipate slaves, considering them a distraction from the intended work of the delegates.

In appearance and personality Huntsman was eccentric: in addition to his distinctive peg leg, he was short in stature and somewhat rotund with a balding head that on occasion was adorned with a hairpiece. While staying at a Nashville boardinghouse, a young boy went to Huntsman's room to retrieve his boots for cleaning. He soon ran from the room and refused to go back. The frightened boy explained that Huntsman "took all the hair off his head and laid it on the table, and took his teeth out, and then took off one of his legs." "I can't stay where that man is," he told the landlord, "he's taking himself all to pieces!"[2]

Huntsman is best remembered for being the "timber toe" lawyer who beat David Crockett for Congress in 1835, leading to his journey to Texas and heroic death at the Alamo. But there was much more to him than the outcome of one election. As a public servant, he prided himself on his independence and serving the interests of his constituents. "I am the partizan of no man," he declared. "I never intended to be so." It was that individualistic spirit which put him at odds with one of the most forceful personalities in American history—Andrew Jackson—and helped bring about the first two-party political system in Tennessee history.

Despite losing his leg, Huntsman never lost his sense of humor. It was an essential ingredient in his writings and speeches, sprinkled with Biblical references and selections from Aesop's Fables. It brought him personal popularity in courtrooms and on the campaign trail, where he never lost a race for public office. It enabled him to negate Crockett's own homespun humor; his satire "The Book of Chronicles West of the Tennessee and East of the Mississippi rivers" was publicized beyond Crockett's congressional district and contributed to his unsuccessful reelection bid in 1831.

Huntsman was not the frontier buffoon that fellow congressman and former president John Quincy Adams labeled him. His writings and speeches reflect a wide-ranging knowledge of American and world history undoubtedly acquired more from his own efforts than what he

---

2. Jane H. Thomas, *Old Days in Nashville, Tennessee* (Nashville: Methodist Episcopal Church South, 1897): 73

learned in the simple Virginia "field schools" of his childhood. In addition to the Bible and Aesop's Fables, his favorite literary work was John Milton's epic poem *Paradise Lost*; he even named one of his daughters Paradise. In summary, one newspaper editor who knew him wrote: "We like Adam. He is an honest, straight ahead, though a queer and unpolished man. He has a wooden leg, a stout heart, and an iron nerve. Alike fearless as to consequences from the iron shoe on his wooden understanding to the top of his quizzically shaped head, he tells what he knows like an honest man, and believes Andrew Jackson the greatest General and statesman in the world."[3]

I WAS FIRST INTRODUCED to Adam Huntsman in a booklet purchased for me by my grandparents at the David Crockett Cabin in Rutherford, Tennessee when I was about twelve. Entitled *The Fabulous David Crockett* by Ernest T. Thompson, it described Huntsman as "a rough and tumble lawyer" who wore a peg leg and was "skilled at writing letters to the papers which were full of biting sarcasm and ridicule."[4] The late Emma Inman Williams, official historian for Madison County, Tennessee and author of *Historic Madison*, recognized his political and literary skills and his colorful personality. She was fascinated with him, describing him with playful exuberance as "the very able criminal lawyer, the artful politician, the distinguished wit and humorist and practical joker." When assigned to write on a local subject for a college history course almost twenty years ago, I chose Huntsman.

There has been only one scholarly article written about him, a well-researched sketch of his political career by Chase C. Mooney, professor at Indiana University. Biographical descriptions are also contained in Miss Williams's book and an article on Madison County, Tennessee by Jay Guy Cisco. This has been the extent to which Huntsman's life has been studied. It did receive five lines of narrative in the first volume of the *Biographical Directory of the Tennessee General Assembly*, of which its co-editor

---

3. Franklin (TN) *Western Weekly Review*, reprinted in Washington D.C. *United States Telegraph*, 21 November 1836

4. Ernest T. Thompson, *The Fabulous David Crockett* (Rutherford, TN: David Crockett Memorial Association, 1956): 39-40

Dan M. Robison later wrote: "I venture the guess…that few would protest the scant attention given to Adam Huntsman."[5]

In fairness to this opinion, information about him has not been readily available to historians. Instead, it has been scattered in a multitude of books, articles, letters, and newspapers. This book is an attempt to bring these far-flung sources together and give an accurate portrait of this frontier lawyer and politician and the role he played in antebellum Tennessee history. Its purpose also is to correct mistakes, the most prevalent being his misidentification as Adam R. Huntsman. There is no instance in any letters or documents that he ever referred to himself with a middle initial. The best explanation for this repetitive mistake is confusing Huntsman with Adam R. Alexander, another early Madison County, Tennessee resident.[6]

By necessity, this book is more a political than a personal biography. No letters between Huntsman and his personal friends or family members that would give insight into his life outside politics have survived. The majority of his extant letters were written to James K. Polk, yet many of them give a glimpse into his personality and sense of humor. Spelling and grammar from quotations have been left as originally written without attempts to add [sic] after each instance.

I am grateful for assistance given to me by staff members at various libraries: the Tennessee State Library and Archives, Nashville, Tennessee; Robert Taylor and Evelyn Keele in the Tennessee Room at the Jackson-Madison County Public Library in Jackson, Tennessee; the Jean and Alexander Heard Library at Vanderbilt University, Nashville; the Knox County Archives in Knoxville, Tennessee; and Christine M. Beauregard, Senior Librarian in Manuscripts and Special Collections at New York State Library.

---

5. Dan M. Robison, "Biographical Directory of the Tennessee General Assembly." *Tennessee Historical Quarterly* 25: 351

6. The earliest instance of him being referred to as "Adam R. Huntsman" is in Emma Inman Williams, *Historic Madison: The Story of Jackson and Madison County Tennessee From the Prehistoric Moundbuilders to 1917* (Jackson, TN: Madison County Historical Society, 1946): 275. It is, however, the only instance in all twenty-five pages of the book in which Huntsman is mentioned as such. I believe it was simply an editorial mistake that confused Adam Huntsman for Adam R. Alexander, yet it seems to have been accepted in subsequent works on him.

Special appreciation goes to a few people who have offered research assistance and moral support. Patricia Grames Pollock, Adam Huntsman's great-great granddaughter, has been this book's biggest supporter. I'm grateful to her for her emails, reading portions of the manuscript, and preserving the portrait of her great-great grandfather, whose image I thought I would never see. I've had the honor to know Jonathan K.T. Smith, historian and genealogist, for twenty years. He always thought of me when inspecting some court minute book working on his own projects and sent me copies of items that he uncovered relating to Huntsman. His letters are always encouraging and uplifting, and I'm thankful for his kindness and support. Jack Darrel Wood, custodian of the important historical resources in the Tennessee Room at the Jackson-Madison County Public Library, has always offered guidance in all my research projects. The full page illustrations in this book are a tribute to him. James R. Boylston and Allen J. Wiener, authors of a great Crockett biography, read several chapters and provided valuable feedback. Wade Dillon's artistic vision and talent helped recreate moments in Huntsman's life and career.

As with all my projects, I'm thankful for the love and support of my wife Cindy and our two children, Braden and Brianna. They've tolerated my work on this book for the past three years and locking myself away in the office for hours at a time to finish it. I love you all.

Kevin D. McCann
Dickson, Tennessee
December 18, 2010

The Peg Leg Politician

Chapter One

Beginnings

1786–1813

Let us give decided evidence that while others talk, we are prepared to act—Let us go to the scene of action, and there present ourselves, ready to share with our brethren, the dangers and glories of the field—Let us not wait for the slow formality of being dragged from home by compulsory orders—Freemen ought to risk something—Let us go on our own expences in the first instance—If we can thus be useful to our country, we will be more than compensated.

—John Williams, November 10, 1812

Born on Saturday, February 11, 1786, Adam Huntsman described his early life as spent in "poverty & indigence." His father—also named Adam Huntsman—was a farmer and tobacco planter in Charlotte County in south-central Virginia. His mother was Jeane Francis Huntsman, daughter of James Francis and Obedience Carrington Francis of Charlotte County.[1]

The elder Adam Huntsman was the oldest of three brothers. As an adolescent, his family was attacked by a Native American Indian raiding

---

1. For further explanation of Huntsman's genealogy, refer to Appendix A.

party in 1764 and his father, grandfather, and an infant brother were killed. Adam, Jacob, John and their mother Barbara Huntsman were abducted and taken back to the tribe's home. As a stipulation for ending hostilities between the British and several tribes in the Ohio Valley caused by Chief Pontiac's Rebellion, British Colonel Henry Bouquet required tribal leaders to free over 200 white captives. Barbara and her sons Adam and John were among ninety Virginians who were returned over several weeks in November 1764 and sent to Augusta County, Virginia.[2] It seems Jacob was not among them, staying with his captors at least four years before he was eventually released. Afterward, Adam and Jacob agreed to share the responsibilities of operating the family farm and taking care of their widowed mother and younger brother. During the Revolutionary War, Jacob and John transported supplies for the Charlotte County militia, and John later served in either the Virginia State Militia or Continental Line.[3]

Young Adam Huntsman was born five years after the war for American independence ended at Yorktown, Virginia some 150 miles from his birthplace. But the United States was only a collection of thirteen independent states at the time, bound to one another simply by a "firm league of friendship." The government was weakened by its inability to collect taxes, which left it unable to pay off its war debt or generate revenue for the fledgling nation. This led men like Alexander Hamilton, James Madison, and George Washington to push for a revision of its governing document, the Articles of Confederation. The result was the creation of a new Constitution in 1787 that became the enduring framework for the country.[4]

It was under this framework that Adam grew up in Charlotte County. He lost his mother at an early age, perhaps younger than seven years old. His father was of Dutch ancestry and Adam and his brothers James and

---

2. The Papers of William Johnson (Albany, NY: University of the State of New York, 1921): 485, 486. Returned Captives <www.wvgenweb.org/hardy/tgart3.htm> May 15, 2010.

3. Jacob Huntsman obituary in *Sparta* (TN) *Review*, May 4, 1825. Jacob Huntsman v. Adam Huntsman, Charlotte County, VA Chancery Court Index No. 1784-010 and 1787-005. Virginia Memory (Library of Virginia) website <www.lva.virginia.gov/chancery> Elizabeth Huntsman Revolutionary War Widow Pension Application. <www.footnote.com>

4. Catherine Drinker Bowen, *Miracle at Philadelphia: The Story of the Constitutional Convention, May to September 1787* (Boston: Little, Brown and Company, 1966): 4-11

John and sister Ann grew up speaking the language of their ancestral home. It was not until the family moved to an English speaking village when he was ten years old that his father "began to try to learn his boys that language."[5] Unable to write his own name, his father paid tuition for him to attend a local "field school." Field schools in Virginia were community funded and typically held in a one-room log cabin or a church. Classes typically lasted from April to September and were taught by a local minister or church leader. In addition to reading, writing, and arithmetic, young Adam remembered learning the principles of republican government that he carried with him into his legal and political careers.[6]

At this time, Charlotte County was the home of Patrick Henry, former governor of Virginia and passionate defender of American liberty before and during the American Revolution. He came to Charlotte County two years after Adam's birth to practice law and retire from politics. Though offered many positions of importance in the fledgling federal government, Henry declined each one, including the honor of serving as chief justice of the United States Supreme Court.[7]

It was a request by former president George Washington that brought Henry—almost sixty-four years old and in poor health—out of retirement in 1799 to campaign for a seat in the Virginia House of Delegates. Word circulated around Charlotte County that he would address the people at the county seat of Marysville (later Charlotte Court House) in March 1799. One onlooker recalled "immense multitudes...pouring in

---

5. Jeane Huntsman (mother of Adam Huntsman) had died by the time her own mother Obedience Francis wrote her will on October 1, 1793. Charlotte County, VA Will Books 2: 40. During the 1834 Tennessee Constitutional Convention, Huntsman apologized at one point to a fellow delegate who misunderstood him and facetiously attributed it to him "having been unfortunately born a Dutchman, and having never spoken a word of English until he was ten years of age." Nashville (TN) Republican, 24 May 1834.

6. *Jackson* (TN) *Gazette*, July 2, 1828. Timothy S. Ailsworth, Ann P. Keller, Lura B. Nichols, Barbara R. Walker, *Charlotte County: Rich Indeed* (Charlotte County, VA 1979): 175. The elder Adam Huntsman left his mark as a witness to the last will and testament of Joseph Oliver on September 7, 1799. Charlotte County, VA Will Book 2: 163. In a letter dated May 16, 1836, written while he sat in "Representative Hall" (the U.S. House of Representatives chamber), Huntsman wrote that he attended school for two years with one Lucy Cook, the daughter of a former Revolutionary War soldier, Rains Cook. Lucy Cook Williamson Revolutionary War Pension Application <www.footnote.com>

7. Ailsworth et al. *Charlotte County*: 259

from all the surrounding country to hear him." Perhaps thirteen-year-old Adam Huntsman too was drawn to Marysville to hear the renowned patriot and orator.[8]

Onlookers gathered in front of a tavern across from the courthouse with its patriotic red shingled roof, white painted frame, and blue doors and window frames.[9] Though "somewhat bowed with age and weakness," Patrick Henry addressed the crowd. His voice was "cracked and tremulous" at first, but grew "clear and melodious" as his spoke. "Let us trust God and our better judgment to set us right hereafter," he said. "United we stand, divided we fall. Let us not split into factions which must destroy that union upon which our existence hangs." As he finished, Henry's strength left him; he did not hear a rebuttal offered by a young Jeffersonian politician named John Randolph of Roanoke, who would represent Virginia in Congress for the next thirty years. The speech would be Henry's last: Three months later, he died at "Red Hill," his home in Charlotte County.[10]

ADAM HUNTSMAN WAS a young man in his early twenties when he left his home in the commonwealth in early 1807 or 1809, a few years after his father's death, to make a new life for himself in Tennessee.[11] He had family in Knox County where his uncles Jacob and John Huntsman both settled as early as 1799. His journey would have taken him down the wagon trail from Abingdon, Virginia to Knoxville, Tennessee. He may have passed a small log tavern in Jefferson County owned by John Crockett, whose

---

8. Ibid: 262
9. Ibid: 76
10. Ibid: 262-264
11. It is uncertain exactly what year Huntsman came to Tennessee. The Nashville (TN) *National Banner and Daily Advertiser*, August 27, 1834, stated that it was 1809, which coincides with the first record of him in Knox County. (No doubt Huntsman himself gave this information to the newspaper.) Yet a letter written by Huntsman and published in the *Knoxville Gazette*, October 19, 1836, stated that when he lived in Knoxville, he voted for Hugh Lawson White for the state senate. The only election that White ran for the seat during Huntsman's residence in Knoxville was in 1807; perhaps his memory was inaccurate and he believed it occurred in 1809. *Knoxville Gazette*, October 19, 1836. Huntsman's father seems to have died by 1803. He is shown in the 1800 Charlotte County tax list, but does not appear in the U.S. Census for Charlotte County ten years later.

fifth son—David Crockett—would figure prominently in the Virginian's future political career.[12]

Knoxville had been the social, economic, and political center of Tennessee since 1791, when territorial governor William Blount made it the capital for the Territory South of the River Ohio. It had served as Tennessee's capital since its admission to the Union in 1796, and was home to many of the state's earliest leaders, including Blount, who was Tennessee's first U.S. senator, and John Sevier, its first governor. By the time Huntsman arrived, westward migration had diminished East Tennessee's population and its influence in state affairs; except for a two-year return in 1817 and 1818, it ceased to be the capital by 1813.[13]

When he first settled in Knoxville, Huntsman described himself as "poor and pennyless." Yet tax lists for 1810 and 1811 show he was not as destitute as he later claimed. Though he owned no acreage, he did have three slaves.[14] The earliest record that mentions him in Knox County is a lawsuit he filed against one John Wright for a debt Wright owed him. It was dismissed on April 12, 1809, after the defendant offered to pay him. Three months later, Huntsman served on a jury for the county court that ruled on about thirty cases.[15]

One promising opportunity for social and economic advancement in frontier society was to practice law. It meant learning the profession from a skilled practitioner who had a library of law books from which to study for the bar examination. For his legal mentor, Huntsman gained the confidence of an ambitious young attorney with marital ties to the founding family of Knoxville. John Williams was born in 1778 to a pros-

---

12. The Crockett tavern was located on the Abingdon-Knoxville Road, the most likely route that Huntsman would have taken to reach Knoxville. David Crockett, *A Narrative of the Life of David Crockett of the State of Tennessee*. James A. Shackford and Stanley J. Folmsbee, eds. (Knoxville: University of Tennessee Press, 1973): 22

13. Lucile Deadrick, ed. *Heart of the Valley: A History of Knoxville, Tennessee* (Knoxville: East Tennessee Historical Society, 1976): 16. William Rule, George F. Mellen, J. Wooldridge, *Standard History of Knoxville, Tennessee* (Chicago: Lewis Publishing Company, 1900): 90. Two-thirds of the state's population resided in West Tennessee (present-day Middle Tennessee) by the gubernatorial election of 1809. Corlew, Tennessee: 136

14. 1810, 1811 Knox County, TN Tax Lists. In both records, Huntsman was listed as being in Captain Dodd's militia company. Knox County, TN County Court Book 7: 13.

15. *Jackson* (TN) *Gazette*, 5 July 1828. Knox County, TN Court Minute Book 7: 13, 69-89.

John Williams, prominent Knoxville attorney and future U.S. Senator in whose law office Huntsman prepared for the bar examination.

Courtesy of the Tennessee State Library and Archives

perous North Carolina family and came to practice law in Knoxville about 1800. Five years later he married Melinda White, the youngest daughter of General James White—the founder of Knoxville—and sister of fellow attorney Hugh Lawson White. Williams prosecuted and defended cases in the Knox County courts and on occasion served as an acting judge for the Superior Court of Law and Equity. He also sat on the board of trustees for East Tennessee College (now known as the University of Tennessee) with such notable state political figures as former governors John Sevier and Archibald Roane and future congressman and U.S. senator George Washington Campbell.[16]

Huntsman's legal apprenticeship would have been like most aspiring lawyers experienced in the early nineteenth century. In addition to reading Sir William Blackstone's *Commentaries on the Laws of England*, *Coke on Littleton*, and other standard legal books of the period, he also would have performed clerical duties, transcribed legal documents, and ran errands. Williams may have taken time to explain the complex legal principles and terminology he had read and test him periodically to gauge his progress. It is likely his apprenticeship lasted at least two years.[17]

To receive a law license, applicants were required to stand before the Tennessee Supreme Court of Errors and Appeals. Huntsman likely did so in the early months of 1811, when it was in session at Knoxville. He would

---

16. Leota Driver Maiden, "Colonel John Williams." *East Tennessee Historical Society's Publications* No. 30 (1958): 7, 10-11. The fact that Huntsman read law under Williams is mentioned in Huntsman's obituary in Jackson *West Tennessee Whig*, 30 August 1849. A notation dated 12 January 1850 written at the top of a letter by Huntsman to Samuel H. Laughlin, (perhaps written by Laughlin) mentions that Huntsman studied law under Williams. Unfortunately, portions of the first line of the notation are missing as a result of the frayed letter, making it impossible to read the entire text. AH to Samuel H. Laughlin, 6 July 1844. Samuel H. Laughlin Papers. Accession No. THS 8, Box 1, Folder 9, TSLA.

17. Information on the apprenticeship of a typical lawyer during the late eighteenth and early nineteenth centuries was taken from various sources. The most useful were: Charles Sellers, *James K. Polk: Jacksonian, 1795-1843* (Norwalk, CT: Easton Press, 1987): 57-59. Hendrik Booraem, *Young Hickory: The Making of Andrew Jackson* (Dallas, TX: Taylor Trade Publishing, 2001): 131-133, 142-144. Lawrence M. Friedman, *A History of American Law* (New York: Simon & Schuster, 2007): 238. One attorney who read law during this time period recalled: "No man in those days applied for a license unless he had devoted two years to the study of law...I read Blackstone carefully ten times before I applied for a license." John C. Guild, *Old Times in Tennessee, with Historical, Personal, and Political Scraps and Sketches* (Nashville, TN: Tavel, Eastman & Howell, 1878): 77-78.

have presented a certificate from the Knox County Court that attested to him being "a man of good reputation" and at least twenty-one years old. His legal knowledge and personal character would have been scrutinized by justices George W. Campbell and Hugh Lawson White. Once they were satisfied with his competence, he was presented with a license to practice law in the state of Tennessee as well as the professional title of Adam Huntsman, Esquire.[18]

RATHER THAN BEGIN in Knoxville, he traveled one hundred miles west to White, Rhea, and surrounding counties to start his fledgling legal practice. Whether it was the promise of new opportunities or the advantage of fewer lawyers to compete against that drew him away from the capital is uncertain. With the confidence of a young man eager to begin his new career, he presented his license to the White County Court at Sparta on May 14, 1811, and received its approval to practice law there. Two months later, he was given the "necessary oaths of qualification" to practice in the Rhea County Court.[19]

Huntsman's decision may have been influenced by an affair with a young woman named Elizabeth Witt and her subsequent pregnancy. She was the daughter of George Witt, who in 1811 owned 300 acres in Knox County and lived in the same militia district as Huntsman. Both men had served jury duty together the previous year in the county court.[20] She and the twenty-five year old Huntsman did not marry. To help care for their child, he sold to Elizabeth and "her Infant now unborn" a fourteen year old slave named Milley "now in possession of George Witt Senr" for fifty dollars on June 6, 1811. He stipulated that Milley would belong to the child should Elizabeth marry or die, but if both mother and child died, Milley would revert back to him.[21]

---

18. John Haywood and Robert L. Cobbs, *The Statute Laws of the State of Tennessee, of a Public and General Nature* (Knoxville, TN: F.S. Heiskell, 1831) 1:14-15

19. White County, TN Court Minute Book, 1806-1811: 250. Rhea County, TN Court of Pleas and Quarter Sessions, Minute Book B (January 1810-April 1813).

20. 1810 and 1811 Knox County, TN Tax Lists. Knox County, TN Court Minutes 7: 69-89. Emma Inman Williams, *Historic Madison: The Story of Jackson and Madison County, Tennessee From the Prehistoric Moundbuilders to 1917* (Jackson, TN: Jackson Service League, 1972): 78.

21. Knox County, TN Deed Book 0-1, page 93

A daughter was born to Elizabeth on Sunday, August 25, 1811, but Elizabeth died four or five months later. Huntsman became the child's legal guardian and on October 9, 1812, he petitioned the Knox County Court to allow him to adopt her and recognize her as his legitimate daughter. He renamed her Melinda Jane Huntsman, perhaps to honor the wife of his legal mentor, Melinda White Williams.[22]

As with many ambitious young attorneys, the law became a stepping-stone to politics. Huntsman's early interest is evident in his appointment as a teller for the Tennessee house of representatives, which convened in Knoxville in September 1811. Responsible for counting the votes of law-makers, the position gave him the opportunity to see the inner workings of state government and interact with members of the General Assembly, who included Pleasant M. Miller, John Cocke, Archibald Roane, and Newton Cannon.[23]

On September 16, the first day of the legislative session, his name was placed in nomination with five other tellers for assistant clerk of the house. Because there were so many candidates, the election went eight ballots without a winner. Huntsman and another teller were eventually dropped from the contest, but it still took three more ballots before an assistant clerk was finally chosen.[24]

MEANWHILE, AMERICA WAS preparing for war with Great Britain. Relations had grown tense between the two nations as the Royal Navy impeded American trade with Europe through continued harassment of its vessels at sea and impressment of its sailors, claiming they were British deserters. The need for America to assert itself in the world and validate its

22. Knox County, TN Settlements and Administrations, Volume 2: 11. Knox County, TN Wills, Inventories, and Settlements Volume 0: 97, 103. Knox County, TN Court Volume 7: 258-259. The child's original name was Rutilia Witt. Knox County, TN Wills, Inventories, Settlements, Volume 0: 96.

23. *Journal of the House of Representatives, at the First Session of the Ninth General Assembly of the State of Tennessee, Begun and Held at Knoxville, on Monday, the Sixteenth Day of September, One Thousand Eight Hundred and Eleven* (Knoxville, TN: George Wilson, 1812): 4. The other tellers were: A.M. Nelson, John G. Eason, John Maze, Richard G. Gillaspie, and George Hale. Nelson was eventually elected house clerk on the eleventh ballot. Ibid. Robert H. White, ed. *Messages of the Governors of Tennessee 1796-1821* (Nashville: Tennessee Historical Commission, 1952): 1: 736.

24. Ibid

independence were the driving sentiments behind the country's first declaration of war on June 18, 1812.

War also offered the prospect of land conquest, and the prizes that settlers in the West sought were the "Floridas"—East and West Florida—which were held by Spain, a British ally. The United States had long coveted them and feared that Spain might allow them to be used by the British as southern bases of operation, or worse cede the provinces to them. The Floridas were also home to the Seminoles, a tribe of Native Americans made up of members from other tribes of the Southeast. Their ranks also included runaway slaves; the fact that East Florida had become a sanctuary for them made it all the more important to slaveholders in the South that it be taken.[25]

In the spring of 1812, President James Madison sent agents to the Spanish provincial government at St. Augustine to determine whether it would cede East Florida to the United States or give it to Great Britain. With Spain unwilling to sell to either country, one of the American agents exceeded his charge in March 1812 and, with the aid of U.S. regular army soldiers, American settlers, Georgia militia, rebellious Spaniards, and American naval gunboats, tried to take it by force.[26] The agent was dismissed a month later and the Navy was ordered to leave, but the regulars and militia were left in the East Florida swamps, continuing to fight the Spanish and the Seminoles (with their African-American allies) as well as sickness, starvation, and sweltering weather throughout the summer of 1812. Georgia was determined to prevent incursions by the Seminoles across its shared southern border and appealed to Congress for assistance.[27]

In October, Madison asked Tennessee Governor Willie Blount for 1,500 volunteers to "defend the lower country," meaning New Orleans but also implying a possible invasion of East and West Florida. Andrew Jackson, newly commissioned as major general of volunteers, responded

---

25. John R. Elting, *Amateurs to Arms! A Military History of the War of 1812* (Chapel Hill, NC: Algonquin Books of Chapel Hill, 1991):156. Daniel F. Littlefield Jr., *Africans and Seminoles: From Removal to Emancipation* (Westport, CT: Greenwood Press, 1977): 6-7.

26. John K. Mahon, *The War of 1812* (Gainesville, FL: University of Florida Press, 1972): 195. Robert E. May, *Manifest Destiny's Underworld: Filibustering in Antebellum America* (Chapel Hill: University of North Carolina Press, 2002): 6.

27. Mahon, *War of 1812*: 195-197.

to the call with two thousand volunteers. By foot and flotilla, he led them toward the Crescent City in January 1813. The expedition camped for several weeks at Natchez, Mississippi to await further orders. Word finally came from the War Department on March 15 that their services were no longer needed. Jackson and his men were left in the wilderness with only an order to dismiss and "the thanks of the President of the United States" for their wasted time and effort.[28]

The militias of East Tennessee commanded by Major General John Cocke were left out of the war preparations. But as adjutant general of the state militia, Colonel John Williams—Huntsman's legal mentor—began formulating his own plan. A strong show of force against the Seminoles in East Florida, he believed, could deter the Creeks in the South and even the tribes of the Northwest from taking up arms with the British.[29] He published a call to arms on November 10, 1812, appealing to the patriotism of East Tennesseans to assist the Georgia militia and conquer East Florida.

> A glorious opportunity is now offered the people of East Tennessee, to evince their patriotism, and prove their right to the liberty they enjoy. *Deeds* and not *Professions* of Patriotism are now wanting! Americans have drank to the dregs of the cup of forbearance—War now rages in our land.—A deranged monarch[,] a venal Prince, and a ministry, have driven us to assert our rights at the point of the bayonet. They have enlisted under their banners, the savages, those hell hounds fitted only for deeds of ferocity, who seek victory by the indiscriminate slaughter of all ages and sexes.
>
> Our families and property are in a place of security— Our brethren in a sister state need our aid, will it be withheld? Heroes of the Revolution, and sons of those

---

28. Robert E. Corlew, *Tennessee: A Short History* (Knoxville: University of Tennessee Press, 1981): 138-139. Elting, *Amateurs to Arms!*: 157. Robert V. Remini, *Andrew Jackson and the Course of American Empire 1767-1821* (New York: Harper & Row, 1977): 170-171, 173-175.

29. Samuel C. Williams, "A Forgotten Campaign." *Tennessee Historical Magazine* (1926) 8.4: 269

FELLOW-CITIZENS OF EAST TENNESSEE.

The last News-Paper accounts shew a want of troops in East Florida to check the hostile Indians. 'Tis shamefull that Georgia alone should bear this burthen.—All those who have enrolled themselves with me, are directed to parade, at Knoxville, on Tuesday, the first day of December next, prepared with a supply of provisions to take them to the point of destination.

The patriotic freemen of Tennessee, who have not enrolled themselves, are requested on that day, to come forward well mounted, and prepared to march to Saint Johns, where the troops of the United States are stationed, and where the Indians are said to be assembled, in such numbers as to threaten the destruction of our troops. A glorious opportunity is now offered the people of East Tennessee, to evince their patriotism, and prove their right to the liberty they enjoy. *Deeds* and not *Professions* of Patriotism are now wanting! Americans have drank to the dregs of the cup of forbearance——War now rages in our land.—A deranged monarch a venal Prince, and a corrupt ministry, have driven us to assert our rights at the point of the bayonet. They have enlisted under their banners, the savages, those hell hounds fitted only for deeds of ferocity, who seek victory by the indiscriminate slaughter of all ages and sexes.

Our families and property are in a place of security—Our brethren in a sister state need our aid, will it be withheld?

Heroes of the Revolution, and sons of those heroes, surely not—Let us march to their relief—Let us give decided evidence that while others talk, we are prepared to act—Let us go to the scene of action, and there present ourselves, ready to share with our brethren, the dangers and glories of the field—Let us not wait the slow formality of being dragged from home by compulsory orders—Freemen ought to risk something——Let us go on our own expences in the first instance—If we can thus be useful to our country, we will be more than compensated.

The necessary arms can be had at Knoxville, from Maj. Gen. John Cocke, who has patriotically enrolled himself as a common soldier——Militia officers imitate your general——Set an honorable example to your troops—Such of you as may march on this emergency, will be permitted to resume your respective commands whenever there is a regular call of the militia.

JOHN WILLIAMS.

Each soldier must be mounted on a strong horse, armed with a musket or rifle (at his election) with a brace of pistols, if to be procured, a Tomahawk, and a butcher knife—Dressed with black hat, black huntingshirt or roundabout, and pantaloons, boots, or shoes and leggings at his election.

JOHN WILLIAMS.

November 10, 1812.

Recruitment broadside distributed by John Williams seeking volunteers to march to East Florida and conquer the Spanish-controlled region in the winter of 1812-1813.

Courtesy of the Library of Congress

heroes, surely not—Let us march to their relief—Let us give decided evidence that while others talk, we are prepared to act—Let us go to the scene of action, and there present ourselves, ready to share with our brethren, the dangers and glories of the field...[30]

Volunteers were instructed to meet in Knoxville on December 1. They would serve without pay and bring their own horses, weapons, and equipment. Their uniforms would be simple: a black hunting shirt, trousers, a hat, and boots or "shoes and leggings"; their weapons should be a rifle or a musket, two pistols, a tomahawk, and a butcher knife. Despite wintry weather, the call was answered initially by "forty or fifty active and enterprising men" who set up camp outside town. Local farmers brought provisions for them and their horses while other residents collected funds to help those would could not afford their own equipment. Within four days, their numbers had increased to about 150 volunteers.[31]

Remarkably, Williams pressed forward with his plan without official authorization. He wrote President Madison a day before leaving Knoxville that he understood volunteers were needed "to check the hostile savages." Confident that the president and Congress would "shortly wish to occupy the Floridas," he had taken the initiative to organize a small army to offer its help. "In executing your orders," he assumed, "not a man in the corps will entertain constitutional scruples on the subject of boundaries"—particularly the one between Georgia and Spanish-held Florida.[32]

There is reason to suppose that Adam Huntsman joined this expedition. His name is absent from court records in counties where he would have practiced law between December 1812 and September 1813. He was almost twenty-seven years old and a bachelor living in Knoxville. It would have been an opportunity for military service—and all the glory it

30. John Williams, "Fellow Citizens of East Tennessee." Printed Ephemera Collection; Portfolio 174, Folder 1. Library of Congress.
31. Ibid. *Raleigh* (NC) *Register and North Carolina Gazette*, January 1, 1813
32. East Florida encompassed much of present-day Florida west to the Chattahoochee River. From the river east to the Mississippi River was considered West Florida, which some believed was part of the Louisiana Purchase. Elting, *Amateurs to Arms!*: 157. Williams's statement about boundaries is a sentiment that Huntsman reiterated later in his political career.

potentially entailed—under his legal mentor from whom he had learned the skills of his chosen profession. It would be difficult to believe that he would not have responded to Williams's patriotic call.[33]

The Volunteer Infantry Regiment of East Tennessee Mounted Infantry left Knoxville on December 4 and marched toward Asheville, North Carolina.[34] At Asheville, Williams wrote to Governor David B. Mitchell of Georgia his intention to "march to the scene of action" and aid his state's militia. All he needed to know was where to take his men. Mitchell suggested that he rendezvous with the 3rd U.S. Infantry under the command of Brigadier General Thomas Flournoy at Point Petre or Colerain on the St. Marys River that divided southeast Georgia and East Florida.[35]

The progress of the Tennesseans through North Carolina and Georgia over the next five weeks was reported in newspapers across the country. They were described in praiseworthy prose as "gentlemen of the first respectability" and "examples of magnanimity and patriotism."[36] The people of Georgia were especially grateful to them, as some of their own militia officers refused to fight outside the state. The state legislature had even asked its U.S. senators to sponsor legislation to construct a road between the two states should Georgians ever need their aid again in the future. Georgians praised their "generous and patriotic conduct," wrote the *Augusta Chronicle*, "and have done everything which could be made their march both comfortable and agreeable."

> This gallant corps is composed of every age, from 18 to 80, of men of independent fortune, liberal education, lucrative professions, men filling with reputation the highest

---

33. No complete roster of those who served in Williams's expedition has survived. Because it was never sanctioned by either Tennessee or the War Department, the volunteers were never paid for their service. The time period of the expedition—December 1812 to March 1813—coincides with Huntsman's noticeable absence from the circuit and county courts he typically travelled. His name is absent from court records until 6 September 1813, when he was appointed solicitor for the White County Court. Such an injury—the loss of his lower leg—required a period of recuperation and might explain his absence.

34. Tennessee Gov. Willie Blount was confident had Williams waited another week, "one thousand men of the same description would have joined them." Williams, "A Forgotten Campaign": 270.

35. Maiden "Williams": 14-15

36. Williams, "A Forgotten Campaign": 273

offices in their country's gift, who, like the Romans in the purest days of that Republic, have cheerfully and promptly abandoned all to aid in supporting the honor and independence of our country.

Indeed, the Volunteer Infantry Regiment consisted of men of various ages and walks of frontier society. There were soldiers such as Major General John Cocke—who had assumed the rank of a private for the expedition—but there were also farmers, merchants, and lawyers. Because they were volunteers and received no pay, most of their names were never recorded.[37]

The volunteers reached the St. Marys River in early January 1813 and were ordered to Camp Pinckney. But General Flournoy was uncertain the War Department would even allow him to use them, so they languished in camp for three weeks until he received further orders. Finally on February 3, the Tennesseans along with regular army soldiers and Georgia militia were ordered to attack the Seminole towns of Payne's Town (near present-day Gainesville) and Bowlegs Town (near present-day Micanopy).[38]

The two-week expedition resulted in the burning of close to four hundred Seminole homes and two thousand bushels of corn in both towns and seizing about 250 horses and about 400 cattle. There were two significant skirmishes in which 53 Seminoles were killed, several wounded, and seven captured, including African-Americans. "The balance of the Seminole Nation is completely in waste," reported Williams. "On all occasions the Tennessee Volunteers supported the toils and dangers of the campaign with the same spirit which animated them in making a tender of their services." Williams's command suffered only one killed and seven wounded. Huntsman may have been among the wounded, suffering a lower leg wound severe enough that led to its partial amputation.[39]

37. Maiden "Williams": 14-15; Williams "Forgotten Campaign": 271; *Raleigh Register and North Carolina Gazette* January 1, 1813. In addition to Williams and Cocke, the expedition included brother Thomas L. Williams and Hugh Lawson White (Williams's brother-in-law), Pleasant M. Miller, Peter Parsons, Enoch Parsons, B.I. White, Alexander Outlaw, and Judge William Cocke.
38. Maiden, "Williams": 15-16. Williams, "Forgotten Campaign": 273-274.
39. Williams, "Forgotten Campaign": 273-274. Maiden "Williams": 15-16.

As the expedition made its way back to Camp Pinckney, General Flournoy learned from the War Department that the Tennesseans were no longer needed. They were officially discharged on February 26 and began the long journey home. They reached Knoxville by late March 1813, where they were mustered out of military service.[40]

HUNTSMAN PAID A STEEP PRICE for his military adventure in the swamps of East Florida. He would have to use a wooden peg leg to stand and walk the rest of his life. But he used it to his advantage, both to show the personal sacrifice he had made for his country and as a prop for his self-directed sense of humor. On one occasion, he was asked by a traveling companion how he lost his leg. Huntsman said it brought back terrible memories, but he would tell him if he promised not to ask another question about it. When the man agreed, Huntsman stoically told him it had been bitten off. The journey continued in silence as the man pondered this scant information until he could no longer hold his curiosity.

"Well stranger, I promised not to ask another question about the loss of your leg, but I'd like very much to know what bit it off."[41]

---

40. Maiden, "Williams": 17

41. Memucan Hunt Howard, "Recollections of Tennessee." <www.tngenweb.org/records/madison/history/misc/recolltn.htm> Accessed May 16, 2010. Microfilm No. 678, H-135 TSLA

Chapter Two

Law and Politics

1813–1821

> ADAM HUNTSMAN, ATTORNEY AT LAW. *Will attend the Circuit Courts at Smith County and manage such business as may be entrusted to his care to the best of his ability.*
> —Carthage Gazette, February 16, 1821

Huntsman left Knoxville in late 1812 or early 1813 and opened a law office ninety miles northwest at Monroe, the county seat of Overton County. Located on the foothills of the Cumberland Mountains, it was part of a region known as the Mountain District, which included Jackson and White counties and encompassed present-day Putnam, Clay, Fentress, and Pickett counties. Monroe was a thriving village at the crossroads of a trail between Fort Blount in Jackson County and Monticello, Kentucky, and the road that linked Danville, Kentucky to Huntsville, Alabama. By the time Huntsman made it his home, it had a log courthouse and jail, a whipping post and stocks for public punishment, wooden plank sidewalks, and a population of about 200 residents. It was here for the next ten years that he built his law practice, forged important relationships, and built his personal fortune.[1]

On October 20, 1812, Huntsman was appointed as one of three commissioners for the town of Monroe by the General Assembly and served until he left Overton County in 1823. He worked with many influential citizens in local and county government, including Benjamin Totten, Charles Robertson Sevier, and sheriff Valentine Matlock. Totten, one of the earliest settlers in the county, partnered with Huntsman in several land speculation ventures. His three sons later became attorneys and practiced law in the Western District; one of them, Archibald O.W. Totten, would work with Huntsman in the Democratic party. Both Sevier and Matlock were nephews of John Sevier, hero of the Battle of King's Mountain in the Revolutionary War and first governor of Tennessee. After his death in 1815, his second wife Katherine Sherrill Sevier joined her siblings and children in Overton County and settled at a homestead called "The Dale." Charles Sevier thought enough of Huntsman to name one of his sons Adam Huntsman Sevier.[2]

Huntsman became the leading lawyer in Monroe. But a law practice in a small community was insufficient; like most attorneys, he supplemented his income by traveling to neighboring counties either alone or with other lawyers, following the circuit court judge to the county seats in his judicial district. Typically, they rode on horseback with saddlebags draped over that contained law books and legal papers on one side and clothing and personal items on the other. A branding iron was a common accessory when livestock was bartered for their services.[3]

---

1. A.V. and W.H. Goodpasture, *Life of Jefferson Dillard Goodpasture* (Nashville TN: Cumberland Presbyterian Publishing House, 1897): 5-6. *John L. Mitchell's Tennessee Gazetter, and Business Directory, for 1860-61* (Nashville, TN: J.L. Mitchell, 1860): 187.

2. Robert M. McBride and Dan M. Robison, eds. *Biographical Directory of the Tennessee General Assembly* (Nashville: Tennessee State Library and Archives and Tennessee Historical Commission, 1975) 1: 658. Cora Bales Sevier and Nancy S. Madden, *Sevier Family History* (Washington D.C.: Self-published, 1961): 420-421.

3. Sellers, *Polk: Jacksonian*: 61-62. Dick Everett, *The Dixie Frontier: A Social History of the Southern Frontier from the First Transmontane Beginnings to the Civil War* (Norman: University of Oklahoma Press, 1993): 230-231.

Huntsman as a circuit lawyer in the Mountain District
Illustration by Wade Dillon

The trips fostered camaraderie among the lawyers, who shared stories and played practical jokes on one another to pass the time. Huntsman had fun at the expense of a young attorney named John Catron, who would later become an associate justice on the U.S. Supreme Court. Catron was particularly fond of a racehorse his father owned named Agricola. He cared for it, showed it off at public events, and boasted of its racing prowess. Huntsman and fellow lawyer Harry H. Brown took great delight in mimicking his excessive pride in the animal—much to Catron's annoyance—and jokingly dubbed him its "groom."[4]

Because they attended court together, ate meals together, and lodged in the same rooms, it was difficult for the lawyers to hold grudges against one another after heated courtroom battles. One attorney who rode the mountain circuit recalled nights spent at roadside taverns indulging in whiskey and card games with his associates. It was understood that disagreements would not end in a duel. "[I]f any one happened to suffer from a smashed bottle, he took it and made up on the spot."[5]

Court day was a festive occasion on the frontier. The local population swelled as citizens from across the county flocked to the seat of justice to mingle and gossip, to buy, sell, or trade goods and merchandise, and to discuss politics. While some attended court to settle debts and lawsuits, most came to hear the eloquent speeches and verbal jousting of the lawyers as they fought for the interests of their respective clients. For an isolated frontier community, such displays of oratory skills and strategy were as entertaining as any theatrical performance.[6]

Huntsman prosecuted and defended clients in the circuit and county courts in Overton, White, Jackson, Smith, and Warren counties, as well as the Tennessee Supreme Court at Sparta in White County, between 1811 and 1823. He was appointed solicitor (or public prosecutor) for White County on September 6, 1813, for which he was paid fifty dollars a year. He

---

4. Frank B. Williams, "Samuel Hervey Laughlin, Polk's Political Handyman." *Tennessee Historical Quarterly* 24 (1965): 358

5. John Livingston, *Portraits of Eminent Americans Now Living; Including President Pierce and His Cabinet; with Biographical and Historical Memoirs of their Lives and Actions* (New York: R. Craighead, 1854): 95.

6. James Grant Wilson and John Fiske, eds. *Appleton's Cyclopedia of American Biography* (New York: D. Appleton and Company, 1887) 3: 374

The Mountain District of Middle Tennessee in 1834

served for close to three years before resigning on July 17, 1815.[7] In addition to his office in Monroe, he may also have had one in the southern portion of his circuit at McMinnville in Warren County. There he met a young store clerk and law apprentice named Samuel Hervey Laughlin, who would later become a political friend and editor of the *Nashville Union*, the official state newspaper of the Democratic party.[8]

HUNTSMAN'S LAW PRACTICE was profitable enough that as early as the spring of 1815, he began acquiring large amounts of acreage in Overton and surrounding counties. Subsequent purchases between 1817 and 1821 totaled twenty-two town lots in Monroe and 22,590 acres in Overton County alone. He would continue to buy and sell land there even after he moved further west. These transactions, as well as buying and selling slaves, would have increased his personal income significantly.[9]

His courtroom speeches and personal popularity earned him notoriety in the region, and his large landholdings enabled him to meet the requirement of owning two hundred acres to qualify for public office. In the summer of 1815, he presented himself as a candidate to represent Overton, White, and Jackson counties in the Tennessee state senate. Three other candidates vied for the seat, but he emerged victorious in his first political contest.[10]

7. White County, TN Court Minute Book 1815: 95, 139. *Carthage Gazette*, February 16, 1820.

8. Walter Womack, *McMinnville at a Milestone* (McMinnville, TN: Standard Publishing Company, 1960): 49. Huntsman's law office stood on the southwest corner of Lot 63 on Morford Street in McMinnville. Stockley D. Rowan, who read law in his office, purchased the lot in 1819 and built a brick home on the southeast corner in 1824. Ibid. Huntsman may also have owned a two-story brick home on Lot 34, which was across the street from his office facing the court square. Womack indicates that Huntsman purchased the home in 1828, which could be a typographical mistake. Ibid: 48. Williams, "Laughlin": 358.

9. Melville M. Bigelow, ed. *Reports of Cases Argued and Adjudged in the Supreme Court Errors and Appeals of Tennessee* (New York: Hurd and Houghton, 1870): 723-733. Overton County, TN Deed Book D: 302-303, 306-307. Ibid, Book E: 59, 63, 66-67, 91-93, 96-97, 99, 144-145, 375-376. Ibid, Book F; 55-56. Overton County History Book Committee, *History of Overton County, Tennessee* (Dallas, TX: Unknown publisher, 1992): 84-85. Huntsman's slave transactions for this period may be found in Overton County, TN Deed Book E: 67, 104, 145-146, 153-155, 576-577. Ibid, Book F: 261-262.

10. Statewide General Elections: Overton, White, Jackson counties. Record Group No. 87, Roll 1815-1 TSLA. The other candidates were Jonas Bedford, Thomas Stone, and a man named Cross. Unofficial results for Overton County show Huntsman carried his home county with 68%

Huntsman traveled to Nashville for the first session of the 11th General Assembly. The senate convened at the Davidson County Courthouse on September 18, 1815, and elected Edward Ward as its speaker, a position he would hold for the next four years. The next day, Huntsman made his first legislative motion, a resolution that the senate create a commission "to enquire if any amendments were necessary in the present state judiciary system." He was later assigned to committees on land claims and a boundary dispute between Tennessee and Kentucky.[11]

On September 20, he introduced a resolution for a joint select committee to report on amendments proposed by the states of Connecticut and Massachusetts to the Constitution. Among them were ones to limit the president to one term and prohibit two individuals from the same state being elected to two consecutive terms. The resolution was adopted; on November 17, the committee rejected the amendments and voted to print copies of their report for the consideration of other states.[12]

Over the course of the legislative session, lawmakers received numerous petitions from constituents addressing various issues and seeking permission or funding for construction projects. Huntsman presented thirteen such petitions in his first session, eight of which concerned internal improvements, particularly the creation of turnpike roads. The first was on behalf of William Marchbanks and James Chisum, who sought authorization to build a turnpike road on Cumberland Mountain that would extend from Overton to Roane County. On October 30, he presented another that would allow George Wallis of Overton County to build a warehouse at the mouth of Obed's River for "inspecting and safekeeping of tobacco and other merchantable commodities." Other petitions included pleas for monetary relief, such as a militia captain named William Evans who sought compensation on behalf of Stephen Oxendine for a rifle Evans had impressed from Oxendine. Huntsman also voted with the majority on a relief bill for Samuel H. Laughlin

---

of the vote. He received 706 votes, with Bedford securing 220, Stone 75, and Cross 68. In the town of Monroe, Huntsman took 314 votes to Stone's 55 and Bedford's 38. Ibid.

11. *Senate Journal of the First Session of the Eleventh General Assembly of the State of Tennessee* (Nashville, TN: M & J Norvel, 1815): 4, 7, 22, 54

12. Ibid: 20, 221-222

seeking compensation while Laughlin served as a judge advocate in the trial of General John Cocke.[13]

The issue of slave emancipation came up a week into the session when a petition was introduced by John Gass of Greene County from a group of his constituents seeking "gradual abolition of slavery." In his first vote on the institution, Huntsman sided with the petitioners in a losing effort to prevent it from being tabled. He believed their appeal should be read and considered by the senate "although we may be opposed to the principles of the petition." Twenty years later, he would have a decidedly different opinion.[14]

A few days later, he voted against a resolution that would ask the state's U.S. senators and representatives to set aside territory for freed slaves within the United States. But on the very next vote, he favored a bill which passed its first reading that would enable owners to free slaves "of a certain description." He later withdrew his support when a colleague added an amendment that Huntsman felt "defeats the best object of the bill." The amended bill failed to pass on its second reading, but he apparently abstained from casting his vote.[15]

On October 23, Huntsman introduced a bill to hold a referendum in the 1817 election asking voters whether or not a convention should be organized to revise the state constitution. Two weeks later, on his motion, both houses of the General Assembly moved into joint session to consider the referendum, but the question was defeated by a narrow 27-29 vote. Nevertheless, a fellow senator insisted that because two-thirds of the legislature had concurred with the decision, voters should be allowed to decide on a convention to revise sections relating to property taxation and the process for amending the document. This final effort in the senate was quelled 3-13, with Huntsman voting in the minority. Though deterred in this instance, he and other convention proponents would continue the debate over the next eighteen years.[16]

---

13. Ibid: 65, 83, 97, 173
14. Ibid: 40-41
15. Ibid: 41-42, 53, 67, 77
16. Ibid: 131, 177, 195-197

On October 26, word reached the General Assembly that former governor John Sevier had died on a surveying trip in Alabama on September 25. Being a friend of his family in Overton County, Huntsman introduced a resolution that lawmakers should wear mourning crape on their left arms for the remainder of the session and thirty days afterward in memory of the "distinguished fellow citizen, statesman, and patriot."[17]

HUNTSMAN WAS ELECTED one of Tennessee's eight electors in the 1816 presidential election. He cast his vote for the Republican candidate, James Monroe of Virginia, in the Electoral College. Monroe won with 183 electoral votes to 34 by the Federalist candidate, Rufus King of New York. Huntsman ran again four years later representing Overton, White, Jackson, Warren, Franklin, Hamilton, Marion, Bledsoe, and Rhea counties, but lost the race.[18]

In 1817, he defeated challenger Sampson Williams to win reelection to the senate.[19] The state capital continued its nomadic existence, returning to Knoxville for the 12th General Assembly that convened on September 15. With only four senators returning from the previous session, Huntsman became one of the senior members. Among the newcomers were Hugh Lawson White of Knox County (though he had served a previous term) and John Bell of Williamson County, who was beginning his forty-three year political career. Governor Joseph McMinn had won a third term and was inaugurated two weeks later.[20]

Huntsman's seniority led to more responsibilities given him by speaker Edward Ward. He was appointed chairman of the committee on claims, which judged the merits of petitions presented by individual citizens seeking financial compensation from the state. Among the claims he approved was one from J.W. Byrne, sheriff of Sumner County, who sought $20 as reimbursement for taxes he paid on a horse named Truxton, presumably

17. Ibid: 163
18. Peter Force, *The National Calendar for MDCCCXXXI [1831]* (Washington D.C.: Peter Force, 1831) 4: 25. Nashville Gazette, 30 September 1820.
19. AH circular to James Chisum, 4 July 1823. Box 1, Folder 4, Chisum and Robinson Small Collections, TSLA. There are no returns available for Huntsman's 1817 and 1819 senatorial elections at TSLA.
20. White, ed. *Messages* 2: 736-737

Knoxville served as the capital of Tennessee for the last time during Huntsman's second term in the state senate in 1817.

Courtesy of Brent Moore and www.seemidtn.com

the thoroughbred owned by Andrew Jackson. Huntsman served on several joint select committees, including ones on the Tennessee-Kentucky boundary, amendments to the state judiciary, anticipated land acquisition from a treaty with Cherokee leaders, congressional funding for colleges and academies in the state, and the encouragement of the arts and manufactures. He was also chairman of a select committee on turnpike roads.[21]

Being a lawyer, he was especially interested in legislation to improve the state judiciary. He also advocated internal improvements to enhance the state's infrastructure. As chairman of the select committee on turnpike roads, he considered many proposals submitted by citizens to build new roads and endorsed the most promising ones. He presented petitions and introduced bills for various turnpike projects in his own district, as well as petitions from sundry citizens of Sumner and Davidson counties to enable one James Stewart to improve grist and saw mills there.[22]

Tennessee's economy flourished in the years after the War of 1812. Its agricultural products were in demand at home and abroad, especially cotton, which fetched thirty-four cents a pound in 1817. With this prosperity came the desire for more financial capital, and citizens clamored for more banks from which to borrow it. In addition to lending money and receiving deposits, banks also issued paper notes that circulated as currency and could be redeemed for gold or silver (called specie) on demand. Speculators like Huntsman were encouraged by the federal government to buy public lands on credit, and banks were eager to oblige. Before 1817, there had been only two in the state: the Nashville Bank and the Bank of the State of Tennessee at Knoxville. By the time the legislature adjourned in late November, ten more had been created, all but three in Middle Tennessee. Huntsman supported new banks and voted in favor of the expansion.[23]

---

21. Senate Journal (1817): 19-20, 25, 27-28, 38, 140

22. Ibid: 31, 38, 54, 86, 112, 125, 140. The petitions for grist and saw mills led to the creation of a joint select committee on November 4, 1817, "for the encouragement of arts and manufactures" on which Huntsman served. Ibid: 140.

23. Paul H. Bergeron, *Paths of the Past: Tennessee, 1770-1970* (Knoxville, TN: University of Tennessee Press, 1979): 28. Thomas Perkins Abernathy, *From Frontier to Plantation in Tennessee: A Study in Frontier Democracy* (Chapel Hill, NC: University of North Carolina Press, 1932): 224. White, ed. *Messages* 1: 513-514.

The possibility of a constitutional convention, which Huntsman had proposed two years earlier, surfaced again in 1817. On November 2, two-thirds of the General Assembly (12-7 for the senate and 28-11 for the house) approved a resolution to put the question on the ballot in the 1819 election. But three-fourths of the electorate saw no need to reform the state's fundamental law and overwhelmingly rejected the referendum, 17,430 to 5,919.[24]

Toward the end of the session, the house of representatives forwarded to the senate a resolution it had passed urging the state's congressional delegation to introduce or support legislation for "colonizing, in some distant country, the free people of color" living in the United States and its territories. Hugh Lawson White and John Bell were among its supporters in the senate, but Huntsman voted against it. The measure fell to defeat by a tied vote, 9-9.[25]

On November 25, before the legislature adjourned, White presented to the senate Huntsman's resignation as senator in order for him to be a candidate for solicitor of the 5th Judicial Circuit, which served Overton, White, Jackson, Bledsoe, and Warren counties. Both houses met in joint session for the election, but Thomas Jefferson Campbell, a former Rhea County attorney and clerk of the house of representatives, was chosen instead.[26]

AS HUNTSMAN CAMPAIGNED for reelection in the summer of 1819, the economic boom went bust. Cotton prices and land values plummeted. Speculators, businessmen, and merchants who owned bank notes rushed to redeem them for hard money. But the banks had overextended themselves and with the exception of the Bank of the State of Tennessee led by Hugh Lawson White, they were forced to suspend specie payments. Middle Tennessee, which at the time grew most of the cotton in the state,

---

24. Senate Journal (1817): 28, 170. Senate Journal (1817): 69, 103-104, 128, 132-133. White, ed. *Messages* 1: 521.

25. Senate Journal (1817): 210-211. The rules of the senate stated that a tied vote would be considered as a rejection.

26. Ibid: 214. Charles A. Miller, *The Official and Political Manual of the State of Tennessee* (Nashville, TN: Marshall & Bruce, 1890): 22.

suffered greatly from the financial collapse, as the effects of the Panic of 1819—America's first economic depression—were felt across the nation.[27]

Under these dire circumstances, the 13th General Assembly convened at Murfreesborough on September 28, 1819. Huntsman had won a third term in the senate and, being one of its senior members, immediately took an active leadership role. He made the first motion of the session that Robert Weakley of Davidson County be unanimously elected speaker, which was approved. The next point of business was the election of a clerk. The candidates were Joseph M. Anderson and an apprentice in Representative Felix Grundy's law office named James Knox Polk. Polk was elected; twenty-five years later, when Polk received the Democratic nomination for President of the United States, Huntsman humorously recalled the small, slender twenty-three year old as being "a Possum looking fellow" when he assumed his duties as senate clerk.[28]

The next day, Huntsman asked that a joint select committee be appointed to consider the Tennessee-Kentucky boundary dispute to which Governor McMinn had alluded in his message to the legislature on September 28. Mention of the disagreement had become commonplace in the governor's communications, and it had become custom for the General Assembly to enact a law each session "to adjust the boundary line between this state and the state of Kentucky." How it would be resolved was a concern for Huntsman's constituents in northern Overton and Jackson counties who owned property in the disputed strip of land.[29]

The squabble with Kentucky began in 1803 when the commonwealth realized that the boundary it shared with Tennessee had not been accurately surveyed. In 1779, before both states were admitted into the Union, commissioners from their parent states, North Carolina and Virginia, were instructed to extend their shared boundary at the 36° 30′ parallel.

---

27. Corlew, *Tennessee*: 142

28. *Journal of the Senate at the First Session of the Thirteenth General Assembly of the State of Tennessee, Begun and Held at Murfreesborough, on Monday the Twentieth Day of September, One Thousand Eight Hundred and Nineteen* (Murfreesborough, TN: G.A. and A.C. Sublett, 1819): 4. AH to JKP, 11 June 1844, Emma Inman Williams, ed. "Letters of Adam Huntsman to James K. Polk" *Tennessee Historical Quarterly* 6 (1947): 360. Adam Huntsman Papers, Accession No. 1967.013, IV-A-5, TSLA.

29. Senate Journal (1819): 20. White, ed. *Messages* 1: 537.

Murfreesboro served as Tennessee's capital during Huntsman's third term in the state senate in 1819 and the special session of 1820.

Courtesy of Brent Moore and www.seemidtn.com

A disagreement between the two surveying parties resulted in two distinct lines being measured: the North Carolinians ran their line—called the Henderson line—to the Cumberland Mountains and stopped in protest; the Virginians ran theirs—the Walker line—south of the Henderson line and extended it westward to the Tennessee River. Although they did not physically survey it or have authority to do it, the Virginia commissioners claimed their line terminated at the Mississippi River. Eventually, after North Carolina ceded to the federal government the territory that became Tennessee, Walker's Line was accepted as the boundary between it and Kentucky.[30]

But Kentucky discovered that Walker's Line actually began at the 36° 34′ parallel and deviated northward to 36° 40′ at the Tennessee River, taking from the commonwealth some 2,500 square miles of territory from six to twelve miles in width north of where the line was supposed to be. The Kentucky legislature in 1818 declared that it would recognize the 36° 30′ boundary and asked Congress to enact legislation that would allow the U.S. Supreme Court to settle the disagreement. "Nothing short of the establishment of the line between this state and the state of Tennessee, according to its true latitude, will now comport with the wishes of this legislature," lawmakers declared. A year later, they appointed commissioners to survey a new line with the determination that they would do so with or without the participation of commissioners from Tennessee.[31]

In October 1819, Huntsman was made chairman of the Tennessee-Kentucky boundary committee. After a month of meticulous examination of available records, he presented the committee's findings to the senate in a report that one historian described as "one of the most exhaustive...ever reported to the Tennessee Legislature." It began with a

---

30. W.R. Garrett, "Northern Boundary of Tennessee." *American Historical Magazine* 6 (1901): 26-27. Joseph H. Parks, *Felix Grundy: Champion of Democracy* (Baton Rogue, LA: Louisiana State University Press, 1940): 122-123.

31. White, ed. *Messages* 1: 639. Garrett, "Northern Boundary": 30-31. Parks, *Grundy*: 122-124. Gabriel Slaughter, *Acts Passed at the First Session of the Twenty-Sixth General Assembly for the Commonwealth of Kentucky, Begun and Held in the Town of Frankfort, on Monday the First Day of December 1817* (Frankfort, KY: Kendall and Russells, 1818): 576-579. Had the Kentucky commissioners ran the line as the commonwealth wanted, the boundary would have extended south of Clarksville, Tennessee. Parks, *Grundy*: 31.

comprehensive history of efforts to determine a boundary line dating back to the initial land grant of King Charles II of England in 1665. As he progressed, Huntsman made the case that regardless whether it was mathematically accurate or not, Walker's Line had been recognized by both states as their shared boundary and used to determine county lines and the center of each county for locating seats of justice. "[H]aving referred to this line," he argued, "which she [Kentucky] and others reputed to be the line, she thereby makes it the real one; no matter where the mathematical line of 36, 30, really is." He added:

> Is not Walker's line the actual southern boundary of all [the Kentucky counties]...and in all the acts for erecting these counties, has it not been called the state line, or the Tennessee line, or the North Carolina line; add these admissions to those of Virginia ... and the body of evidence which they form in support of Walker's line, will prove itself worthy of the highest consideration.[32]

Although confident that Tennessee would prevail should the dispute ever reach the Supreme Court, Huntsman believed both states should avoid inevitable bitterness and settle a disagreement which involved "such few difficulties." He cautioned Kentucky that should it go to court, other miscalculations not in the commonwealth's favor might be discovered. Instead, he advocated "the propriety of one more attempt at amicable adjustment" of the boundary. If the matter still could not be settled, he recommended legal action to resolve the matter and passage of a bill that would move it forward.[33]

Fortunately, the General Assembly agreed to send two commissioners to meet with their Kentucky counterparts in 1819 and settle the dispute. The commonwealth relinquished its claim to territory below 36° 30′ and agreed that Walker's Line would be the border from East Tennessee westward to the Tennessee River. From there, a line would run up the river

---

32. White, ed. *Messages* 1: 544-549
33. Ibid: 551

to meet the Alexander-Munsell Line (commissioned by Kentucky in 1819 at 36° 30′) and extend west to the Mississippi River. As chairman of the joint select committee on the boundary during a special session in 1820, Huntsman acknowledged that the agreement "was as good as could have been obtained, or reasonable expected under all the circumstances" and recommended its approval.[34]

IN AN EFFORT to help alleviate the financial suffering of many citizens, the General Assembly passed the Endorsement Act in 1819, which prevented debtors from being taken to court for two years unless creditors accepted depreciated bank notes as payment. Huntsman felt this legislation was "indispensable to the country, as an exaction of specie, at this time, would be a total sacrifice of property without either paying the debt, or leaving the defendant the means of ever paying it."[35]

But Governor McMinn felt more drastic measures were needed to deal with the crisis. He called the legislature into special session on June 26, 1820, and proposed the creation of a loan office that would allow citizens to borrow money from the state using circulated treasury certificates backed by public credit and sustained through land sales and unappropriated state funds. Felix Grundy championed the governor's plan and guided it through the house. Huntsman agreed that the legislature should provide relief measures within the framework of the state constitution and protect landholders from "the monied speculator, with all his merciless rapecity" who would take advantage of the economic situation "[to] purchase up the property of the unfortunate part of the community for one fifteenth of its value, and thereby enrich himself upon the miseries of others." Opponents argued that a loan office would be unconstitutional because the state was prohibited from issuing money, and the treasury

---

34. Parks, *Grundy*: 124, 131-132. White, ed. *Messages* 1: 638. For a thorough explanation of the Tennessee-Kentucky boundary dispute and documents related to it, see White, ed. *Messages* 1: 537-559, 624-639.

35. Corlew, *Tennessee*: 142-143. Adam Huntsman and John B. Cross circular to "Fellow Citizens," 27 November 1819. Early American Imprints (2nd Series). Shaw-Shoemaker Bibliography, 1801-1819. Jean and Alexander Heard Library, Vanderbilt University, Nashville TN.

certificates would circulate as a form of currency. One lawmaker contended that it would simply "take one mans property to pay anothers debts."[36]

The most conspicuous and vocal critic of the loan office bill was General Andrew Jackson, hero of the Battle of New Orleans and a member of the wealthy land gentry of Davidson County.[37] It was "such a corrupt, base, wicked and unconstitutional law" that he traveled to Murfreesborough to personally chastise lawmakers who supported the bill—including Huntsman—and declared they would violate their oaths of office and commit perjury if they passed it. When a friend later rebuked him for his behavior, Jackson defended himself. "I know I was warm...It is my foible to Such Topics to get two warm & I often regret it; but Sir it is time for every man who wishes to perpetuate the constitutional government of our choice to Speak out."[38]

Jackson took part in public meetings against the loan office bill and helped articulate a "memorial of remonstrance" signed by Davidson County voters that was presented to the house of representatives on July 17. The lengthy petition stated their opposition to the bill as a violation of both the state and federal constitutions. The bill was "inexpedient and contrary to sound policy," it declared, and would do more harm than good in alleviating the suffering of Tennesseans. The remonstrance also scolded legislators with a word-for-word reminder of the oath each man had taken, stressing that they would not consent "to any act...that shall... lessen or abridge the rights and priviledges, as declared by the constitution of this state."[39]

---

36. *Nashville Whig*, August 9, 1820. White, ed. *Messages* 1: 595.

37. Another critic was William Carroll, also from Davidson County, who would be elected governor in 1821. Nine years later, when he advocated the closing of the Bank of the State of Tennessee, he felt the 1820 special session had worked "under the delusive hope that the distresses of the people could be removed by legislative enactments." White, ed. *Messages* 2: 261.

38. AJ to William B. Lewis, July 16, 1820. Harold D. Moser, David R. Hoth, George H. Hoemann, eds. *The Papers of Andrew Jackson* (Knoxville, TN: University of Tennessee Press, 1994) 4: 379. Jackson's rebuke against members of the legislature took place in Murfreesborough on July 12, 1820.

39. White, ed. *Messages* 1: 600. *Nashville Clarion*, July 25, 1820. According to state senator Abram P. Maury Sr. of Williamson County, Huntsman told Jackson "he'el [sic] be dammed, if he did not make as much money as he could and spend it too if he chose." It is not stated, however, under what context he made the statement. Abram P. Maury Sr. to Abram P. Maury Jr., July 16, 1820. "Letters from Forgotten Ancestors, Pre-1920 Letters." <www.tngenweb.org/tnletters/will-l-2.htm>

Andrew Jackson, hero of the Battle of New Orleans, clashed with Huntsman and other state senators during the Loan Office bill fight in 1820.

Courtesy of the Library of Congress

When the remonstrance was presented to the house, Grundy motioned that it be received. But when it was brought to the senate, it met with a less cordial reception. Huntsman moved that it be laid on the table until the first day of January 1821, essentially disregarding it for the remainder of the special session. The vote was 11-4 in favor of his motion. Then he asked that the reasons he and fellow senator David Wallace of Smith County voted to table the remonstrance be recorded in the Senate Journal. He acknowledged the right of citizens to petition their representatives and express their sentiments on legislation "in a mild, temperate, respectful manner." But he objected strongly to Jackson's attempt to intimidate lawmakers and "in the most indecorous manner...[state]...that any member who voted for it [the loan office bill] would perjure himself, & that if the law did pass, twelve honest jurymen upon oath would convict those who voted for the measure of perjury." The remonstrance, coupled with Jackson's tirade, represented "a direct and unwarranted attack upon the dignity of the Senate." He concluded:

> the insinuations of perjury cast in said memorial is neither reason nor argument to convince any rational mind of any principle whatever—and further the undersigned [Huntsman and Wallace] humbly sensible to the exalted and responsible situation they have been called to, by the voice of their country think that the indignity offered, extends through then to those whom they have the honor to represent, and therefore feel bound in behalf of themselves and their constituents to protest most solemnly against that part of said memorial as dictatorial, indecorous and intemperate.[40]

On July 20, the senate proposed a joint select committee to examine the loan office bill and reach a consensus. Four senators (including Huntsman) were appointed along with eight representatives, among them Grundy, Pleasant M. Miller of Knox County, and William Williams of

---

40. *Nashville Clarion*, July 25, 1820

Davidson County, who had presented the remonstrance. The committee's deliberations were brief; the only significant change made was to its title. Rather than create a state loan office, it would now establish "a Bank of the State of Tennessee."[41] The amended bill was approved by the senate, but it had a harder time in the house. Eventually, it was accepted with minor amendments by the narrow margin of 20-19. Several more days of passing the bill between the two chambers followed and more amendments were added by the senate. On July 26 it adopted the amended bill by a 13-7 vote, authorizing a new state-sponsored bank.[42]

The new Bank of the State of Tennessee—created "for the purpose of relieving the distresses of the community and improving the revenue of the state"—was established on one million dollars in capital derived from anticipated land sales south of the French Broad and Holston rivers (with interest) and unappropriated state revenue. Certificates were issued in denominations from one dollar to one hundred dollars borrowed at six percent interest. No individual was allowed more than a $500 loan. The main bank was established at Nashville with a branch at Knoxville and agencies in each county of the state.[43]

Yet even after the bill became law, Huntsman was still targeted by its critics. Using the pseudonyms of "One of the People" and "A Republican" in newspaper articles, they defended the people's right to protest to their elected representatives in whatever language and manner they saw fit. Both Huntsman and Wallace's constituents were encouraged to throw them out of office in the next election. Their opposition to the Davidson County remonstrance had made it a case of "Adam Huntsman and David Wallace versus the people of Tennessee."[44]

Huntsman addressed his anonymous critics in a letter to the *Nashville Whig* on August 9. He insisted that his motive had been to help his suffering constituents. But while trying to do so, he and his fellow legislators were accused of committing perjury and lectured about their

---

41. According to one legislative historian, the title revision was made by the senators on the joint committee, as the bill had been returned to that chamber. White, *Messages* 1: 606-607.
42. Ibid: 610-611
43. Ibid: 611-612
44. *Nashville Whig*, July 26, August 2, 1820

constitutional oaths in a condescending and demeaning manner, both in person by Andrew Jackson and on paper in the Davidson County remonstrance. Taken together, both insinuated that lawmakers "have not understanding sufficient to appreciate the obligation of an oath; and that unless we act in a certain way therein declared, we shall commit perjury." Huntsman conceded that the remonstrance had been well written by intelligent and talented individuals; nonetheless, he regretted that legislators were abused by the petitioners "in the course vulgar language of a bully" in order to convey their disapproval of the loan office bill. He and his senate colleagues who tabled the remonstrance believed it to be an insult to their constituents and themselves. "Every principle of manly independence, both as citizens and representatives of a high minded people, irresistibly impelled us to the course we pursued."[45]

When "A Republican" claimed Huntsman's official response to the remonstrance contained "secret personal or political feelings," Huntsman acknowledged that he felt more insulted and disrespected by Jackson and former senate speaker Edward Ward than any of the other seventy-three signers of the petition. Jackson had used "degrading and abusive" language toward members of the legislature and the remonstrance that followed "embodied…the same ideas, though differently dressed." Huntsman regretted that Ward, whom he considered "to be a man of transcendent talents, high political information, and sterling integrity," would allow himself—"perhaps by the force of great example"—to be involved with the remonstrance.[46]

He denied any personal hostility toward Jackson. In the 1819 session, he had voted with the General Assembly to commend Jackson for conquering Spanish-held Florida in 1818, award him a sword, and instruct the state's congressional delegation to thwart the efforts of an investigation that would "tarnish" his reputation. "But it seems if we differ in opinion from some of the great people in this land, we are perjured," Huntsman lamented. The "independent principles" asserted in his stand against Jackson were recognized later by James P. Erwin in a letter to his father-

---

45. Ibid, August 9, 1820
46. Ibid

in-law, Henry Clay of Kentucky. It would not be the last time Huntsman would have to deal with the bank he helped create, which soon earned the unflattering moniker of the "Saddle Bags Bank."[47]

BY 1820, HUNTSMAN WAS THIRTY-FOUR YEARS OLD with a successful law practice and a promising political career. Much of his time and energy was devoted to these endeavors as well as his land speculations. He remained a bachelor, though he had taken in his widowed brother James Huntsman and James's son Stephen to live with him. At some point before he left the Mountain District, however, he asked Sarah Wesley Quarles for her hand in marriage. The date of their wedding is not known, but it is presumed that the ceremony was performed between 1820 and 1822.[48]

Sarah Quarles was born in Bedford County, Virginia about 1792, and was close to twenty-nine years old when she married Huntsman. She was the sixth of ten children born to William Pennington Quarles and Ann Hawes. Her father had served during the American Revolution as an ensign and lieutenant in the 1st Virginia Regiment and was later promoted to major in the Virginia State Militia. He brought his large family to Tennessee in the winter of 1809 and settled in northwest White County near the boundaries of Jackson and Overton counties, three miles east of present-day Cookeville. Here he spent the next four years building a large house for his family and smaller ones for his married daughters. He also built an inn, a blacksmith shop, and a mercantile store, calling his new home place "White Plains."[49]

---

47. Ibid. James P. Erwin to Henry Clay, August 12, 1827. Mary W.M. Hargreaves and James F. Hopkins, ed. *The Papers of Henry Clay, Volume 6, Secretary of State 1827* (Lexington, KY: University of Kentucky Press, 1981): 893. In the same letter, Erwin also mentioned the election of David Crockett to Congress in the 1827 elections: "Crockett the bear hunter who voted for Colo. [John] Williams for Senator, in opposition to Genl J[ackson] is elected 2 to 1." Ibid.

48. The marriage of Adam and Sarah Huntsman is estimated between 1820 and 1822 because the 1820 U.S. Census for Overton County, Tennessee showed him with no females in his household and the fact that their only child was born on October 25, 1823.

49. Paula Phillips, "The Military Career of Lieutenant William Pennington Quarles." William Pennington Quarles genealogical website <www.wpquarles2009.info>. Phillips, "William P. Quarles Civilian Career Tennessee." Ibid. Dr. Walter Stephens and Ernest H. Boyd, "White Plains Was First Post Office, County Seat of [Putnam] County for 3 Years." *Putnam County Herald*, March 12, 1953. Ibid.

Historical marker for "White Plains," the home of Huntsman's first wife, Sarah Wesley Quarles Huntsman.

Courtesy of Brian Stansberry

Major Quarles was an active leader of the community in the short time he lived there. He served as postmaster for White Plains as well as a justice of the peace and coroner for White County. He operated a "house of entertainment" that offered food and drink and rest for weary travelers along the one hundred mile Walton Road that connected East and Middle Tennessee. It may have been as an innkeeper or an attorney in the White County court that he first met his daughter's future husband.[50]

Huntsman was acquainted with the Quarles family before his marriage to Sarah. The tabulations of his first senatorial victory were certified at their home by Jackson County election officials on August 7, 1815. As a senator, he had presented a petition on their behalf asking that their home be annexed to Overton County and serve as the boundary between it and White County. The request was passed by the General Assembly on September 15, 1817.[51] Unfortunately, Major Quarles never lived to see his daughter's marriage to Huntsman. On his way home from a militia meeting at Sparta, he was murdered on the road near White Plains on

---

50. Phillips, "Quarles Civilian Career." Ibid.

51. Statewide General Election returns, 1815-1 (Overton, Jackson, White), Record Group No. 87 (microfilm), TSLA. Senate Journal (1817): 46. *Acts Passed at the First Session of the Twelfth General Assembly* (Knoxville, TN: George Wilson, 1817): 11.

April 2, 1814. His horse returned home without him; his family went to search for him and found him dead from a head wound. His alleged murderer, William Phillips, was apprehended but twice escaped his captors and was never tried for the crime. It was never determined whether the motive was personal animosity or simple robbery.[52]

AS LATE AS MARCH 1821, Huntsman seemed intent on a fourth term in the senate. But at some point before the election, he withdrew his candidacy and his challenger, James Chisum, won the seat.[53] He did not seek elected office in Overton County again, but instead focused his attention on his law practice. But in recent years, business was harder to find in Monroe and many attorneys were leaving for better opportunities further west.[54] Huntsman cast his own eyes toward virgin territory between the Tennessee and Mississippi rivers that three years earlier had been opened for settlement after its purchase from the Chickasaw Indian tribe. Land hungry settlers traveled to this new wilderness to stake their claims and make their homes in the region known as the Western District.

---

52. Paula Phillips, "William Pennington Quarles: A Summary of His Murder, 1814." <www.wpquarles2009.info.>

53. *Nashville Gazette*, March 31, 1821. There was no extant vote tabulation found for the 1821 election that gives the candidates who competed for Huntsman's senate seat in Tennessee Election Returns, Statewide General Election, August 2-3, 1821. Record Group 87, Box 9 at TSLA. Chisum served two terms (1821-25) before settling in Hardeman County, Tennessee by 1828. McBride and Robison, eds. *Biographical Directory* 1: 142.

54. Interestingly, even after moving to Madison County, Tennessee permanently in 1823, Huntsman still participated in Overton County government. On August 10, 1833, he was one of seven commissioners who for $200 purchased forty acres from Joseph and Ambrose Gore to start the town of Livingston. Two years later, it superseded Monroe as the county seat. Overton County, TN Deed Book F: 406.

Adam and Sarah Huntsman settled in the Cotton Grove community northeast of Jackson, Tennessee in 1823.

Photograph by the author

Chapter Three

Return to the Senate

1821–1831

That there are some assumptions of facts in said argument, which are founded upon newspaper criminations and recriminations, and controversies which originated in great political excitement, and which I do not know to be true or untrue; therefore, the oath I have taken as a senator in this General Assembly, in my own estimation requires me to be satisfied of the truth of every proposition before I assent to it.
—Adam Huntsman, October 20, 1827

In the spring of 1823, Adam Huntsman and his wife Sarah, who was about two or three months pregnant, left Overton County to begin a new life some 240 miles away in the Western District.[1] He bought land from one George Hicks and built a home in the Cotton Gin Grove

---

1. Huntsman was not listed in the 1822 Madison County, TN tax list contained in Jonathan K.T. Smith, *Antebellum Militia, Justices and Some Early Taxpayers, Madison County, Tennessee* (Jackson, TN: Self-published, 1998): 27-41. As late as March 1823, he was shown on a land deed being a resident of Overton County. Overton County, TN Deed Book E: 364-365. He still received mail at Monroe, Tennessee as late as April 1, 1824. *Sparta* (TN) *Review*, April 14, 1824, in Sherida K. Eddlemann, ed. *Genealogical Abstracts from Tennessee Newspapers, 1821-1828* (Bowie, MD: Self-published, 1991): 10.

community, the first settlement in Madison County, located about four miles northeast of the county seat at Jackson. That autumn, on Saturday, October 25, Sarah gave birth to a daughter, Ann, who was likely named for her maternal grandmother, Ann Quarles.[2]

For the past two years, Huntsman had been involved with the development of Madison County while keeping his home and law practice in Overton County. On November 7, 1821, the General Assembly enacted legislation that created Carroll, Henderson, and Madison counties, the latter named in honor of James Madison, the "Father of the Constitution" and fourth President of the United States. Two weeks later, Huntsman was appointed one of eight commissioners for the new county and served on the town commission for the county seat of Alexandria. To raise funds for additional land, a new courthouse, and a jail, the commissioners sold town lots beginning the first two days of August 1822. Bids were encouraged over the next week with an ample supply of whiskey on hand. That month, an act of the General Assembly renamed the county seat Jackson to honor General Andrew Jackson, whose relatives were among the earliest settlers in Madison County. Streets were named for the commissioners. Huntsman's name was attached to one avenue that is now known as Lafayette Street.[3]

On April 22, 1823, Huntsman walked into the rustic seat of justice in Jackson, a single-story, clapboard covered log courthouse, and took the oath that enabled him to practice law in the court.[4] He traveled the 8th Judicial Circuit the remainder of the year representing clients in cases throughout the Western District. According to one historian, he "brought with him a high reputation, particularly as a criminal lawyer,

---

2. Jonathan K.T. Smith, *My Riverside Cemetery Tombstone Inscriptions Scrapbook* (Jackson, TN: Self-published, 1992) 1: 28. There is no deed recorded for this initial land purchase, though it is alluded to as "a twenty-five acre tract of land bought of George Hicks by Adam Huntsman" in Madison County Deed Book 14: 3.

3. Huntsman lived in Overton County as late as March 12, 1823, when he sold 107 acres to Menan M. Martin. Overton County, TN Deed Book E: 364-365. He had settled in Madison County as early as November 1, 1823. Ibid: 576-577.

4. Jay Guy Cisco, "Madison County." *American Historical Magazine* 7.2 (Oct. 1902): 342

> **Adam Huntsman,**
> *(Attorney at Law,)*
>
> HAS opened an office at his own house, four miles east of Jackson, on the Ross' Ferry road, where he can be found at all times unless absent on professional business. Those who wish his services will call at his own house instead of Jackson, where he formerly kept his office. People who are not able to pay can get his assistance gratis. Those who are able must pay well, or get some other lawyer.
>
> July 1, 1826.—4t

Advertisement for Huntsman's legal sevices published in the *Jackson Gazette*, July 1, 1826

and…while he resided in Middle Tennessee was second only to the distinguished Felix Grundy."[5]

Throughout his legal career, Huntsman offered advice and assistance to younger attorneys. Archibald W.O. Totten, a son of his Overton County friend Benjamin Totten, once asked for his help with a troublesome opponent. During a circuit court trial, a Gibson County lawyer named Colonel M.R. Hill had intimidated him so much that he lost. Totten asked his disgruntled client to appeal his case to the state supreme court and hire Huntsman to assist him. If he lost again, he would waive his legal fees. The client agreed. When the case came before the supreme court and Totten began his opening statement, Hill stood ready to fluster him once again. But Huntsman responded in kind, rising to his feet and stomping his peg leg on the floor. "Sit down," he told Hill. "I am in this case." With Huntsman's presence as a deterrent, Totten won the case.[6]

5. Cisco, "Madison County": 337
6. Frederick M. Culp and Mrs. Robert E. Ross, *Gibson County, Past and Present* (Jackson, TN: McCowat-Mercer Press, 1961): 254

In addition to his reputation as a statute and criminal lawyer, Huntsman also brought with him to the Western District his propensity for fun. One evening in Huntingdon, he and his fellow attorneys orchestrated a makeshift trial in the court square to prosecute a nefarious criminal who pillaged local cornfields. Prosecution and defense attorneys were assembled and witnesses testified. Huntsman, Berry Gillespie, and Andrew L. Martin argued the case for much of the evening while the accused, a hapless bull owned by the court clerk, was tied to a stump awaiting its fate. On another occasion, Huntsman took part in an unorthodox group called the "Sacrificial Club" that included several prominent men in the community. While "worshiping at the shrine of Bacchus"—no doubt a Jackson tavern—members discussed how they wanted to engage in professions other than their own. One had the novel idea of offering a human sacrifice as payment for their professional sins. They drew lots to determine who should be sacrificed, and John Bolling Cross—a former legal apprentice of Huntsman in Overton County—"won" the bizarre lottery. He was stripped of his clothing, clad in a white robe, and taken to be sacrificed at the corner of Lafayette and Liberty streets. A makeshift altar was prepared of penned logs and "filled with the most combustible material that could be found." Two members acting as "priests" placed Cross on the altar and were preparing to set it ablaze when a passerby stopped the ceremony.[7]

Huntsman enjoyed telling stories. One he often told occurred when he was a young man in Virginia. Word had spread among the inhabitants of the town of Abingdon that the most wanted man in America had been captured in their own community. Curiosity led them to the Washington County Courthouse, where they crowded into the courtroom to see the notorious fugitive for themselves. The man sat in the courtroom with his face buried in his hands, refusing to yield to their intrusive stares. He was a disgraced former vice president of the United States implicated in a conspiracy to capture the city of New Orleans and make the Louisiana Territory his own personal empire. During the winter of 1806-1807, he

---

7. Samuel Cole Williams, *Beginnings of West Tennessee, 1541-1841* (Johnson City, TN: The Watauga Press, 1930): 221-222. Emma Inman Williams Collection, Box 7. Tennessee Room, JMCPL. Cisco, "Madison County": 33-34.

was declared a traitor to his country and a reward was offered for his capture by President Thomas Jefferson.

The man seated in the courtroom had sought the trust of a tavern owner from a neighboring village. Having overheard a discussion about Aaron Burr and the reward offered for his capture, he approached the owner and after gaining his trust, confided in him a dark secret. He had been falsely accused of a crime and was making his way east to escape his pursuers, hoping to secure passage on a vessel that would take him overseas to freedom. The tavern owner promised his assistance, but was curious who he was. "I feel that I can confide both in your promise and your honor," the stranger told him. "You see before you that unfortunate man, Aaron Burr." But the secret—and the reward offered for his capture—proved to be too great a temptation for the tavern owner. That night, the stranger was awakened from his sleep by local authorities and arrested.

The judge entered the courtroom and took his seat at the bench. He directed the sheriff to begin court, and for the first time looked at the man who had caused so much excitement. Strangely, there was something familiar about him. The judge watched as the man raised his head from his hands to finally reveal his face. The puzzled look on the judge's face quickly changed to recognition and bewilderment. He knew this man—ever they were children!

"Why Adam Huntsman," he exclaimed, "what on earth are you doing here, and under arrest?"

Huntsman rose from his chair. "If your honor pleases, I am here to move the court to issue a bench warrant for the arrest of these scoundrels for false arrest and imprisonment." Turning to the tavern owner, he added: "And particularly that treacherous villain there under whose roof this outrage upon the rights of a free citizen was committed."

After several minutes of confusion, the elaborate trick played on the tavern owner was revealed and the courtroom erupted in laughter. The judge tried unsuccessfully to restore order before giving up and adjourning court for the day "that everybody might have an opportunity to laugh as much as they please."[8]

---

8. Cisco, "Madison County": 337-339

IN THE SPRING of 1824, Huntsman formed a law partnership with a young attorney named William Stoddert, who served with him on the town commission. Together they attended the county and circuit courts of the Western District as well as the state supreme court at Charlotte, Tennessee. An advertisement they placed in the *Jackson Gazette* promised "their joint attention will be given for the ordinary fees." The partnership ended two years later by mutual agreement.[9]

In July 1826, Huntsman resumed his independent law practice from an office at his home. He advertised his services in the *Gazette*, but cautioned potential clients how he conducted his business: "People who are not able to pay can get his assistance gratis. Those who are able must pay well, or get some other lawyer." He also placed notices in the paper for the return of lost items like a book or a saw to draw attention to himself. On one occasion, he advertised prices for timber cut from his property and asked any trespasser who chose not to compensate him "be sufficiently polite to keep his feet and hands off my land" and "probably get clear of a lawsuit."[10]

Huntsman became an active member of the community. He renewed his membership in Freemasonry and was a master mason at the Jackson Lodge No. 45 of Free and Accepted Masons.[11] The Madison County Court periodically assigned men to repair and maintain the roads in their neighborhoods. Despite his physical handicap, Huntsman did his share of work on "the road from the town of Jackson to the bridge on Butlers Creek, below Hearndon Haralson" where he lived. He and neighbor Roderick McIver built a mill on Butler's Creek where it crossed the Lexington road.[12]

---

9. *Jackson Gazette*, May 29, 1824. Cisco, "Madison County": 47. Smith, *Riverside Cemetery* 1:22. Huntsman and Stoddert's law office may have been located on Lafayette Street in Jackson, as Stoddert and Huntsman's neighbor Duncan McIver jointly owned lots 44 and 74. These lots were two blocks northeast of the public square. Williams, *Historic Madison*: 41.

10. *Jackson Gazette*, April 2, November 5, 1825; April 15, April 29, July 1, 1826

11. "Return of Jackson Lodge No. 45 from the 1st Monday in October 1824 to 1st Monday in October 1825." Grand Lodge of Tennessee Free and Accepted Masons records in Nashville, Tennessee. Copy sent to the author by Jonathan K.T. Smith, April 11, 1994. Huntsman had been a charter member of the Masonic Lodge at Sparta, Tennessee in 1820. Rev. Monroe Seals, *History of White County, Tennessee* (Spartanburg, SC: The Reprint Company, 1974): 94.

12. Madison County, Tennessee Court Minute Book 1: 116, 155, 167, 229

An advocate of internal improvements while in the state senate, he put his support into practice with several endeavors to improve transportation on the roads and waterways of the Western District. He served as a commissioner with David Jarrett and Thomas Lacy in 1824 to supervise the construction of a road and bridge over the Forked Deer River at Shannon's Landing. At the same time, he was appointed by the legislature as one of three trustees to oversee navigational improvements to the Forked Deer, Obion, and Hatchie rivers.[13] In November 1824, another commission that included Huntsman was created with members from Madison, Dyer, and Haywood counties to improve navigation on the Forked Deer River. The six commissioners held a lottery to acquire the funds necessary to finance the project. In 1830, Huntsman and Henry H. Brown were awarded a contract from the town of Huntingdon in Carroll County to build and maintain a turnpike bridge over Beaver Creek that allowed them to collect toll fees for its use.[14]

Huntsman renewed his interest in land speculation and purchased acreage in the Western District. He became partners in separate ventures with several prominent figures in Jackson and surrounding counties such as Robert I. Chester, Benjamin Totten (his friend from Overton County), and fellow attorney Alexander B. Bradford. In the *Jackson Gazette*, he advertised land for sale in Madison, Gibson, Dyer, Obion, and Weakley counties "on good terms for cash or negro property." Even though taxes were low—he and Totten owed only $21.40 for 3,500 acres in Henry County—he and his partners still were cited on several occasions by various county courts for delinquent taxes on their holdings. How successful he and his partners were in their land acquisitions is not known, but his profits reselling them no doubt supplemented his legal income considerably.[15]

---

13. In 1825, a grand jury concluded that no actual work had been done on the project. Huntsman tried to organize his fellow trustees again a year later, asking them to meet at Jackson in early April to "organize a board" and conduct "other business of said Commission."

14. Williams, *Historic Madison*: 122-123. *Jackson Gazette*, March 12, 1825. Carroll County, TN County Court Minutes, 1826-1833: 347-348, 410, 453.

15. *Jackson Gazette*, July 28, August 5, September 9, September 16, 1826; January 20, February 7, 1827.

Sarah Quarles Huntsman tomsbtone, Old Salem Cemetery.
Photograph by the author

IN LATE SUMMER 1825, the town of Jackson received a special guest when General Andrew Jackson accepted an invitation to visit the frontier community named for him. A welcoming committee of Huntsman, Dr. William E. Butler, and Duncan McIver spent the summer making preparations for his arrival. On September 10, the Old Hero reached Jackson with his wife Rachel, U.S. Senator John H. Eaton, and Judge John Overton. Huntsman's law partner, William Stoddert, officially welcomed them with prepared remarks at the Madison County Courthouse. A large dinner was held in the General's honor and toasts were offered by the gentlemen in attendance. Huntsman remarked: "The General and State Governments—May concord and harmony forever unite them." Jackson and his party stayed for three weeks, after which a special delegation escorted them to the town limits on the first of October as they left for a dinner at Paris, Tennessee.[16]

It is not known if Sarah Huntsman attended the festivities with her husband. In October 1825, she died at the age of thirty-three and was buried less than a mile from her home on a small hill called Salem Campground. Because his legal work frequently took him away from home, Huntsman sent his two-year old daughter Ann to live with her maternal grandmother in Overton County. Ann remained with her grandmother until she reached adolescence, even though her father remarried four years after her mother's death.[17] Ten months after Sarah's death, Huntsman suffered another personal loss when his oldest daughter Melinda, who may have been living with her maternal uncle Thomas Witt in Lincoln County, Tennessee, died after a short illness on August 3, 1826. She was fifteen years old.[18]

---

16. Williams, *Historic Madison*: 3-4. At a dinner held in Jackson's honor at the Madison County Courthouse on September 18, 1825, Huntsman toasted: "The General and State Governments—May concord and harmony forever unite them; the political phrenzy of Governor Troup, to the contrary notwithstanding." *Jackson Gazette*, September 24, 1825. Georgia Gov. George M. Troup challenged the federal government over his state's right to forcefully remove the Creek Indians.

17. Sarah Huntsman tombstone inscription, Old Salem Cemetery, Jackson, Tennessee. Zola Pointer, *Pointer and Quarles Families* (Gateway Press, 1986): 255.

18. *Fayetteville* (TN) *Village Messenger*, August 9, 1826. Melinda Huntsman's obituary acknowledged her father as "Adam Huntsman, Esq., of Madison County." Her funeral was held at the home of Thomas Witt and officiated by Rev. S.D. Sansum. Ibid.

IN THE SPRING of 1827, Huntsman became a candidate for the state senate representing Madison, Haywood, Tipton, Hardeman, Fayette, and Shelby counties. Three other candidates also entered the race, including his neighbor George Todd. Huntsman won the election and returned to the legislature after a six-year absence. Although the Western District had been represented in the senate since 1823, he became the first senator who actually lived west of the Tennessee River.[19]

The 17th General Assembly convened on September 17, 1827. The state capital finally ceased its transient existence that year and found a permanent home—albeit unofficially—in Nashville. Huntsman presented a bill on November 15 to use interest from one and a half million dollars in land sales in the Hiwassee District of East Tennessee to fund common schools across the state. He estimated that if $100,000 a year were raised, it could provide for five to six schools in each county. Should the bill be passed, he said, "the light of science would dawn on the benighted minds of the children of the country, and they would then not be endangered by the arts and intrigues of politicians, or the glare of great military fame; they would understand their rights and know how to perpetuate them." Children in the state would "be more benefited by appropriating the funds to common schools than by keeping them in a bank." The bill was defeated on December 12 by the narrow margin of 10-8, but a similar measure was later enacted.[20]

Contempt for President John Quincy Adams and the "corrupt bargain" he allegedly made with Henry Clay in 1825 to win the presidency (and make Clay secretary of state) was prevalent among the supporters of Andrew Jackson a year before the 1828 presidential election. They

---

19. Returns for the 1827 senatorial election are incomplete; the only county whose return is extant is Haywood County, which gave Huntsman 207 votes. His opponents—James Tisdale, George Todd, and J. Watson—tallied only eight votes combined. The sheriffs of Madison, Hardeman, Haywood, Tipton, Fayette, and Shelby counties certified Huntsman's victory on August 6, 1827. Statewide General Election Returns, 1827-1, Box 13, Folders 24 and 63, TSLA. The Western District had been represented in the senate by two Middle Tennesseans—Thomas Williamson and Joel Walker—beginning in 1823. Huntsman's neighbor Duncan McIver served in the state house of representatives (the seat last held by David Crockett) 1825-29. White, ed. *Messages* 2: 681-683.

20. Senate Journal (1827): 292. *National Banner and Nashville Whig*, November 24, 1827. Chase C. Mooney, "The Political Career of Adam Huntsman." *Tennessee Historical Quarterly* 10.2 (June 1951): 110.

Huntsman opposed resolutions presented by Sen. Aaron V. Brown that criticized President John Quincy Adams. Brown later became governor of Tennessee.

Biographical Album of Tennessee's Governors

decided to use the legislature as their podium to condemn the president and exalt his challenger. Aaron V. Brown of Giles County, a law partner of Congressman James K. Polk, presented three resolutions to the senate on October 18, calling for an amendment to the U.S. Constitution that would allow for the direct election of the president and vice president rather than through the Electoral College. More importantly, they declared the policies of the Adams administration to be "dangerous to the liberties of the country" and advocated the election of Jackson as "the surest remedy for these evils." In addition, Brown attached a copious diatribe in support of each resolution, implying the alleged "corrupt bargain" and alluding to personal attacks and slanders against Jackson and his wife purportedly instigated by the administration.[21]

When the resolutions were brought up for adoption the next day, Huntsman objected. He did not endorse Adams and though he agreed

21. White, ed. *Messages* 2: 232-237. Aaron V. Brown would later serve as governor of Tennessee (1845-47).

with the sentiments expressed in the resolutions, the arguments to support them were undignified and based "upon mere presumptive evidence" against the president. He hoped the arguments "might be modified, for he was not willing to subscribe, under oath, to statements he did not *know* to be true." After further debate, Huntsman offered a fourth resolution that would ask the state's congressional delegation "to use all fair and honourable means to promote" Jackson's election. Brown said it was "substantially the same" as his own resolution. Huntsman countered that the resolution was meant "as an addition, that the original ones should not be deprived of any of their dress and finery," but it was still voted down.[22]

Brown's resolutions were adopted on October 20, and Huntsman reluctantly cast his vote for them.[23] Yet he continued to express his concern over the arguments, which he felt were "founded upon newspaper criminations and recriminations, and controversies which originated in great political excitement." The oath he had taken as a senator obligated him to "be satisfied with the truth of every proposition before I assent to it," and he believed the arguments unfairly maligned the president.

> I cannot…give a vote of condemnation upon the highest characters now in the country, because, it is possible, if they are guilty, are so in a much less degree than asserted in the argument. Nor do I believe the cause of Gen. Jackson, requires a vote of censure or condemnation upon others. He stands preeminently conspicuous for talents, firmness and a thorough knowledge of the human character, with a patriotism and love of country, seldom equalled, never surpassed; together with a long list of meritorious services, which presents his claims upon much higher grounds than a legislative re-iteration of newspaper charges. His own claims are all powerful

---

22. Senate Journal (1827): 164-165. *National Banner and Nashville Whig*, October 27, 1827.
23. Senate Journal (1827): 177. Brown's resolutions were adopted by an 18-2 vote, with Theodorick T. Bradford of Bedford County and John Williams of Smith County dissenting. Huntsman and other opponents tried earlier for separate votes on the resolutions and the arguments, but their motion for a division of the question was voted down, 6-14. Ibid.

and will prevail, without condescending to notice the weakness of his adversaries. His cause requires no such sacrifice of magnanimity and independence; I shall therefore speak evil of none."[24]

Eleven years later, when several legislators who had enthusiastically supported the Brown resolutions converted to the Whig party—led by Henry Clay—Huntsman reminded them of his initial opposition. He reiterated that the resolutions contained "the most rare and exquisite dose of vituperative abuse (and perhaps a little slander) upon Mr. Clay and Adams...I could not swallow the dose, because I did not believe the half of it, although I was a Jackson man." In light of their abandonment of Jackson, he facetiously advised Clay's new allies in the General Assembly that the offensive resolutions should be expunged from the senate journal.[25]

FOUR YEARS AFTER the death of his wife, Huntsman remarried on June 14, 1829, to twenty-three year old daughter Elizabeth Todd, daughter of his neighbor and former political opponent George Todd. She was born about 1809 in either North Carolina or Montgomery County, Tennessee. Over the next ten years, Elizabeth gave birth to five children: America, George, Paradise, Adam, and Susan. In a curious twist, two months later, her sister's brother-in-law Duncan McIver (who at the time was a state representative) opposed her new husband in his reelection bid for the senate. Huntsman defeated his new kinsman 2,287 votes to 1,950, a majority of 665 votes. He carried four of the six counties in his district, losing only Shelby and Tipton. The contest was closer in their home county, where Huntsman prevailed by only 44 votes in the town of Denmark and 62 in Jackson. One constituent foresaw a higher office for him in the future,

---

24. Ibid: 178-179. *Jackson Gazette*, November 13, 1827. White, ed. *Messages* 2: 237-238. Huntsman's hesitance to accept the "corrupt bargain" charge against Adams and Clay as factual was brought up by the Whig party during the 1844 presidential election. William G. Brownlow, *A Political Register, Setting Forth the Principles of the Whig and Locofoco Parties in the United States, with the Life and Public Services of Henry Clay* (Spartanburg, SC: The Reprint Company, 1974): 311-312.

25. *Nashville Union*, November 12, 1838.

believing "he has been faithful over a few things, we will make him ruler over many."[26]

While the General Assembly was in recess, Sam Houston unexpectedly resigned as governor in April 1829 following a controversial separation from his new wife. William Hall, who had served as speaker of the senate, assumed the office until a new governor, William Carroll, was elected in August. When it convened in mid September, Huntsman took an active role and was involved in several important issues facing the 18th General Assembly. He was appointed chairman of the committees on banks and the judiciary and was a member of several select committees, including education, a state penitentiary, and criminal jurisprudence.[27]

Governor Carroll's first message to the legislature after his inauguration on October 5 made clear his desire for legislators to close the controversial Bank of the State of Tennessee. He had opposed its enactment nine years earlier and regarded the institution as the product of "the unwise, unjust and ruinous policy of legislative interference between debtor and collector." As the financial circumstances that led to its creation had subsided, he supported legislation that would give borrowers enough time to repay their loans and bank officials sufficient time to account for funds at its main Nashville office, its Knoxville branch, and at agencies in each county.[28]

As chairman of the senate committee on banks, Huntsman was responsible for following through on the governor's recommendation. A week into the session, he believed a careful examination of the bank was needed to determine its financial condition, and his committee received authority to question bank officials and examine their documents. Immediately, he sensed resistance to his inquiries and based on

26. Byron and Barbara Sistler, eds. *Early West Tennessee Marriages* (Nashville, TN: Self-published, 1989) 1: 146. Elizabeth Huntsman tombstone, Old Salem Cemetery, Jackson, TN. McBride and Robison, eds. *Biographical Directory* 1: 480-481. *Jackson Gazette*, August 8, 15, 1829. During a Fourth of July dinner at Brownsville, Huntsman toasted: "The original purity of Elections—May it be preserved in manly independence, without robbing the Rackoon on the range, the Otter of his slide, or the Doggery of its tenants." *Jackson Gazette*, August 8, 1829.

27. White, ed. *Messages* 2: 212, 269-270. *Journal of the Senate of the State of Tennessee at the Eighteenth General Assembly Held at Nashville* (Knoxville, TN: F.S. Heiskell and A.A. Hall, 1829): 6, 17, 33, 38. Mooney, "Huntsman": 110.

28. White, ed. *Messages* 2: 261-263

the initial cashier's report and what information was sparingly given his committee by bank officials, he suspected there might be embezzlement taking place. When pressed further, the cashier, Joel Parrish (who was a former state senator from Williamson County), stole all the accounting books to protect the names of friends and persons with no deposits at the bank whom he had allowed to overdraft about $80,000. Though he denied it at the time, it was later found that Parrish himself had embezzled over $47,000.[29]

The embattled cashier refused to disclose the location of the record books to the committee. Huntsman could not overstate their importance: "Their destruction would have greatly deranged, if not totally prostrated the institution, consequently, to obtain possession of them was of vital importance to the State; without them, all was disorder in the most important operations of the Government." Desperate to secure the records, the threat of criminal prosecution was taken away and Parrish produced the books. Huntsman delegated a two-man committee[30] to examine them with the new cashier in the short amount of time left in the session. They reported that while the books had not been altered during their absence, the accounts had not been balanced for at least two years and there was not enough time to calculate the financial losses to the bank.[31]

Huntsman gave his committee's report of the "arduous and unpleasant investigation" to the senate on January 13, 1830. Based on what information was known, he concluded that the Bank of the State of Tennessee was solvent, though its "affairs are greatly disorganized and deranged" at the main bank and its county agencies. "To arrive at the actual loss which the State may suffer," he reported, "would require the books to be balanced, and all the Specie and Bank paper to be counted, and the amount of solvent debt due the Bank ascertained." He speculated that a thorough audit by a future committee would take twenty to thirty

---

29. Ibid: 273-274. Parrish had been appointed as cashier of the Bank of the State of Tennessee when it began operation in 1820. He was a nephew of Senator Abram P. Maury Sr. of Williamson County. McBride and Robison, eds. *Biographical Directory* 1: 570-571.

30. The members of the committee were Senator James Campbell of Franklin and Warren counties and Representative Ephraim H. Foster of Davidson County. Ibid: 275.

31. White, ed. *Messages* 2: 274-275

Huntsman's copy of *Acts of the 18th Tennessee General Assembly*.
Courtesy of the Tennessee Room, Jackson-Madison County Library

days at the expense of all other legislative responsibilities. He believed "the loss must be considerable" and recommended that the General Assembly make preparations to close the bank and secure funds from the county agencies that were intended for education and internal improvements. The committee found no fault with the bank president or its directors, except for their "misplaced confidence" in the cashier. As a result of the investigation, future cashiers were appointed by a joint session of the legislature rather than by the bank directors. The bank itself would exist until 1832, when it was replaced by yet another state bank, the Union Bank of the State of Tennessee.[32]

Huntsman continued his efforts to bring funds for internal improvements to his district. He introduced bills to remove obstructions from rivers in the Western District, declare others navigable, and construct

---

32. Ibid: 275-276. Phelan, *Tennessee*: 266-267.

bridges, canals, and roads. On October 23, 1829, he proposed the creation of a four-man commission to dispense state funding for such projects. His initial plan called for three of the four commissioners to come from the Western District, one from Middle Tennessee, but no one to represent East Tennessee! To reiterate his insistence on such an unbalanced alignment, he wrote in his bill's margin a blunt warning: "Let every d—n committee keep its fingers off this bill." Nevertheless his colleagues rejected this stipulation, though the rest of his bill was enacted to establish a commission with a budget of $150,000. But the senator from the Western District did ensure that one-fifth of the funds went toward projects in his section.[33]

As part of Governor Carroll's attempt to reform the state penal system, a bill was presented to the senate in 1829 to authorize the construction of a state penitentiary. It passed by a vote of 12-7 on October 22, but Huntsman opposed it. While he agreed that a penitentiary was needed, he voted against this particular bill because it failed to specify where it would be built and left the decision in the hands of a commission. "And I cannot place interests of so much importance to my constituents in irresponsible hands," he wrote. Despite his objection, the bill was enacted and the commission selected a site at Nashville for its construction, which was completed by the first day of January 1831.[34]

In 1829, the house of representatives passed a bill with recommendations to reform the state judicial system. As chairman of the senate judiciary committee, Huntsman submitted a comprehensive examination of the bill with reasons why each recommendation was needed. In his estimation, the Tennessee judiciary was "the most expensive and least efficient of any in the United States."[35] He argued against various tribunals—justices of the peace, county court, circuit court, and the supreme court—which essentially handled cases with the same subject matter. Such a judicial structure encouraged litigants to incessantly appeal their cases to the next court, much to the inconvenience of jury members who had

---

33. Ibid: 288 fn. Mooney, "Huntsman": 110-111. Owing to the colorful notation made by Huntsman, the author tried unsuccessfully to locate this particular bill at TSLA.

34. White, ed. *Messages* 2: 282-283. Corlew, *Tennessee*: 163-164.

35. Ibid: 292-293. Historian Robert H. White complimented this report by Huntsman on the judiciary bill as "the first really exhaustive report on the court system and its actual modus operandi ever submitted to a Tennessee Legislature." Ibid: 292.

to leave their farms to serve "at the most busy season of the year." "The cause may be continued from term to term for years," he wrote, "during which time, ill will, strife and party animosity not only prevail between the parties litigant, but unfortunately the surrounding neighbors often engage in feuds in consequence of it." Such cases resulted in bankruptcy and ruin for both parties through court expenses while "fattening the officers of the law." The solution Huntsman proposed was to hold jury trials in the circuit courts and eliminate them in the county courts. Should a litigant seek a jury trial in the county court, he would be obligated to pay the expenses for it. He believed there were few justices of the peace with the necessary education and legal knowledge to administer justice in their communities. Appointees were chosen based on their support of the sheriff in his election rather than being "the most enlightened, and best qualified of our citizens." If such patronage continued, he predicted, "the more incompetent will be the county courts."[36]

Huntsman attributed the "great delay" of court cases to attorneys who wasted time "unnecessarily consumed in argument" and judges who would not curtail them. Such time-consuming cases increased court expenses considerably. Estimating the number of days per court term, the number of jurors and constables, and the solicitors' fees, he determined the county courts spent as much as $58,652 a year, some $3,800 more than the expenses of the entire state government—including a session of the General Assembly—during the same period. The figure would increase, he noted, if the costs of incessant appeals were added.[37]

As chairman of the judiciary committee, Huntsman recommended passage of the bill by the senate along with amendments to add three judges and provide twelve circuit courts with original jurisdiction in every criminal case. The bill was initially rejected by an 11-8 vote on November 26, 1829, but the senate voted to reconsider its decision by an identical vote. It lingered for several weeks without a follow-up vote until the house rejected it on December 12 by a vote of 20-17. There was sentiment among constituents and lawmakers that the bill would benefit only

36. Ibid: 293-294
37. Ibid: 294-295

the legal profession because it had been crafted primarily by lawyers and included an amendment for three new judicial circuits.[38]

AS IF TO STRESS the need for judicial reform, the house of representatives approved articles of impeachment in 1829 against Judge Nathaniel W. Williams of the 3rd Judicial Circuit, who was subsequently tried by the senate acting as a Court of Impeachment. Among the charges he faced were carelessness, impulsiveness, falling asleep in court, failing to hold court, and failing to read the court minutes from the previous session. The tumultuous trial began on October 27 and lasted more than two months, resulting in his acquittal by one vote. It was alleged that the proceedings stemmed from personal animosity between Williams and Representative Hopkins L. Turney.[39]

The senators had not even concluded the Williams trial before receiving word in late December that the house had also passed articles of impeachment against Judge Joshua Haskell of the 8th Judicial Circuit in the Western District. Haskell was a popular judge both for his personality and his efficient style of dispensing justice from the bench. At one time he presided over forty cases in seven days, after which he dismissed court for half a day to allow everyone to enjoy refreshments. But the judge was also known to wander outside the courtroom and engage in conversations or personal business while court was still in session.[40]

With the Haskell trial ready to begin, Huntsman asked to be excused as a member of the court because he believed he might be called as a witness by the investigating committee. Such a scenario would require him to determine the credibility of his own testimony, which he felt would be a conflict of interest. Senator James Campbell moved that Huntsman be excused, but the motion was overwhelmingly rejected by a 1-17 vote. As it turned out, Huntsman did not have to judge his own testimony after

---

38. Ibid: 296-297
39. Ibid: 296, 313-314. Huntsman's daughter Paradise later married Nathaniel Washington Williams, a son of Judge Williams, in Madison County, Tennessee on May 30, 1855. Williams family research courtesy of Margaret White.
40. Ibid: 301. Journal of the Court of Impeachment, the State of Tennessee vs. Joshua Haskell contained in Senate Journal (1831). Williams, *Historic Madison*: 67.

all. The legislative session having extended past its regular adjournment time, Representative Andrew L. Martin of Madison County presented a resolution on Christmas Day that Haskell's trial be postponed until the next General Assembly. After an attempt for an indefinite postponement failed, the resolution was eventually approved on January 4, 1830.[41]

When the trial resumed in 1831, Huntsman was no longer a senator, having chosen not to seek reelection. He was called as a witness along with fellow Western District lawyers Joseph H. Talbot, Andrew L. Martin, Alexander B. Bradford, and William Stoddert. He testified that during the trial of one William Walden at Lexington, Tennessee, Judge Haskell left the courtroom for more than an hour and walked to a nearby tavern. He was also seen "looking at some horses" some eighty or one hundred yards from the Henderson County Courthouse. When a problem arose during the trial, someone brought Haskell back to the courtroom. On another occasion, the judge was seen "at a stall where cakes and cider were sold" while court was in session. In the end, he was acquitted by a tied vote and returned to the bench, where he paid more attention to his judicial duties the remainder of his career.[42]

LIKE MOST AMBITIOUS MEN of his day, Huntsman speculated in land—buying and selling large tracts in Madison and other counties in the Western District and elsewhere—to build his wealth. Sometimes he incurred debts for which he was sued by his creditors. In this regard he was not unlike other respected members of the community, many of whom were also susceptible to indebtedness and were brought into court. It was a burden that would plague him for the next nineteen years. One historian who extensively studied circuit and county court records for Madison County noted: "It would take a wizard to untangle the record of indebtedness of the talented and prominent Adam Huntsman. The public records of Madison County for his time are filled with references to indebtedness he owed and for which he was taken to court time and again."[43]

---

41. Senate Journal (1829): 368. White, ed. *Messages* 2: 328-329.
42. White, ed. *Messages* 2: 402-403. Williams, *Historic Madison*: 69.
43. Jonathan K.T. Smith, *Genealogical Abstracts from Antebellum Circuit Court Records, Madison County, Tennessee* (Jackson, TN: Self-published, 1997): 12

One entreprenurial venture almost led to his financial ruin. In July 1829, he invested in a mercantile business with John K. Chester at Chester's corner in Jackson. "Chester & Huntsman" carried an inventory that included cloths, shoes, boots, saddles, saddlebags, books, stationary, and "gentlemen's hats." In December, they advertised the arrival of "winter goods" and "a handsome stock of DOMESTIC GOODS" that included "leather shoes for ladies and children, embroidered belts, [and] belt buckles." An advertisement in the *Jackson Gazette* on December 19 invited "friends and customers to call and see—and [they] promise good goods and fair bargains."[44]

By the spring of 1830, however, Chester & Huntsman had gone out of business and Huntsman was saddled with most of its debts, in addition to those he already owed personally. A friend estimated his total debts from the failed business between $12,000 and $15,000.

In addition to entering into at least two deeds of trust in 1831 and 1832 (likely involving his home and property), Huntsman also had to sell many of his slaves. As executor for the estate of his father-in-law George Todd, Roderick McIver paid $650 from the estate to help Huntsman settle a debt owed to the Second Bank of the United States.[45] A sample of other court judgments against him for personal debts during this period,

---

44. *Jackson Gazette*, January 3, August 8, December 19, 1829; March 13, 1830. Six months before going into business with Huntsman, Chester ended a partnership with F.C. Dulaney at the same location. Dulaney is not listed in the 1830 census for Madison County.

45. Mention of these deeds of trust between Huntsman and Bartholomew Stewart and Andrew L. Martin and James Vaulx is made in Madison County, Tennessee Circuit Court Minute Book Vol. 3: 274, 368. Huntsman's friend Andrew Stewart, a brother of Bartholemew Stewart, an early lawyer in Madison County, recalled that Huntsman was "very much in debt" between 1829 and 1832, as a result of the business failure. "I heard it said by many persons that it would break him," he recalled. "He told me that it would injure him very much." Andrew Stewart document in author's collection. Mention of his debt owed to the Second Bank of the United States is made in Madison County, Tennessee Deed Book 3: 22-23. Five judgments were found against Huntsman and John K. Chester between August 3, 1830, and May 8, 1832 totaling $2,443.07 (or close to $49,334 in modern U.S. dollars accounting for inflation). Madison County, Tennessee Court Minute Book 3: 264, 294, 376. Madison County, Tennessee Circuit Court Minute Book 2: 202, 203, 253, 254. The modern currency calculation was obtained through "The Inflation Calculator" <www.westegg.com/inflation>.

> **ENTIRELY NEW.**
>
> THE undersigned have much pleasure in announcing to their friends and the public generally, that they have just received, and are now opening in the house on Chester's corner, formerly occupied by Chester & Dulaney, an entirely new and general stock of
>
> **Merchandize,**
>
> consisting, in part, of Super black, blue and brown cloths and cassimeres; a great variety of sattinets and cassimeres; black and gray lastings; bleached and brown drillings; Irish linens, linen cambrics, and linen cambric handkerchiefs; super Italian lutestring, and gros de Naples; seashawls, florences, ass'd colours, Canton & Italian crape; a large and splendid stock of fancy prints, newest style; berage, gauze, Italian lutestring; gros de naples; fancy and madrass handkerchiefs; fancy garnetures, painted belts, belt and cap ribbonds; 3, 4, 5 & 6-4 bleached and brown sheetings & shirtings; plaid and stripe domestics; brown linens, ticklenburgs & ducks of every description; silk and cotton hasury, umbrellas, parasols, leghorn bonnets, patent stocks, ladie's prunella and lasting shoes & boots; gentlemen's hats; boots, shoes & pumps; saddles, bridles, martingales and saddle bags; books & stationary; together with
>
> **Queensware, Groceries, &c. &c.**
>
> all of which they offer cheap for cash, or on accommodating terms to punctual men.
>
> Jackson, july 11-tf   CHESTER & HUNTSMAN.

Advertisement for Chester & Huntsman published in the *Jackson Gazette*, July 11, 1829

both individually and jointly with others, totaled $4,038.88, or $81,558.77 in modern funds.[46]

---

46. Thirteen judgments against Huntsman between May 5, 1829, and November 12, 1832, were found in Madison County, Tennessee Court Minute Book 3: 76, 134, 164, 179, 204, 205, 221, 283, 310, 460, 463,

Chapter Four

Davy of the River Country

1831–1833

And it came to pass in those days when Andrew was chief ruler over the children of Columbia, that there arose a mighty man in the river country, whose name was David: he belonging to the tribe of Tennessee, which lay upon the border of the Mississippi and over against Kentucky.

David was a man wise in council, smooth in speech, valiant in war, and of fair countenance and goodly stature, such was the terror of his exploits, that thousands of wild cats and panthers did quake and tremble at his name.

—The Book of Chronicles, 1831

On June 21, 1828, a letter written by "A Voter" was published in the *Jackson Gazette*. It stated that voters in the Spring Creek community of northeast Madison County would support Adam Huntsman if he would be a candidate for representative of the 9th Congressional District in the 1829 election. At the time, it was the second largest district in the country with 22,000 voters. It contained eighteen counties, fifteen between the Mississippi and Tennessee rivers and the remainder

David Crockett had been on friendly terms with Huntsman before turning against President Jackson in 1831. Afterward, Huntsman became his primary antagonist both in the newspapers and on the campaign trail in the 1831, 1833, and 1835 congressional elections.

Courtesy of the Library of Congress

stretching across the Tennessee to include Hardin, Wayne, and Lawrence counties in southwest Middle Tennessee.[1]

The incumbent representative was David Crockett, who ten months earlier had been elected to his first term. His prior experience had been two terms served in the state house of representatives, where his backwoods background earned him the unflattering moniker from a more refined colleague as the "gentleman from the cane." But it was his humble background and homespun humor that made him such a popular figure in the Western District. Many voters saw in him a reflection of themselves, an honest yeoman farmer and hunter with a straight forward personality, a self-directed sense of humor, and a talent for telling funny stories. Professing his loyalty to the presidential aspirations of General Andrew Jackson, Crockett beat incumbent Adam Rankin Alexander in the 1827 election and rode the crest of Old Hickory's popularity that won a majority for the Jacksonians in both houses of Congress.[2]

Huntsman responded to the appeal for his candidacy in a letter published in the *Jackson Gazette* on July 5. He declined to run, claiming his private affairs had been neglected in service to his constituents both in the Western District and in the Mountain District for the past thirteen years; they would need his attention "for sometime to come." He reasoned that if a man could not properly take care of his own business, he should not accept responsibility for the people's business, "nor is he the man who should be trusted" with it. But he did use the forum to take issue with what he felt was the "disgraceful" style of political campaigning that had become accepted practice "on the part of some candidates" in the Western District. Without naming him specifically, Huntsman expounded upon the "degrading and contemptible" tactics of courting voters with liquor, tactics similar to those Crockett had employed several months earlier:

> To go up creeks, down valleys, over hills, and into dales
> for the purpose of collecting votes, as a tax gatherer would

---

1. *Jackson Gazette* June 21, 1828, July 5, 1828. Mark Derr, *The Frontiersman: The Real Life and Many Legends of Davy Crockett* (New York: William Morrow and Company, 1993): 128.

2. William C. Davis, *Three Roads to the Alamo: The Lives and Fortunes of David Crockett, James Bowie, and William Barret Travis* (New York: HarperCollins, 1998): 77-78.

his tax, or a cow driver to buy cattle; and in doing this, frequently propagates or gives currency to lies, slanders, and detractions against other candidates, is so far descending beneath the dignity of man, or the independence of a correct politician, that I would not condescend to such an act of degradation to be President of the United States. Add to this the pitiful practice of endeavoring to buy up free men's votes with a half pint of *white-face* CORN WHISKEY; all of which, sooner or later, meets with the merited condemnation of an enlightened public.[3]

The candidate who adopted such tricks to win votes could not be trusted, he reasoned. "Does he not want to serve himself at the expense of the public? I have no doubt if sufficient temptations were thrown in his way, he would sacrifice the interest of his constituents to his own advantage; for it is impossible that he can have either dignity of mind or independence of character, which would form safeguards or protections to our rights and liberties." Huntsman was not opposed to a candidate "mixing with the people" to learn their thoughts on the issues and give them the opportunity to determine the qualifications of the candidate. But it was wrong to gain one's vote for the price of "a half pint of *still burnt whiskey*," he argued, and "cheat him out of his birth right"—the right to vote without outside influence or coercion.

But in the end, Huntsman attributed his decision not to oppose Crockett to his modest belief that his meager education and his inability to abandon his legal practice to study the "science of government and politics in all its aspects" made him unqualified to serve as a congressman. The fact that he was undoubtedly more qualified than the incumbent was not lost on readers of his letter. In truth, his decision had

---

3. *Jackson Gazette* July 5, 1828. The editor of the *Gazette* disagreed with Huntsman's opinion about mixing liquor and politics."We are opposed to drinking whiskey, or treating as it is termed, to excess; but for all our lives we cannot see the evil that can result from the candidates associating with the people, and if an opportunity occurs, taking a small 'horn' with them." Using such tools, he noted that "most of our candidates are pretty good hands at 'electioneering.'" Ibid March 7, 1829.

more to do with Crockett's popularity at the time than Huntsman's purported sense of legislative inferiority.[4]

CROCKETT'S PRIMARY FOCUS in Congress was to secure a land bill favorable to the occupant settlers in the Western District, enabling them to secure clear titles to lands on which they had settled and improved. It was a common goal he shared with other members of the Tennessee congressional delegation who wanted the federal government to relinquish its claims to the unappropriated lands. But they disagreed about who should receive them. His colleagues wanted the lands turned over to the Tennessee General Assembly, which would likely sell them to the highest bidders and use the proceeds to finance public education in the state. Crockett knew such an arrangement would exclude the cash poor occupants whom he wanted to help, who could not afford to pay twelve-and-one-half cents per acre and an additional fifty cents per acre to have it surveyed. They would be forced to leave the land they had worked to clear and cultivate and where they had built their homes. And thanks to speculators who held North Carolina land warrants bought from Revolutionary War veterans and their families, it would not be the first time they had been forced from their homes. Instead, he wanted the lands either to be sold or given directly to the occupants who already lived on them.[5]

Over the next four years, Crockett worked to enact a land bill that would benefit the occupants and not the speculators. He no longer trusted that the state legislature would use the proceeds toward public education, believing instead they would go to colleges and universities where the children of the poor squatters he represented would never attend. Public and often heated disagreements with members of his own state delegation, much to the delight of General Jackson's enemies in the House, revealed fractures in the Jackson ranks. Crockett began associating with the allies of President John Quincy Adams, including Joseph Gales, co-publisher of the pro-Adams newspaper in Washington, the *National Intelligencer,* and *Gales and Seaton's Register of Debates in Congress.* Fellow Tennessean

---

4. Ibid
5. James R. Boylston and Allen J. Wiener, *David Crockett in Congress: The Rise and Fall of the Poor Man's Friend* (Houston, TX: Bright Sky Press, 2009): 27-31. Davis, *Three Roads*: 130-131, 137-139.

James K. Polk claimed Gates was rewriting speeches for Crockett "which he never delivered as reported, & which all who know him, know he never did." To a fellow Jacksonian back home, Polk wrote: "Rely upon it he can be and has been operated upon by our enemies. We cant trust him an inch."[6]

Despite his break with the Jacksonians in his delegation, Crockett still professed his loyalty to the man himself, newly-inaugurated President Andrew Jackson, and remained a popular incumbent going into his reelection campaign in 1829. Initially, the Jacksonians had trouble drafting a candidate to oppose him. Huntsman's name along with a Dresden attorney named William Fitzgerald, General John W. Cooke, and former congressman Adam Rankin Alexander were brought up in the *Jackson Gazette*. Once again Huntsman declined, stating he was already a candidate for reelection to the state senate. Alexander eventually accepted the challenge. Despite the fact that Crockett had failed to secure the land bill he had promised, he handily defeated his old nemesis a second time, 6,773 votes to 3,641.[7]

Crockett tried several times during his second term to pass his own version of the land bill, an effort that now dominated his legislative agenda. In December 1829, he managed to remove it from Polk's Committee on Public Lands to a select committee that he himself chaired, thanks to support from the National Republicans loyal to Henry Clay. Despite backing down and returning to his initial proposals of an endowment for public education and twelve-and-one-half cents per acre instead of free acreage, his bill was tabled until the House reconvened for the second session. It was another political failure for Crockett and left him little to show his constituents as he prepared for his reelection campaign back home in 1831.[8]

IF THERE WAS ANY DOUBT in the voters' minds that Crockett had indeed left the Jacksonians, it was confirmed by a sixteen-page circular he published on February 28, 1831. It was a scathing attack against the Jackson administration that criticized the president's position against national

---

6. Derr, *Frontiersman*: 152. Davis, *Three Roads*: 139
7. *Jackson Gazette*, April 4, 1829. Davis, *Three Roads*: 170.
8. Davis, *Three Roads*: 172-174, 179.

internal improvements, his desire to seek reelection after disavowing the practice, and his determination to remove the remaining Native American Indian tribes from their lands and force them west of the Mississippi River. Crockett defended his position:

> I thought with him, as he thought before he was President: he has altered his opinion—I have not changed mine. I have not left the principles which led me to support General Jackson: he has left them and me; and I will not surrender my independence to follow his new opinions, taught by interested and selfish advisors, and which may again be remolded under the influence of passion and cunning.[9]

At the time, Crockett believed Huntsman shared his distrust of Andrew Jackson. Both men were on friendly terms and had exchanged letters while Crockett was in Washington. Huntsman had told him about Old Hickory's condemnation of state legislators in 1820 who supported the proposed state-owned bank and his own strongly worded response to it.[10]

But Huntsman's attitude had softened by the time Jackson became a presidential candidate in 1824. The Old Hero was invited in 1825 to visit Jackson, the town named for him, and Huntsman was among community leaders who welcomed him. Two years later, at a dinner held at Vauxhall Garden in Nashville attended by such notable state political figures as U.S. Senators Hugh Lawson White and John H. Eaton, Congressman John Bell, Governor Sam Houston, his predecessor William Carroll, and Jackson himself, Huntsman raised his glass and toasted: "May the next administration be composed of a tough Hickory with two prongs, one to whip the Hartford Conventionists, the other the anti-republicans, out of

---

9. James Atkins Shackford, *David Crockett: The Man and the Legend* (Lincoln, NE: University of Nebraska Press, 1986): 130.

10. Jackson *Southern Statesman*, July 30, 1831. Crockett alludes to correspondence between himself and Huntsman, but no letters between them have survived. In hindsight, Crockett called Huntsman's letters "deceitful," as Huntsman used them publicly alongside ones written by Andrew Jackson to discredit Crockett during the 1831 congressional campaign.

the United States." In 1828, he once again supported Jackson's candidacy and "used every *honorable means* to promote it."[11]

In the fall of 1830, the president wanted a new voice to promote his administration to the Democratic party faithful. The *United States Telegraph*, edited by Duff Green, held this honor for the first two years of Jackson's presidency. But he felt Green did not effectively or enthusiastically defend his administration, and the opinions expressed in his editorials ran counter to Jackson's positions on nullification and the Second Bank of the United States. With the president's blessing, his advisor Amos Kendall and editor Francis P. Blair created a new Washington-based newspaper called the *Globe* that would eventually wrest the mantle of administration mouthpiece from the *Telegraph*.[12]

The Washington *Daily National Journal*, an anti-Jackson paper, charged the president with abusing his franking privilege to solicit subscribers for the *Globe*. Its editor, Peter Force, used as evidence a letter Jackson had written to "a distinguished Senator of the Legislature of Tennessee" in December 1830, that reportedly sought the unnamed senator's help procuring subscribers and included a prospectus for the newspaper.[13]

When he learned of the allegation, Huntsman presumed the editor of the *Daily National Journal* was referring to him. He denied the charge made against Jackson, insisting that the president had sent him a copy of the *Globe* in order to read his Annual Message to Congress. While acknowledging that franking "is most corruptly used" by some politicians, Huntsman did not know whether the president had done so. But based on what he had seen in his travels throughout the Western District in the spring of 1831, David Crockett had done his part to import anti-Jackson documents into the region utilizing this taxpayer funded method. "I have seen hundreds of Holmes', Clayton's, Everett's, and Chilton's circulars, in pamphlet form, most from twenty to thirty pages, also Burgess's

---

11. Washington D.C. *United States Telegraph*, October 30, 1827. The dinner for White in Nashville was held on September 29, 1827.

12. Robert V. Remini, *Andrew Jackson and the Course of American Freedom* (New York: Harper & Row, 1981): 292

13. Washington D.C. *Daily National Journal*, May 6, 1831

speeches, distributed every where, and piles of them in the post-offices, all of which have been franked all the way here to abuse General Jackson."[14]

Interestingly, Huntsman conceded that the same mail which brought Jackson's letter—by coincidence—had also included copies of the prospectus for the *Globe*. And he had indeed recruited subscribers for the fledgling Washington paper, but for personal reasons and not at the urging of the president. "There is such a spirit of licentiousness, slander, and vituperation" in both the *Telegraph* and the *National Journal*, he felt, that "if I was sitting as a juror, and any political subject was submitted to me for determination...I would not believe [editors] Duff Green or Peter Force upon oath." Therefore, he "was anxious for the establishment of another paper at Washington City." The fact that Jackson's letter to him had become public knowledge he attributed to "a Clay Lawyer among us" when he shared it with colleagues attending the Supreme Court session at Jackson in December 1830.[15]

Because of the implications against Jackson, portions of Huntsman's letter received national attention in various newspapers. One New York correspondent took Huntsman to task for assuming "he must be the Senator referred to, because...he thought himself the only 'distinguished' one...Such was his droll logic."[16] Thomas Washington, a Nashville attorney who had seen Jackson's letter, came forward to contradict Huntsman's claim that it was "a private letter." In fact, it had been passed around freely among members of the bar attending the Supreme Court, he stated, and its implications for the future of the *Telegraph* as Jackson's official organ had been a topic of discussion among them.

> It is really amusing, to one who knows Mr. Huntsman, and witnessed the use of the letter in question, now to see him make such a flourish of trumpets about the

---

14. *Richmond Enquirer*, June 17, 1831. Huntsman refers to congressmen John Holmes of Maine, John M. Clayton of Delaware, Edward Everett of Massachusetts, Thomas Chilton of Kentucky, and Tristam Burges of Rhode Island, all opponents of the Jackson administration.

15. *Washington* (D.C.) *Globe*, June 15, 1831. Huntsman also noted: "I was anxious for another paper; I thought it [the Globe] would be better—I knew it could not be worse." Ibid.

16. Ibid. *Richmond Enquirer*, June 17, 1831. *New York Spectator*, June 28, 1831.

sacredness of private confidence. So far from its having been confidentially shown...he seemed to take pleasure in exhibiting it, and that his vanity was sensibly operated upon, by the simple circumstance of having received a letter from the President of the United States.[17]

Washington challenged Huntsman to produce the letter and reveal whether it actually contained the *Globe* prospectus in question. It was a challenge that went unanswered. Although he wished no ill feelings by Huntsman toward him, he concluded that "the most material misrepresentation...[is] that in which Mr. Huntsman is spoken of as a distinguished Senator—the writer meant thereby, *elevated* distinction."[18]

NOW THAT DAVID CROCKETT had finally revealed his true feelings toward Andrew Jackson, the president's supporters were ready for his return to the Western District in the spring of 1831. Their candidate, William Fitzgerald, had declared his intention to oppose Crockett exactly one year before the election. The campaign would be a referendum whether the voters supported President Jackson or their independent-minded congressman. As for Jackson himself, he made his wishes clear to his nephew-in-law Samuel Jackson Hays, who lived in Madison County: "I trust for the honor of the state, your Congressional District will not disgrace themselves longer by sending that profligate man Crockett back to Congress."[19]

The Jacksonians did everything they could to ensure it would not happen, and the campaign on both sides became personal and vindictive. Battles were waged on the stump and in the press, with Huntsman leading the fight for Fitzgerald on the pages of the Jackson *Southern Statesman*. Crockett now knew what it felt like to be the prey and not the hunter. "I was hunted down like a wild varment and in this hunt every little newspaper in the district, and every pin-hook lawyer was engaged. Indeed,

---

17. Washington D.C. *Daily National Journal*, June 30, 1831
18. Ibid
19. AJ to Samuel Jackson Hays, April 23, 1831, published in Williams, *Historic Madison*: 403

they were ready to print any and every thing that the ingenuity of man could invent against me."[20]

The most ingenious contributions were made by Huntsman in the form of political satires designed to use Crockett's most effective weapon—humor—against him. His first creation was a humorous twist on Crockett's declaration of independence from Jackson. He placed a mock advertisement in the *Southern Statesman* on March 26, 1831, under the name of "Western District." In the style of notices seeking the recovery of a lost horse or slave, he anxiously sought the whereabouts of the wayward representative who had left the Jackson fold.

> GOING! GOING! GONE!
>
> Strayed or stolen from the Jackson ranks, a certain Member of Congress, from the Western District, named **DAVID CROCKETT**. Davy is upwards of six feet high, erect in his posture, and has a nose extremely red, after taking some spirits. He possesses vast bodily powers; great activity, and can leap the Ohio, wade the Mississippi, and carry one stream and two flat boats upon his back. He can vault across a streak of lightning, ride it down a honey locust; grease his heels, stake down a rainbow, and whip his weight in wildcats and panthers. Davy took the bounty in the Western District, enlisted in the Jackson ranks, and performed prodigies of valour, in divers engagements, between the Jacksonites and the Adams boys. He defeated and put to flight the celebrated John C. Wright, by comparing him to a Monkey, with spectacles on.[21] He demolished the "Little Prince," by telling him

---

20. Crockett, *Narrative*: 207

21. John C. Wright served with Crockett in the 20th Congress (1827-29). In the winter of 1827, Crockett and Wright were among a group of lawmakers who attended an exhibit of wild animals in Washington. One colleague pointed out a monkey riding a pony and asked, "Crockett, don't that monkey favour General Jackson?" Crockett responded, "It looks like one of your boarders, Mr. [Wright] of Ohio." When he turned around, Wright was standing there. "I was in a right awkward fix," he recalled, "but I bowed...and told 'em, 'I had either slandered the monkey, or Mr. [Wright], of Ohio, and if they would tell me which, I would beg his pardon.'" James Strange French, *Sketches*

that the people in the Western District danced all their toe nails off, at Saturday night frolics;[22] & grinned a panther to death at Washington city (as he says).

From the above description, it is presumed he will be well known. Some twelve or eighteen months ago, it was observed that certain uncercumcised Politicians, to wit: [Daniel] Webster, [David] Barton, and [Thomas] Chilton, who are famous for their political thieveries, were hovering round upon the outskirts of the Jackson ranks, in order, as it is supposed, to pilfer whatever they could lay their hands upon, and steal, take and carry away the aforesaid Davy. Whether they have succeeded in the *felony*, or whether Davy has strayed away of his own accord, is yet unknown. The last that has been heard of him, he was riding towards Yankee land, upon a broken poney, which he called **OCCUPANT**. Occupant is a noble little fellow; he has made many daring plunges, and would (if he had been well kept) performed several journies to Congress; but this daring animal he is getting lean and gaunt, for the want of more substantial food, for it seems he can get nothing out of Uncle Sam's crib.

Whoever will bring the said Davy back, chaste and sound, to the Jackson ranks, shall be entitled to receive a reward

---

and Eccentricities of Colonel David Crockett, of West Tennessee (New York: J. & J. Harper, 1833): 178. According to another account, Crockett had said about the monkey, "If he only wore a pair of goggles, he would be as much like Mr. W. as two peas." *Haverhill* (MA) *Gazette*, December 20, 1839.

22. Huntsman refers to a conversation between Crockett and a son of President John Quincy Adams (perhaps his private secretary, John Adams II) after a dinner party at the Executive Mansion. The younger Adams (the "Little Prince") asked Crockett how people entertained themselves "in the backwoods." Believing his intention was to make fun of him, Crockett facetiously explained that there were four classes of people on the frontier. Their particular forms of entertainment ranged from men playing billiards to women who liked "to frolic" and dance in the woods to the sounds of a banjo. "May be, you think they don't go their death upon a jib," said Crockett, "but they do, for I have frequently gone there the next morning, and raked up my two hands full of toe nails," French, *Sketches and Eccentricities*: 172-173.

therefor[e] fifty copies of Hull's surrender to the British, at Detroit; fifty copies of Governor [Caleb] Strong's proclamation, forbidding the Militia of Massachusetts to fight for their country; twenty-five copies of the proceedings of the Hartford convention, and by way of good measure, I will throw in a few copies of the Harrisburg letter and Coffin Handbills. And if the taker up will bring little *Occupant*, he shall, in addition to the above receive one hundred newly manufactured bluelights."[23]

Huntsman's parody was reprinted in newspapers outside the Western District. One editor, keeping with its narrative spirit, felt obligated to warn his readers about Crockett: "We thought it our duty, to give publicity to the foregoing, that a man who can perform such terrible feats, may be at once arrested, and restrained from kicking up a dust with steamboats, thunder and lightning, and the Jackson Party."[24]

But his most effective literary contribution was the satire entitled "The Book of Chronicles, West of the Tennessee, and East of the Mississippi Rivers," which appeared in the *Southern Statesman* on June 25. Its prose resembled those of the Bible, describing the rise and fall of David who "belonged to the tribe of Tennessee, which lay upon the border of the Mississippi and over against Kentucky." He was "a man wise in council, smooth in speech, valiant in war, and of fair countenance and goodly

---

23. *Southern Statesman*, March 26, 1831. The rewards Huntsman offers are various acts of deception and cowardice during the War of 1812: Brig. Gen. William Hull's surrender of Detroit to British and Native American forces that he actually outnumbered; Massachusetts Gov. Caleb Strong's refusal to allow his state's militia to serve in America's defense; and the Hartford Convention, a secret meeting of New England Federalists opposed to the war that advocated secession from the Union. The "Harrisburg letter" may refer to a memorial drafted by a convention at Harrisburg, PA in August 1827, that supported a tariff beneficial to New England manufacturers and farmers. The Coffin Handbills were campaign propaganda used in the 1828 presidential campaign by supporters of John Quincy Adams describing the executions of six militiamen during the Creek Indian War that were ordered by General Andrew Jackson. "Bluelights" likely refers to members of the old Federalist party who were now aligned with Henry Clay and the National Republicans. During the War of 1812, U.S. naval officer Stephen Decatur believed his nighttime attempt to break through the British blockade at New London, Connecticut had been thwarted by anti-war Federalists who shined blue lights from the shore.

24. *Southern Statesman*, May 21, 1831, reprinted from a newspaper called the *Sun*.

stature, such was the terror of his exploits, that thousands of wild cats and panthers did quake and tremble at his name." David had been sent to "the grand Sanhedrim" (Congress) where he was "beguiled" by lawmakers who were opposed to "Andrew [who] was chief Ruler over the Children of Columbia." He then spread lies and deceit about Andrew among the people to advance his own reelection. But the people saw through them, for they "were a stiff-necked generation, and would not agree that David should bring Henry [Clay] to be chief ruler over the children of Columbia." Instead they were determined to "vote for William, whose surname is Fitzgerald—and the people all said AMEN!" It was such an effective and humorous piece that it was reprinted in pamphlet form for wider distribution as well as in the book *The Life and Adventures of Colonel David Crockett of West Tennessee*, the first biography of Crockett, published in 1833.[25]

Huntsman composed a second chapter to his Chronicles that appeared in the *Southern Statesman* on July 16. Now claiming its creation as "Adam the scribe," he continued the story of David, who sought spiritual counsel from a Baptist minister in Gibson County named Roland Cook (whom Huntsman called "Roland the High Priest") to learn "what I must do to be saved in this election." According to Adam's tale, Roland went out amongst David's followers and told them that the Tennessee legislature was against the occupants. Roland himself opposed public education, Adam wrote, because "if the people get learning and education, they will quickly discover that David is unqualified to be our wise man" in Congress. David distributed campaign literature to the people in order to discredit William, while denying them the truth as recorded in the journals of Congress. But once again, the people would not allow themselves to be deceived or permit David to turn them over to "the uncircumcized Yankees and the Claytonites, the Websterites and the Chiltonites." William was their choice, while David was sent back to "the Priestly land of wild cats and Panthers."[26]

---

25. *Southern Statesman*, June 25, 1831. A subsequent edition of *Life and Adventures of Crockett* was French, *Sketches and Eccentricities*: 129-136.

26. *Southern Statesman*, July 16, 1831. Huntsman refers to Rep. John M. Clayton of Delaware, Sen. Daniel Webster of Massachusetts, and Rep. Thomas Chilton of Kentucky.

David Crockett giving a stump speech
Life of David Crockett (1860)

The Chronicles were such an effective campaign tool that Crockett responded to them in like fashion. Writing in the third person and using a similar Biblical dialect, he pointed out Huntsman's hypocrisy regarding his recent support of President Jackson. "Will thee be so good as to tell David," he wrote, "what is to be thy reward for this strange somerset of this distinguished Senator, who was carrying on a correspondence with Andrew the Chief ruler, during the last Congress, and at the same time was writing deceitful letters to David and exhibiting David's letters and Andrew's publicly, and saying that David or the President had one or the other lied." He denied a charge made against him by Huntsman that he had franked $130 in postage for books sent to a friend and demanded that he retract it. "David did have a better opinion of Adam," he wrote, "than to believe he would have joined the little yelpers, which have been after his heels for the last four years." He promised in the future "not to neglect Adam: no not even when Adam shall make the attempt to go to the great Sanhedrim."[27]

The hostility of the newspaper war only intensified on the campaign trail. At one point it was even rumored in a neighboring state that Crockett had been shot while making a speech, but the report was soon refuted.[28]

---

27. *Southern Statesman*, July 30, 1831. An anonymous writer claiming to be "William" chastised "his friend Adam" for making "false, foolish, and insignificant" charges against Crockett in the Chronicles. If Adam did not know the statements were false, "he certainly is a much greater ass than I ever thought him to be." Whether it was written by Crockett or one of his supporters is uncertain. Jackson Southern Statesman, July 9, 1831.

28. *Florence* (AL) *Gazette*, May 1831, reprinted in the Jackson *Southern Statesman*, May 20, 1831. *Rhode Island American and Gazette*, June 3, 1831. In Shackford, *Crockett*: 132-133, the author relates an incident that supposedly occurred in Paris, Tennessee during the campaign. Fitzgerald had accused Crockett of certain misdeeds and Crockett threatened to "thrash" him if the accusations were repeated. At the joint speaking engagement, Fitzgerald rose to speak and placed an object concealed by a handkerchief on the table in front of him. He repeated the charges and claimed he could prove them. Sitting in the audience, Crockett said he would refute them "and whip the little lawyer that would repeat [them]." Fitzgerald reiterated his claim and Crockett rose from his seat and charged the platform. When Crockett was three feet from him, Fitzgerald retrieved the object hidden beneath the handkerchief, a pistol that he pointed at his opponent's chest and threatened to fire if he came any closer. Crockett stepped back off the platform and returned to his seat. This incident is questionable and thus excluded from the narrative. The source cited by Shackford—written by a "correspondent of the Nashville Banner" from Paris, Tennessee and published forty years after the election—by his own admission contains many inaccuracies. For further details, see Shackford, *Crockett*: 305, footnote 21.

As the campaign drew to a close, Crockett claimed Fitzgerald and his supporters—"the little four-pence-ha' penny limbs of the law"—would advertise his appearance at speaking engagements without his knowledge. When the people would gather to hear him, the "small fry of lawyers would be there, with their saddle-bags full of the little newspapers and their journals of Congress" and proclaim that he was afraid to show. Crockett blamed this scheme for his defeat to Fitzgerald, 8,534 votes to 7,948.[29]

BY THE TIME Crockett challenged Fitzgerald again in 1833, the General Assembly had divided the cumbersome 9th Congressional District into two separate districts. But the one for which Crockett would now run, the 12th District, had obviously been designed to favor the incumbent. It was comprised of the northern counties of the Western District—Obion, Dyer, Weakley, Gibson, Henry, and Carroll—and Madison County, which had voted against Crockett in the previous election. "The liberal legislature, of course, gave [Fitzgerald] that county," Crockett remarked, "and it is too clear to admit of dispute, that it was done to make a marsh of me." With the gerrymandered Madison County included, it was "the most unreasonably laidoff [district] of any in the state or perhaps in the nation, or even in the te-total creation."[30]

Crockett approached Huntsman in March 1833 and asked that he not write any Chronicles and other newspaper articles against him in the upcoming election. Huntsman agreed, but only if Crockett promised to conduct his campaign in a "gentlemanly" manner and "quit all slanders, charges and vituperations" against Fitzgerald as he had done in the previous election. A month later, Crockett sought his help to mediate a truce between himself and Fitzgerald. Crockett suggested that Fitzgerald make speaking engagements where he had already spoken in Dyer, Obion, and Henry counties, and then both candidates could hold joint

---

29. Crockett, *Narrative*: 208. When the election concluded, the editor of the *Southern Statesman* apologized to his readers, admitting that his and other newspapers in the Western District had been used as "vehicles of transportation" for each candidates' "baggage." As a result, he had lost many subscribers and promised in the future to "be devoted to subjects affording more amusement and instruction to our readers." *Southern Statesman*, August 6, 1831.

30. Shackford, *Crockett*: 141. Crockett, *Narrative*: 208-209.

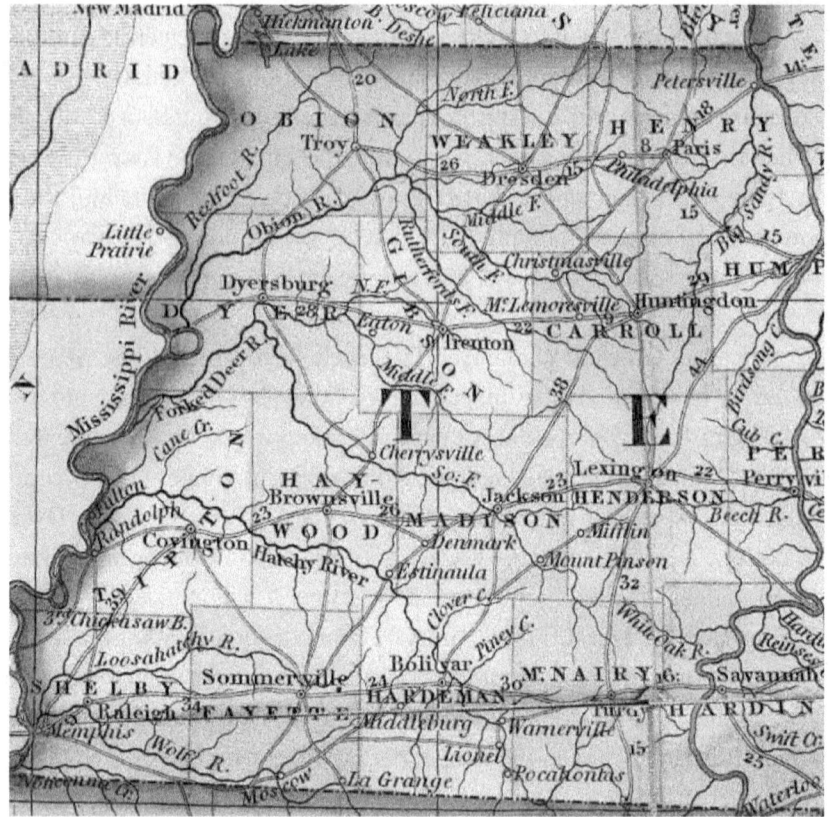

The Western District (present-day West Tennessee) in 1834

engagements in Gibson, Madison, and Haywood counties before mutually ending their campaigns. Though Fitzgerald and his supporters doubted he would uphold the agreement, Huntsman reassured them that he saw no deception in Crockett's proposal and Fitzgerald agreed to abide by it.[31]

The campaign proceeded through the spring and both candidates respected the truce, sticking to the issues and resisting personal attacks. In May, according to Huntsman, Crockett made a speech in Jackson that "went beyond what I considered a friendly canvass but not so much as to produce a rupture." But a rupture was not long in coming. During a speech at Brownsville, Crockett produced a letter written by an anonymous source that claimed Fitzgerald had swindled "a

31. AH to William R. Harris, June 19, 1833, published in the *Southern Statesman*, June 29, 1833.

good deal of money" from the federal government. Huntsman labeled it "a gross violation of every principle of honorable electioneering" and "a palpable violation of the agreement what I was instrumental in making." He felt betrayed by Crockett and released Fitzgerald from the agreement. When word reached him that Crockett had boasted on the stump that he was friendly toward his campaign, Huntsman made it clear that such was not the case. "I cannot support any man who changes his politics as often as he changes his coat," he wrote, "for if he is with me today, there is no certainty that he will be tomorrow."

> When I first knew Col. Crockett, say ten of 12 years ago, he was a thorough going anti-Jackson man, and voted against Gen. Jackson for Senator in Congress. Shortly afterwards he turned a somerset, and came out a *whole-hog* Jacksonian, and offered for Congress...But you find him in 1829-30, turning a somerset again, and going over to the opposition *horse foot and dragoon*. He then wrote a circular against Gen. Jackson, denounced him in his speeches, and franked a great many abusive pamphlets against him, which I saw myself. Now he has thrown another somerset; he has come out for Gen. Jackson's Proclamation [against nullification], for the enforcing bill, and against the doctrines of nullification, and has got to be a good and true Jackson man again—so far as his professions go.[32]

Absolving himself from the promise he had made to Crockett, Huntsman penned a letter under the name of "A Citizen of Madison," seeking to discredit the anonymous letter that Crockett insisted "every man in the District should see...before the election" and expose its mysterious author. The letter charged Fitzgerald with fraudulently overcharging the federal government some four or five hundred dollars for mileage between his home in Weakley County and Washington. But Huntsman

32. Ibid

argued that the informant had miscalculated. According to his own figures, Fitzgerald lived 834 miles from Washington by the stage route, which doubled would have been 1,668 miles and not 1,800 as Crockett's anonymous informant claimed. "This miserable trickery cannot be played off upon any well informed man, but it may do to gull the ignorant," he wrote. As for the identity of the letter writer, Huntsman speculated that it was one Dennis Nally, a Washington attorney who had accompanied Crockett back home and for a short time practiced law and taught school in Trenton. Nally was a dishonest man as well as a "female slanderer and money filcher," Huntsman claimed, who left town owing money to several local attorneys.[33]

Huntsman then scrutinized Crockett's mileage records to and from Washington in the 21st Congress, which had been five weeks shorter than Fitzgerald's tenure in the 22nd Congress. Crockett had received $2,200, some $192 more than Fitzgerald was credited with receiving in the anonymous letter. Still, Huntsman was certain "those incorrigible Crockettites," when presented with such deception, would remain loyal to him even "if father Abraham was to descend from above and tell them."[34]

Crockett responded to both Fitzgerald and Huntsman in a letter published in the *Southern Statesman* on July 20. He claimed the anonymous letter was retaliation after Fitzgerald told a gathering at Denmark in Madison County "that he had been laying up artillery and ammunition for the political war with me, for the last two years." Crockett challenged Fitzgerald "to fire the biggest gun he had," confident that the charges would be baseless. The next day in Brownsville, he put Fitzgerald on the spot and in front of three hundred voters pressed him to answer if the mileage figures given in the letter were correct. "I never charged Mr. Fitzgerald with swindling," Crockett disingenuously wrote. "I only asked him if it was true or false."

Turning his attention to Fitzgerald's accomplice, Crockett bestowed upon Huntsman a new moniker in place of the one he had used in the paper. "I can only say, that Black Hawk is not the man that I thought

33. *Southern Statesman*, July 6, 1833
34. Ibid

he was," he wrote. "I did think that piece [in the *Southern Statesman*] emenated from some poor little possum headed lawyer. I have cut open many possum's heads to hunt for brains and I never found any; therefore, I considered some little pin hook lawyer without brains was the author of that piece, and that old Black Hawk believing in his mental powers, took it on himself."

Crockett admitted that Dennis Nally had traveled with him from Washington to Tennessee, but he did not attribute the anonymous letter to him. He charged Fitzgerald with overextending his congressional franking privilege past the time period allotted to lawmakers in order to mail copies of his speeches to voters in Madison and Haywood counties a month before the election. He even speculated facetiously that Huntsman supported Fitzgerald simply because "he thought he could get the law extended to frank these little possum headed lawyers from one court to another as they cannot get fees enough to pay their expenses."[35]

A week later, Huntsman responded in a letter published under his own name. "I never meddle in elections except when *principal* and *truth* require me to speak," he declared. He held no personal animosity toward Crockett and thanked him for the new name. "[A]s you have named me after a distinguished Indian Chief," he wrote, "I hope you will become more kind to me, as I recollect on a certain former occasion you talked much about your 'heart bleeding for the poor Indians.'"

Keeping with Native American custom, Huntsman proposed that he and Crockett "light up the *pipe of friendship* while I tell over your political sins, which have rendered you unworthy of the favor of the people of this District." Among them were breaking the agreement with Fitzgerald to conduct an honest campaign and not mutually ending the canvass at the same time. Even Crockett's religious conversion could not keep him from returning to his "old way," which was to slander his opponent. "Your mode of electioneering is to claim the votes of the people because your competitor is a rogue," Huntsman wrote. "It matters not what opinions you may entertain, or what course you pursue, your competitor is kept continually on his trial for crimes and misdemeanors charged against

---

35. *Southern Statesman*, July 20, 1833

him by you! That this is the true character of every canvass with you, I appeal to the people."[36]

When voters asked Crockett to substantiate his allegation that Fitzgerald had overcharged his mileage, he claimed he had written to officials in Washington asking for evidence but without success so close to the August election.[37] Huntsman refuted his claim, stating that Secretary of the Treasury William J. Duane had sent both Crockett and Fitzgerald the mileage calculations in question in late June 1833. He argued that Crockett had the information necessary to support or discredit his allegation, yet he chose not to disclose its existence to the voters. "Now sir, could you have acted more unfairly and dishonestly, if you had tried?"[38]

The heated campaign came down to a close finish. Only 173 votes separated the candidates, but it was Crockett who prevailed over Fitzgerald, 3,985 votes to 3,812. Despite the close margin of victory, Crockett boasted like it had been a landslide. He claimed it was a victory over the Jacksonians' attempt to reapportion the 12th Congressional District to Fitzgerald's advantage. The voters, he wrote, "were not to be transferred like hogs…in the market." Although it was Fitzgerald who had been his "open competitor" in the campaign, Crockett recognized that his opponent "was helped along by all his little lawyers again, headed by old Black Hawk, as he is sometimes called, (alias) Adam Huntsman, with all his talents for writing '*Chronicles*,' and such like foolish stuff."[39]

---

36. Ibid July 27, 1833
37. Ibid July 20, 1833
38. Ibid July 27, 1833
39. *Congressional Quarterly's Guide to U.S. Elections* (Washington D.C.: Congressional Quarterly, 1985): 713. Crockett, *Narrative*: 209-210.

Chapter Five

A Good Constitution

1834–1835

> MR. HUNTSMAN *said that the subject of taxation comes home to every man's door. You may talk about other subjects, and you may be told that the one whom you address may tell you that he cares nothing about it...but when you send your tax-gatherer to his door, every man on your poorest knoll will feel sensibly on this subject.*
> —Nashville Republican, June 21, 1834

ALTHOUGH DAVID CROCKETT had regained his congressional seat, there was still good news for Adam Huntsman in the August 1833 election results. Voters had approved a statewide referendum for a convention to revise Tennessee's thirty-seven year old constitution. It was a hard-fought victory for advocates like Huntsman who believed fundamental revisions were needed to the document, especially the sections dealing with property taxation and the state judiciary.

The constitution of 1796 had been considered by Thomas Jefferson to be "the least imperfect and most republican" of state constitutions. While it gave voting rights to all adult males—including free blacks— it placed land ownership restrictions upon those men who wanted to serve in the legislature. The interests of large landholders were further protected as the constitution required equal taxation regardless of the value, location, or condition of one's property.[1] The judiciary in Tennessee was not its own separate and independent branch of government. The power to create and abolish courts—including the Supreme Court—was held by the legislature and judges were appointed and removed from the bench at its discretion. It was not uncommon for judges to be impeached for questionable conduct and removed from office. A vindictive legislator could also push for impeachment to settle some personal animosity, as reportedly occurred against Judge Nathaniel W. Williams while Huntsman was a member of the senate. These were among the most important reasons that many Tennesseans wanted the constitution amended.[2]

Huntsman had advocated changes since his first term in the state senate in 1815, and he brought this mind-set with him to the Western District. On November 20, 1830, he placed a notice in the *Jackson Gazette* asking county representatives to meet at Jackson on December 28. They would express their preference for or against a constitutional convention and "adopt such rules and regulations as shall be best calculated to carry the same into effect."[3] Supporters of a convention were primarily from the rural areas of the Western District and Middle Tennessee, while its opponents were the wealthy landowners of Middle and East Tennessee who benefited from the existing tax system. Some voters feared giving power to a select few to alter the state's fundamental law. The cry for reform that began during the Panic of 1819 took five referendums before a convention was finally approved by the voters and adopted by the legislature on November 27, 1833.[4]

Huntsman wanted to represent Madison County at the convention. He was opposed in the special election by Thomas Henderson, a former

---

1. Corlew, *Tennessee*: 97-98. William H. Masterson, *William Blount* (New York: Greenwood Press, 1969): 289-290.
2. White, ed. *Messages* 2: 558
3. *Jackson Gazette*, November 20, 27; December 4, 1830
4. Corlew, *Tennessee*: 164-165. Paul H. Bergeron, *Antebellum Politics in Tennessee* (Lexington: University of Kentucky Press, 1982): 38. John Trotwood Moore and Austin Powers Foster, *Tennessee, the Volunteer State* (Chicago: S.J. Clarke Publishing Company, 1923): 405.

North Carolina newspaper editor who counted David Crockett among his supporters. The congressman believed Huntsman's determination to be at the convention was the primary reason he had opposed him so forcefully in his last two elections. Crockett hoped Henderson would "beat old Blackhawk to death" and the voters would "lay him away among the unfinished business." But the Madison County electorate thought differently and chose Huntsman to be their delegate.[5]

THE CONVENTION WAS HELD in Nashville beginning on May 19, 1834. Sixty delegates from across the state presented their credentials and were seated in the representative hall of the Nashville Inn. Unlike the 1796 convention whose members included distinguished leaders such as William Blount, James Robertson, Daniel Smith, and Andrew Jackson, this gathering— with the exceptions of former governor Willie Blount of Montgomery County, future governor Newton Cannon of Williamson County, and Robert Weakley of Davidson County—was a rather ordinary group of men. Two-thirds of the delegates identified themselves as farmers, the rest being primarily lawyers, doctors, and merchants. Less than half had served in public office before the convention. One historian described them as "plain but worthy men, who were genuinely representative of the people"; though "wanting in brilliancy, [they] were rich in common sense." Issac Walton of Sumner County held the distinction of being the only member who had served at the 1796 convention.[6]

The first order of business was to select a president, and William B. Carter of Carter County was elected on the seventh ballot. As a conservative voice in the delegation, he advised restraint in making changes to the state's fundamental law, "to touch the Constitution with a cautious and circumspect hand, and to deface that instrument, formed with so much wisdom and foresight by our ancestors as little as possible." It was

---

5. Williams, *Historic Madison*: 423

6. White, ed. *Messages* 2: 466-469. Among the delegates were William G. Childress, a cousin of James K. Polk, and Julius Caesar Nichols Robertson, a great-great nephew of James Robertson, considered the "Father of Middle Tennessee" and a delegate to the 1796 convention. McBride, ed. *Biographical Directory* 1:140, 631-632, 757. Joshua W. Caldwell, *Studies in the Constitutional History of Tennessee* (Cincinnati, OH: The Robert Clarke Company, 1907): 194.

The Tennessee Constitutional Convention was held at the Nashville Inn during the sweltering summer months of 1834.

Courtesy of the Tennessee State Library and Archives

decided that members would enter into a Committee of the Whole each day presided over by Newton Cannon to present resolutions for amendments that would be discussed and debated.[7]

There were both conservative and progressive factions within the delegation on how much of the document should be changed and to what extent. Huntsman was among the progressive leaders and an active participant early in the convention. He introduced motions and resolutions that helped get its work started. He proposed the creation of various committees and was named chair for two of them, the rules committee and the Committee on Privileges and Elections. He also moved that copies of the constitution and Declaration of Rights be provided to the members for their use.[8]

Contention arose on the second day over the need for the delegates to take an oath. One had been administered to the secretary and assis-

---

7. S.H. Laughlin and J.F. Henderson. *Journal of the Convention of the State of Tennessee Convened for the Purpose of Revising and Amending the Constitution Thereof. Held in Nashville* (Nashville: W. Haskell Hunt and Company, 1834): 4-5, 10, 15-16, 33

8. Ibid: 6-7, 9-10

tant secretary (who were not members), but many delegates felt it was an unnecessary formality for them. Huntsman—who had voted against an oath for the secretaries—argued that while requirements for a convention were given in the constitution, no mention was made about an oath that should be administered to its delegates. Regardless, no court could punish a member should he commit perjury. "[I]f members of the Convention had no moral principles enough to keep them to their duty," he said, "they might kiss all the skin from the bible in taking oaths and it would be of no benefit." The question was rejected by a 25-35 vote.[9]

Early in the convention, he took steps to ensure that members would be compensated for their time and expenses. Having learned beforehand that the treasurer for Middle Tennessee had no money available, he presented a resolution on May 24 that the treasurer make arrangements to transfer state funds from his counterpart in the Western District, which was adopted. Two days later, some members had second thoughts— "[W]e had done nothing as yet to earn our pay," one remarked—and sought to reconsider the resolution. Huntsman was unapologetic about his reasons for advancing it: "[S]ome gentlemen said they were not in a hurry; but he was in a hurry, and would tell his reasons. He wanted money." It was common practice for lawmakers to obtain expenses from the state treasury when needed, and he saw no reason that it should not be done for convention delegates as well. If the state needed more funds, he knew there were banks in Nashville willing to loan it. He warned that if the "wealthy gentlemen" were successful in reconsidering his resolution, "he gave them due notice that he should call on them for a loan of what money he should need for his individual use." The vote to reconsider fell short, 28-32.[10]

---

9. Ibid: 7-9. *Nashville Republican*, May 20, 1834.

10. *Nashville Republican*, May 27, 1834. Huntsman later elaborated that "it had always been customary for the members [of the legislature] who stood in need of it, to draw small sums from the Treasury, from time to time, to meet the demands of boarding, washing, &c. before the compensation bill was passed" at the end of each session. He pushed the resolution because "I wanted some money, and intended to have it, if it could be got." AH to Editor of the *Nashville Republican*, June 13, 1834, published in the *Nashville Republican*, June 14, 1834.

WITH PRELIMINARY WORK COMPLETED, delegates began confronting the problems that necessitated a constitutional convention. Huntsman was a lively participant in the debates, utilizing his knowledge of the issues with a mixture of intelligence, wit, and sarcasm—and at times a touch of Aesop's Fables[11]—to the enjoyment and annoyance of his fellow delegates. During one exchange, a colleague misunderstood what he meant and Huntsman apologized that he spoke Dutch as a child and learned English when he was older. "He would, however, try as much as he could to make himself understood" and "furnish him [his colleague] with a Dutch dictionary, which, together with his own excellent knowledge of the English language, would enable him to make out the meaning."[12]

The primary issue that brought the convention into existence was the constitutional requirements for property taxation. Article 1, Section 26 of the 1796 constitution stated: "All lands held by deed, grant or entry, shall be taxed equal and uniform in such a manner that no one hundred acres of land shall be taxed higher than another except town lots, which shall not be taxed higher than two hundred acres of land each." The intent of the framers was to encourage landowners to clear and develop their properties and make improvements upon them without fear of increased taxes. But it also meant property (with the exception of town lots) was taxed the same regardless of its condition. The owner of swampy bottom lands in the Western District paid as much as the owner of rich farmland in Middle Tennessee. The unfairness of the clause became the driving force some two decades later for constitutional revision.[13]

Huntsman was among the outspoken leaders for taxation reform. In late June he gave a practical and articulate speech on the subject, which he confessed was "a much longer speech than I am accustomed to make." Using real life circumstances and three fictitious sons named

---

11. Huntsman sometimes alluded to particular selections from Aesop's Fables that he felt pertained to the topic under discussion. On one occasion, Terry H. Cahal of Maury County—whether in good humor or not is uncertain—shared his own fable and added: "The gentleman [Huntsman] knows it by heart. His course here shows that he understands what happened in Aesop's days." *Nashville Republican*, June 21, 1834.

12. *Nashville Republican*, May 24, 1834. This exchange was with Joseph Kincaid of Bedford County.

13. White, ed. *Messages* 2: 525

for the counties of Davidson, Montgomery, and Wilson to illustrate his point,[14] he addressed the "gross injustice" of a clause that for tax purposes placed all lands upon the same footing, regardless of their location or topographical conditions.

> He [the taxpayer] will inquire why is it, that my neighbor...who has a tract of land joining my own, which possesses fertility of soil, a salubrious air and refreshing streams...and possessing all those conveniences which are calculated to make him comfortable and happy, and which is worth twenty five dollars per acre, is compelled to pay no more tax for this, than I have to pay for the barren soil I have to cultivate, which requires that I should toil throughout the days and months and years of my life, and it will scarcely produce a scanty and lean subsistence...and I cannot sell it for one dollar per acre? Why is it that I have to pay twenty five times as much tax in proportion to the value of my property as my wealthy neighbor has to pay upon his? Does a different sun rise and set upon him?[15]

Huntsman wanted a tax structure that was fair to all citizens. "[A]ccording to the principles of everlasting justice," he said, "the proposition to tax every man in society in proportion to his means and ability, is the only just, true, and republican principle that should be adopted in an organic law."[16] He estimated Tennessee's wealth in land, town lots, slaves, and merchandise at $200 million dollars and government expenses at less than $75,000. He proposed that 6 ¼ cents per $100 worth of property or 42 ½ cents per $1,000 could be taxed to finance it. What would be subject to taxation—land, lots, slaves, horses, cattle—should be at the legislature's

---

14. Ibid: 529-530. Huntsman's example of the unfairness of the existing tax structure using sons named Davidson, Montgomery, and Wilson counties is reminiscent of Jesus's Parable of the Talents in Matthew 25:14-30 and Luke 19:12-28.
15. White, ed. *Messages* 2: 526-533
16. Ibid: 531

discretion, but the people would hold their legislators accountable should they abuse their power. "[T]he representatives are so directly under the control of the people, and the people are so sensitive upon the subject of taxation, that I apprehend no lasting evils on this subject," he said. Progressives won the battle and property taxation based on its value was approved by a vote of 43 to 13. All but one of the dissenting votes were cast by delegates from Middle Tennessee. The new law became Article 2, Section 28 of the revised constitution.[17]

Another major struggle that evoked passionate debate was the basis for representation in the General Assembly. While conservatives wanted the number of representatives and senators determined by population as laid out in the existing constitution, progressives such as Huntsman promoted a plan that would allow each county to have one member in the house of representatives while the number of senators would still be determined by population. Huntsman believed county representation would end the disgraceful electioneering practices by some candidates to which he had long objected. "Each county would know its man," he reasoned, "and give a vote on merit alone, without subjecting their candidate to the mean and degrading arts of the demagogue."[18] Delegates from the larger and wealthier counties argued that it would be unfair for the smaller counties—which contributed less in taxes than the larger ones— to have an equal voice in the house. To abandon the principle of majority rule as laid out in the present constitution, one Middle Tennessee delegate lamented, would mean "the days of the republic will soon be numbered."[19] Eventually, it was decided that representation would be apportioned based

---

17. Ibid: 532. Article 2, Section 28 of the 1835 constitution gives the revised taxation provision (with amended portions in italics): "All lands liable to taxation, held by deed, grant or entry, town lots, bank stock, slaves between the ages of twelve and fifty years, *and such other property as the Legislature may from time to time deem expedient,* shall be taxable. All property shall be taxed according to its value; that value to be ascertained in such manner as the Legislature shall direct, so that the same shall be equal and uniform throughout the State. No species of property from which a tax may be collected, shall be taxed higher than any other species of property of equal value. But the Legislature shall have power to tax merchants, pedlars, and privileges, in such manner as they may, from time to time, direct. A tax on white polls shall be laid, in such manner and of such an amount, as may be prescribed by law." 1835 Tennessee Constitution.

18. *Nashville Republican*, June 14, 1834

19. White, ed. *Messages* 2: 494

Adam Huntsman as he may have looked at the time of the 1834 Tennessee Constitutional Convention.
Illustration by Wade Dillon

on the number of "qualified voters" rather than "taxable inhabitants" as originally specified in Article 1, Sections 2 and 4. Population remained the basis for representation, but progressives increased the number of representatives from forty to ninety-nine (once the state's population reached 1.5 million) and senators from twenty to one-third the number of representatives.[20]

As a longtime advocate for reform of the judiciary system, Huntsman insisted that the supreme court be an independent branch of state government in order "to survive the storm of passion" that might result from verdicts unpopular with the people. This was accomplished. Initially, he felt three justices would be sufficient, but later reconsidered and proposed that the bench be expanded in anticipation of a larger population and a higher case load in the future. In the end, the number of justices was placed at three, one from each of the three grand divisions.[21]

Among other successful amendments Huntsman proposed were disqualification of persons who had participated in duels from holding public office, withholding voting rights from convicted felons, and new requirements for the boundaries of old and new counties. He also suggested an amendment to encourage the legislature to pursue internal improvements that would "develop the resources of the State, and promote the happiness and prosperity of her citizens." Revisions offered by his colleagues included the popular election of county officials, the requirement of a majority vote rather than a two-thirds majority for amendments, and the requirement that the next General Assembly determine a permanent location for the state capital.[22]

Naturally, not every proposal Huntsman made was accepted. He tried to take from the senate the authority to act as a court of impeachment, believing that body's "expensive and unwieldy character" was detrimental to it serving in such capacity and making it susceptible to partisan influences. He proposed instead that "three men of character and law talents" be appointed to hold court with a jury in the county or district where the alleged crime was committed. Portions of his resolutions—

---

20. Corlew, *Tennessee*: 166
21. *Nashville Republican*, July 12, 1834
22. Corlew, *Tennessee*: 166-167. Bergeron, *Paths*: 41-42.

with slight alterations—were accepted as Article 5, Sections 4 and 5; the court of impeachment, however, remained in the senate.[23] He argued in favor of giving the governor the power to veto legislation and believed the lieutenant governor—"as a man liable to be called to exercise the highest executive power in the State"—should be chosen by popular election, but these proposals failed as well.[24]

Perhaps with Job 12:12 in mind—"Is not wisdom found among the aged?"—Huntsman believed that senators and judges should be men of a certain age. Whereas the 1796 constitution specified that all members of the General Assembly be at least twenty-one years old, he thought senators should be at least thirty years old. "Let the young go to their proper branch, and stay there five or ten years," he said, "and then when the heat and fervor of their youthful blood had abated, let them come into the Senate."[25] He expressed a similar opinion regarding the justices of the state supreme court, whom he felt should be at least forty years old. At the same time, he acknowledged the limitations of old age and believed judges should not preside past the age of sixty. Some colleagues disagreed with the age restrictions he proposed, though one fellow delegate humorously deferred to the forty-eight year old Huntsman "for age and experience." Robert M. Burton of Wilson County declared that he would "rather have a boy of 25, of bright native talents, to decide upon his rights, than a man of 75 years of age, who had never had any brains." Huntsman and Burton had a lively exchange on the subject, reported the *Nashville Republican*, "in which the shafts of wit and satire fell as thick and keen as the meteors of last November."[26] Minimum age requirements of thirty years old for senators and twenty-one for representatives were amended in Article

---

23. *Nashville Republican*, July 3, 1834. 1835 Tennessee Constitution.
24. *Nashville Republican*, June 24, 28, 1834.
25. *Nashville Republican*, June 19, 1834. Huntsman quoted from one of Aesop's Fables "that while 'young folks thought that old people were fools, the old knew the young to be so.'" Ibid.
26. Ibid: July 15, 1834. The *Republican*'s convention reporter referred to a spectacular and memorable meteor shower that brightened the skies over Nashville in the early morning hours of November 12-13, 1833. *The Western Methodist*, November 15, 1833, contained in Jonathan K.T. Smith, *Genealogical Information from The Western Methodist 1833-1834* (Jackson, TN: Self-published, 2003): 4.

2, Sections 9 and 10, and thirty-five years old for supreme court justices in Article 6, Section 3.[27]

Overall, Huntsman was pleased with what the convention had accomplished thus far. "From the great harmony and good feeling which prevails amongst the members," he wrote on July 5, "I think the prospects are brighter for a good constitution than I thought they were at the first of the session."[28]

He spent considerable time on a controversy that had nothing to do with the constitution. As chairman of the Committee on Privileges and Elections, he had to investigate the contested election of Shelby County delegate Adam Rankin Alexander. Alexander's opponent and former state senate speaker Edward Ward believed ineligible voters had influenced the results. The committee gathered depositions and certificates from voters and election officials and issued subpoenas for witnesses to testify. On June 30, Huntsman reported to the convention that conflicting voter certificates pertaining to voting requirements led to the conclusion that the election results should be voided and a second election held to decide a new delegate for Shelby County. "[I]t was not within the compass of human comprehension to come to a different conclusion…from the conflicting mass of testimony laid before them," he explained. A hearing between the two sides consumed the delegates' time until Ward ended his protest on July 12, allowing Alexander to serve as the uncontested Shelby County delegate for the remainder of the convention.[29]

ONE DEBATE THAT delegates did not expect was the emancipation of slaves living in the state. In its first weeks, memorials from citizens of East Tennessee were presented to the convention, thirty of which called for the gradual abolition of slavery. While Huntsman advocated reform on various issues that faced the convention, like most of his fellow del-

27. 1835 Tennessee Constitution
28. AH to Editor of the *Truth Teller*, July 5, 1834, published in Jackson *Truth Teller and Sentinel*, July 11, 1834.
29. Journal of the Convention: 116. Jonathan K.T. Smith, *Adam Rankin Alexander, A Life Sketch* (Jackson, TN: Self-published, 1992): 18.

egates, he was decidedly conservative on this topic. He offered his perspective on June 6 that the memorials were needless distractions from the intended purposes of the convention. "I did not expect that I should have engaged in the discussion of a question which seems to have created a thrilling interest in the eastern portions of this State," he said. The same "excitement" that had generated them in that section had not "spread its blighting influence as far west as the county in which I live. No fanatic has been preaching impracticable schemes of emancipation."[30]

For Huntsman, it was a question of property rights rather than the morality of human bondage. The Fifth Amendment to the U.S. Constitution guaranteed that private property could not "be taken for public use, without just compensation"; to slaveholders such as Huntsman, slaves were indeed private property. Because the petitions could offer no solutions for financial compensation, he was confident that a provision abolishing slavery would be unconstitutional. "I verily believe," he said, "we have no more authority to regulate or disturb the rights of property in relation to this species, than we have to regulate the progeny of any other description of live property that is owned by any individual in the State."[31]

Huntsman saw the endeavors of the American Colonization Society to send freed slaves to the African colony of Liberia as a possible remedy to the predicament. As early as 1831, he had served as a vice president of the Tennessee State Colonization Society at Nashville.[32] Like many Southerners who belonged to the organization, he supported colonization not as a method of gradual emancipation, but as a way to separate free blacks from their enslaved brethren. He advocated legislation that would assist anyone who might want to voluntarily free their slaves, with the stipulation that "they do not thereafter encumber society." He added a surprisingly personal revelation: "I will also assert that at those

---

30. *Nashville Republican*, June 10, 1834
31. Ibid
32. *The American Colonization Society, The African Repository, and Colonial Journal* (Washington D.C.: James C. Dunn, 1831): 6:179. Though his name is not listed, Huntsman was likely a member of the Jackson Auxiliary Colonization Society, which was established at Jackson, Tennessee on February 25, 1830. *Jackson Gazette*, March 13, 1830.

The emancipation of slaves in Tennessee became a divisive issue during the 1834 Constitutional Convention.

Courtesy of the Library of Congress

periods of my life, when I was a large owner of this description of property, I would at any time have taken two thirds of their value, if they could have been taken to some country where they could have enjoyed rational liberty and republican government."[33]

It was the first time in his political career that Huntsman had publicly expressed his views on slavery. Aside from the number of slaves he owned at various times of his life, few details are known about his personal involvement. It is known that one of the crops grown on his land in Madison County—which was described as "one of the best farms in West Tennessee"—was cotton. In the mid 1830s, he employed the services

---

33. *Nashville Republican*, June 10, 1834. Robert V. Remini, *Henry Clay: Statesman for the Union* (New York: W.W. Norton and Company, 1991): 179.

of one Dr. Joseph Powell of Carter County, Tennessee to buy slaves on his behalf, for which Powell received two percent of their cost.[34] Huntsman seems to have been a modest slave owner, certainly not on the scale of wealthier men of his time such as Andrew Jackson. He owned three slaves as early as 1810 when he lived in Knoxville, 17 slaves after living in Madison County for seven years, and 30 slaves in 1840. As "a great reader and lover of history," he accepted that slavery was part of the culture "in every nation almost, and in every age from the days of Nimrod down to the present—and so it would probably ever be."[35]

Huntsman favored the convention "getting clear of the subject" of emancipation altogether, and he moved that the petitions and memorials be tabled until the first day of January 1835. The motion passed by a 38 to 20 vote. Subsequently, he was appointed to a select committee with Robert Allen of Smith County and chaired by John A. McKinney of Hawkins County—each representing one of the three grand divisions—to articulate the convention's reasons for opposing the memorials. Though McKinney crafted the final report, it undoubtedly contained the attitudes and opinions of Huntsman and Allen as well.[36]

Their report was presented to the convention on June 19. What the memorials proposed—freeing the children of slaves born after 1835 or all slaves in the next twenty or thirty years—was impractical, and debating it would "produce no result except the waste of time, the expenditure of money, and the destruction of that harmony" necessary for delegates to complete their intended work. The committee members did not dispute the fact that "slavery is an evil…but to tell how that evil can be removed, is a question that the wisest heads and the most benevolent hearts have not been able to answer in a satisfactory manner." Particular attention was given to the free black man, whom the report depicted as living under the oppression of white society, "a stranger in the land of his nativity…an

---

34. *National Banner and Nashville Whig*, April 29, 1835. In an advertisement for his particular services, Powell listed among his references Huntsman and Ephraim H. Foster, who would later become a U.S. senator and a Whig rival of Huntsman during the 1840 presidential campaign.

35. 1810, 1811 Knox County, TN tax lists. 1830 Madison County, TN tax list, published in Smith, *Antebellum Militia*: 81. 1840 U.S. Census for Madison County, TN. *Nashville Republican*, July 24, 1834. Refer to pages 232-239 for information on slavery at Huntsman's farm.

36. Journal of the Convention: 71-72

outcast in the place of his residence...beset with temptations...degraded, despised and trampled upon by the rest of the community.

Remarkably, it contended that the life of a slave was "better than the condition of the free man of colour in the midst of a community of white men, with whom he has no common interest, no fellow feeling, no equality." Slaves in Tennessee were treated well, the report argued. They received food and clothing and their work "is not grievous nor burdensome." They were allowed to worship in white congregations and taught to read in Sunday school. If slaves were freed at a specific date, it feared, nothing would prevent their owners from taking them as far south as Louisiana, where they would labor in a harsher climate and be susceptible to illness such as cholera. The committee believed: "If the prayer of the slave population of this State could be heard on this subject, it would be that the prayer of the memorialists might not be granted."[37]

The report contended that once slaves gained their freedom, it would be impossible for them to integrate into white society; the color of their skin would be a constant reminder of their servitude. The result would be a social class with freedom but "without the real blessings of liberty, or the real privileges of the freeman," leading to "perpetual hostility and mutual distrust" between the two. Such animosity, it feared, would eventually lead free blacks to unite with slaves in other Southern states "to exterminate the white man and take possession of the country." The report acknowledged that colonization in Africa had been proposed in some memorials, but left unresolved was the financial cost, who would pay to transport them, and whether freed slaves would leave voluntarily. Instead, the committee concluded that the American Colonization Society—a private enterprise which offered colonization in Liberia as a stipulation for freedom—was the best alternative: "In this way...slavery will yet be extinguished, in a way that will work no evil to the white man, while it produces the happiest effects on the whole African race." The "meddling" and ill-considered efforts of "misguided fanatics" in other

---

37. Ibid: 87-90. Chase C. Mooney, "The Question of Slavery and the Free Negro in the Tennessee Constitutional Convention of 1834." *Tennessee Historical Quarterly* 12 (1946): 493-494. Lacy K. Ford, *Deliver Us from Evil: The Slavery Question in the Old South* (New York: Oxford University Press, 2009): 401.

parts of the country only hindered what the committee believed would be the inevitable end of slavery.[38]

The convention approved the select committee's report by a vote of 44 to 10. Subsequently, four East Tennessee delegates[39] asked that their protest be recorded in the official journal. The signers of the memorials—most of whom they claimed were slaveholders—deserved more consideration than a three-man committee explaining why their beliefs were being dismissed. The report itself was "subversive of the true principles of republicanism" and "at variance with the spirit of the Gospel... found in the Bible" in espousing the benevolence of the institution. "[N]otwithstanding the beautiful description...of the benefits of slavery," they wrote, "yet on reflection we are free to say, we have not fallen quite so much in love with it as to desire it for ourselves." Rather than offering definite steps to achieve emancipation, they believed the memorials asked the convention to consider ways in which the state could eventually "be delivered from the curse and evil of slavery." Just because other states chose not to confront it did not prevent Tennessee from exploring the possibility. They objected in particular to the report's description of the lives of free blacks and believed the color of their skin was no reason to deny them "the common rights of man." Despite the sentiments of the committee, the delegates were convinced that "they would be happier and safer subjects of our government, as free men than as slaves." They concluded that the report essentially "was a kind of apology for slavery."[40]

On July 9, the select committee submitted a second report to answer its critics. It denied being disrespectful toward the memorial signers or maligning their opinions; each memorial was read on the floor of the convention and referred to their committee. Regarding the claim that the report conflicted with Biblical principles, the committee felt they should be obeyed by each individual rather than "telling him to take his neighbor by the throat to compel him to obey them." The report disagreed with the claim that "a large portion" of the memorials' signers were slaveholders,

---

38. Journal of the Convention: 88, 90, 92-93
39. Matthew Stephenson of Washington County, John McGaughey of Greene County, Richard Bradshaw of Jefferson County, and James Gillespy of Blount County.
40. Journal of the Convention: 102-104. Ford, *Deliver*: 403-405.

believing instead "their number to be very inconsiderable, if any." All but one of the memorials advocated a plan for emancipation and promoted the "absurdity" that 150,000 slaves and their children could be set free and sent to the Liberian colony in twenty-one or thirty-two years. The committee asserted that a republican government was created "to promote peace, protect property, and to preserve all the rights and privileges of every member of the community," and emancipation "would inevitably destroy the happiness of the white population" and "sap the very foundation of a republican government."[41]

Eventually, a provision was added to the state constitution—overcoming a close 30-27 vote—that prohibited any law passed by the legislature to abolish slavery. In addition, the right to vote held by free blacks under the original constitution was taken from them in the revised document when the word "white" was inserted in Article 4, Section 1.[42]

DELEGATES ENJOYED A FEW welcome diversions from their work over the course of the convention. They adjourned on the Fourth of July and marched in a procession to the Methodist Episcopal Church, where the Declaration of Independence was read and "a handsome, eloquent, and appropriate Address" was given by the church's pastor, Rev. James Gwin.[43] On July 17, General Edmund P. Gaines of the U.S. Army was seated during the proceedings and former Tennessee governor Sam Houston attended the next day. An unwelcome diversion occurred when Huntsman and three fellow delegates were approached individually by "a link-jawed, villainous looking fellow, with a penitentiary cast in his countenance" who claimed to be a resident of their respective counties. Pleading hard-

---

41. Journal of the Convention: 125-129. For a broader discussion of the slavery debate in the convention, see Ford, *Deliver*: 390-417.

42. The provision against emancipation became Article 2, Section 31. 1835 Tennessee Constitution.

43. Journal of the Convention: 121. Washington D.C. *United States Telegraph*, July 24, 1834. At Vauxhall Garden later in the day, Huntsman toasted Rev. Gwin: "May he live a thousand years, and preach a fourth of July sermon on each recurring anniversary." Ibid.

ship, he had gained their sympathy and swindled from each man a small amount of money.[44]

On August 14 the convention welcomed President Andrew Jackson, who was spending the summer away from Washington. He hoped the efforts of the delegates would "be crowned with success, and that the free people of Tennessee, whilst enjoying the prosperity and happiness which are the reward of wise and equal laws and a steady and virtuous administration of them, may remember each and all of you as their benefactors." Each delegate greeted him as they adjourned for the day. They followed him in a procession that included Governor William Carroll and members of the state congressional delegation leading to Vauxhall Garden, where everyone enjoyed an early afternoon dinner.[45]

After almost fifty days of deliberation over proposed alterations and amendments, the work of the Committee of the Whole was completed on July 24. All that remained to be done was to pass the amended constitution on three readings. With most of its work completed, Huntsman rose from his seat and praised Newton Cannon for his "upright, faithful, and able services" as chairman of the Committee, which drew the appreciative applause of the convention. The Williamson County delegate thanked his colleague for the "very flattering sentiments."[46] The convention adjourned on August 30 after 104 days in meticulous review of Tennessee's fundamental law, almost ten weeks longer than the 1796 convention. Huntsman was appointed to a five-man committee responsible for the final structure and language of the revised document. For his efforts in the convention, he received a salary of $416 (four dollars a day) and $48 in mileage.[47]

---

44. Journal of the Convention: 142. Huntsman and three convention delegates—William Ledbetter, Issac Walton, and Joseph Kincaid—placed a notice in the *Murfreesborough* (TN) *Central Monitor*, July 19, 1834, about the incident with one John Cullender, who claimed to be from Warren County, Tennessee. "We therefore caution the public against this fellow for twelve months next ensuing," the notice read, "for it is our opinion, that by that time he will take up his lodgings in the penitentiary." As Huntsman is the first man listed, he was likely the one who placed it in the newspaper.

45. *Arkansas Gazette*, August 26, 1834. Robert V. Remini, *Andrew Jackson and the Course of American Democracy 1833-1845* (New York: Harper & Row, 1984): 212.

46. *Nashville Republican*, July 31, 1834

47. Journal of the Convention: 413. Huntsman claimed 300 miles travelled to and from Nashville for the convention. Ibid.

Unlike the 1796 document, the amended constitution had to meet the approval of the qualified voters of the state. As the delegates debated, Huntsman asked them to try and seek common ground on the myriad of issues before them. Once they returned home, it would be their responsibility to convince their constituents to vote for it. "[E]ach [delegate] would depend on each [other] to recommend to his friends the work in which all had had a hand, and which would be for a century, he hoped, the monument of their united skill and labor."[48] He did his part among the voters of Madison County to ensure its passage, even writing letters for publication to settle misconceptions about what had been changed.[49] It is possible he may also have written more detailed articles under a fictitious name in support of the new constitution.[50]

WHILE CAMPAIGNING FOR the constitution, in October 1834, Huntsman also announced his intention to oppose David Crockett for the 12th Congressional seat in the 1835 election. A third candidate, former state senator James R. McMeans of Paris, Tennessee, entered the race a few weeks later. By this time, President Jackson had enough of Crockett and was anxious to see his congressional career come to an end. The fact that Crockett had conspired with fellow Tennessean and Speaker of the House of Representatives John Bell and others in the state's congressio-

48. *Nashville Republican*, July 24, 1834

49. AH to Editor of the Jackson *Truth Teller and Sentinel*, reprinted in *Randolph* (TN) *Recorder*, January 2, 1835. Huntsman clarified that neither free blacks, Native Americans, or people of interracial lineage—"until he gets as far off as the fourth generation" from his ancestor—could give testimony in court under the new constitution. "The constitution does not change the law as it has stood for forty years," he added. Ibid.

50. The author believes Huntsman could have anonymously written a series of articles under the name of "Madison" that were published in the *Nashville Whig* on September 8, 11, 16, 22, 26 and October 1, 6, 1834. In the article entitled "The New Constitution, No. V," the writer discusses changes that had been made to the state judiciary. He was familiar with legal proceedings in the Mountain District where Huntsman practiced law and also made reference to various Supreme Court cases at Sparta. One of these was "Philips, for the murder of Quarles on the highway"; this was Huntsman's future father-in-law. At times, the writer speaks as one who is more familiar with the obstacles faced by the delegates than an ordinary citizen would be, mentioning the "oppressiveness from heat" in the spring and summer months. Historian Robert H. White noted his inability to identify this mysterious writer whose "grasp of the basic philosophy of government approached the phenomenal, and the vigor, clarity, and soundness of his statements may very properly arouse envy on the part of myriads of present-day political scribblers." White, ed. *Messages* 2: 637-657.

nal delegation to entice Jackson stalwart and U.S. Senator Hugh Lawson White to run for the presidency only fueled the president's desire to see "Mr Bell Davy Crockett & Co, hurled as they ought, from the confidence of the people."[51]

On New Year's Day 1835, Huntsman renewed an old acquaintance with Congressman James K. Polk of Columbia, Tennessee. He first met Polk in 1819 when he was a state senator and the twenty-five year old Polk was clerk for the senate. Over the next sixteen years, the young clerk had become a practicing attorney, served a term in the state house of representatives, and was now in his fifth term as representative for the 9th Congressional District. Polk enjoyed the support of President Jackson and was considered his choice for House speaker, a position he lost a few weeks earlier to Bell. Perhaps Huntsman felt it was time to communicate with the president's trusted House leader as he embarked on his own congressional campaign.

Writing to Polk in his facetious style, he hoped the congressman was not "so tightly stuffed with Christmas pudding" that he could not respond to his letter. Because his own congressman, David Crockett, would not write to him, he would have to correspond with one from another district instead. "I should like to hear from you occasionally in relation to the actings and doings of your great folks at Washington…[in] return for which I will give you some nonsense." Striking a more serious tone, Huntsman reported that he had already been in all but one of the counties in the 12th Congressional District and felt confident he could "beat Davy" even with McMeans in the race. He believed Crockett was losing support, despite his best efforts to spread anti-Jackson mailings throughout the district. Hope for an August victory would depend upon Crockett's success with his land bill. "If he carries his land Bill I will give him strength," he wrote. "Otherwise the conflict will not be a difficult one."[52]

On March 5 and 6, 1835, the qualified voters of Tennessee went to the polls to decide the fate of the amended version of the state constitution. Close to three-fourths of them rewarded the efforts of the convention

---

51. AJ to JKP, May 12, 1835. CJKP 3: 191. McMeans dropped out in late March or early April 1835. Nashville Union, April 9, 1835.

52. AH to JKP, January 1, 1835. CJKP 3: 3.

and voted in its favor, 42,644 to 17,091. In Madison County, it passed with 87% of the vote, 837 to 125. Only four counties in Middle Tennessee voted it down. On March 30, Governor William Carroll declared the revised constitution to be ratified and adopted. For Huntsman, it was the culmination of a twenty-year struggle and his first political victory of the year. He hoped for reason to celebrate again in August.[53]

---

53. White, ed. *Messages* 2: 659-660

Chapter Six

Campaign for Congress

1835

A HUNTSMAN BEATEN, YET VICTORIOUS.—*The Hon.* DAVID CROCKETT, *of hunting fame renowned, has at length been* **beaten** *on his own* **beaten** *track, and by one of his own kith, bone and persuasion. A. Huntsman, Esq. has been elected member to Congress from West Tennessee, vice* DAVY CROCKETT, *Esq.* "**grinned off.**"
—St. Louis Daily Commercial Bulletin, August 24, 1835

Adam Huntsman, I believe if I were to go to hell you'd follow me there.
—David Crockett, August 1835

The election for Tennessee's 12th Congressional seat in 1835 drew attention across the country. In stereotypical backwoods dialect, one New England newspaper told its readers: "This department of coons, canebreaks and airthquakes, is beginning to make somewhat of a stir. First of all, the Colonel has a rival for popular favor in a candidate named Huntsman, who, on a trace or track, is not slow, and it is expected will give the roarer a severe pull for the lead at the next meeting on the congressional course." A New York City paper noted that Crockett was opposed "by a gentleman of the primitive name of Adam Huntsman…[H]e must be a bold huntsman indeed who undertakes to contend with such an animal as Colonel Crockett." Back home, the *National Banner and Nashville Whig* believed "[a] *skinning* contest may be expected between the great Huntsman of Madison, and 'the mighty Hunter of Weakley.'" The *McMinnville Gazette* favored "our old friend" Huntsman who once practiced law there: "We hope to see him 'go ahead' of Davy at the Polls."[1]

In the two years since he regained his seat in Congress, Crockett had become a national celebrity. His autobiography entitled *A Narrative of the Life of David Crockett of the State of Tennessee* was published in 1834, and became a best seller. It was written in order for Crockett to gain control over the "half-horse, half-alligator" superhuman exaggerations of his frontier persona and profit from his life story. The public was enamoured by his tall tales of life on the frontier and the fascination transferred to other mediums as well. A Crockettesque character named Nimrod Wildfire entertained audiences in a play called *Lion of the West*. A fictitious New Englander named Major Jack Downing exchanged letters in the newspapers with "Davy Crockett," whose responses written in outlandish backwoods dialect amused readers across the country. Davy was even the subject of a series of almanacs beginning in 1835. In addition to information typically found in such publications, the Crockett Almanacks featured far-fetched stories drawn from books on Crockett, the Nimrod Wildfire character, and other imaginative sources, with crude woodcut illustrations that compliment them. Huntsman was mentioned in both the *Narrative* and the 1836 Nashville edition of the Crockett Almanack.[2]

NATIONAL POLITICS PLAYED a decisive role in Tennessee's congressional and gubernatorial elections in 1835. President Jackson's choice to be his successor and the Democratic nominee in the 1836 election was Vice President Martin Van Buren. But many of Jackson's followers in his home state were not enthusiastic about promoting the New Yorker's candidacy.

---

1. *Vermont Gazette*, January 6, 1835. *New York Transcript*, October 31, 1834. *National Banner and Nashville Whig*, October 8, 1834. Reprint from the *McMinnville* (TN) *Gazette* published in the *Richmond Inquirer*, October 28, 1834.

2. Boylston and Wiener, *Crockett in Congress*: 109-110. Franklin J. Meine, ed. *The Crockett Almanacks: Nashville Series, 1835-1838* (Chicago: The Claxton Club, 1955): xi-xiii, xvi-xviii, 43-44. Michael A. Lofaro, ed. *Davy Crockett: The Man, the Legend, the Legacy 1786-1986* (Knoxville: University of Tennessee Press, 1985): 25-26. Crockett, *Narrative*: 7, 210.

Huntsman—minus his trademark peg leg—scales a tree in pursuit of a panther in this fanciful woodcut illustration.

1836 Crockett Almanack (Nashville Series)

They saw "The Little Magician" as a cunning politician who had beguiled the Old Hero and manipulated himself into the presidential succession. Jackson's opponents within his own party used this dissatisfaction to their advantage and offered an alternative candidate. In December 1833, a movement began in the General Assembly to nominate fellow Tennessean and U.S. Senator Hugh Lawson White for the presidency. A year later, John Bell and other members of the state's congressional delegation (with the exception of Jackson loyalists James K. Polk and Cave Johnson in the House of Representatives and Felix Grundy in the Senate) signed a letter asking if White would allow his name to be considered for the Democratic nomination. Despite being a loyal Jacksonian and a personal friend of the president, the East Tennessean agreed and set into motion a political revolt in Old Hickory's home state.[3]

The White bandwagon gained momentum leading up to the 1835 statewide elections, making each contest a referendum on his candidacy. The question was raised early in the campaign between Crockett and Huntsman. On May 25, a letter written by "the friends of Judge White" was published in the Jackson *Truth Teller*, asking each candidate if he would support the reelection of John Bell as House speaker in the next congress. It was a veiled attempt to gauge their support for White or Van Buren publicly: "That he [Bell] will be strenuously opposed by the open and *secret* friends of Mr. Van Buren, no person can doubt," the anonymous writer noted.[4]

Crockett responded first, pledging his wholehearted support for Bell and vowing that he would vote for him "against any man in the United States." He believed the outcome of the election for House speaker would

---

3. Jonathan M. Atkins, *Parties, Politics, and the Sectional Conflict in Tennessee 1832-1861* (Knoxville: University of Tennessee Press, 1997): 38-39. Nancy N. Scott, ed. *A Memoir of Hugh Lawson White* (Philadelphia: J.B. Lippincott & Co., 1856): 329-330. A.O.P Nicholson to JKP, December 5, 1835. CJKP 2: 157. L. Paul Gresham, "The Public Career of Hugh Lawson White." *Tennessee Historical Quarterly* (Dec. 1944): 3: 310.

4. Michael F. Holt, *The Rise and Fall of the American Whig Party: Jacksonian Politics and the Onset of the Civil War* (New York: Oxford University Press, 1999): 56. *National Banner and Nashville Whig*, June 12, 1835. Two years later, an anonymous writer using the name "The People" charged John Bell with interfering in the 12th District campaign in 1835. Bell "dictated or procured the dictation of a letter to the [Jackson] Truth Teller, calling upon the candidates for Congress to vote for him for speaker." *Nashville Union*, May 5, 1837.

influence the presidential election a year later. Regarding the selection of Van Buren for the Democratic presidential nomination a few days earlier, Crockett added: "[W]e may expect to see the collar-dogs of *little Van* turned loose and set on Judge White and Mr. Bell. I now hope to see my countrymen do their duty, and stand by the country against dictation."[5]

Despite being the Jacksonian candidate, Huntsman endorsed White's presidential aspirations without hesitation; for speaker, he would support Bell "or any other that may be agreed upon to be supported by Judge White's friends." His position was based on the assumption that "both White and Bell support the main principles of Jackson's administration." (When it later became apparent that this was not the case with Bell, he labeled this statement as being his *"saving clause."*[6]) Because both candidates shared identical positions on Bell's reelection—and thus White's candidacy—the issue was settled in the minds of voters for the remainder of the campaign.[7]

THE CANVASS BETWEEN Crockett and Huntsman began in earnest when the incumbent returned from Washington in the spring of 1835. It was now a two-man race after James R. McMeans withdrew his candidacy in late March. Crockett's failure to pass his occupant land bill the previous session and the lack of legislative accomplishments after six years in Congress made him vulnerable. His opposition to the Jackson administration and his personal vendetta against both the president and vice president had become repetitive and tiresome. Moreover, he went on an ill-timed political tour in the spring of 1834 to New York, Philadelphia, Boston, and other Northeastern cities when he should have been attending to congressional business in Washington.[8]

---

5. *National Banner and Nashville Whig*, June 26, 1835
6. Ibid. Samuel H. Laughlin, editor of the state Democratic newspaper, the *Nashville Union*, wrote James K. Polk: "We [Huntsman and Laughlin] had a hearty laugh over the saving clause appended to his letter in answer to the questions propounded to him through the Truth Teller on the subject of is support for Judge White and Speaker Bell." Laughlin to JKP, November 18, 1835. CJKP 3:364.
7. *National Banner and Nashville Whig*, June 26, 1835
8. *Nashville Union*, April 9, 1835. Shackford, *Crockett*: 156.

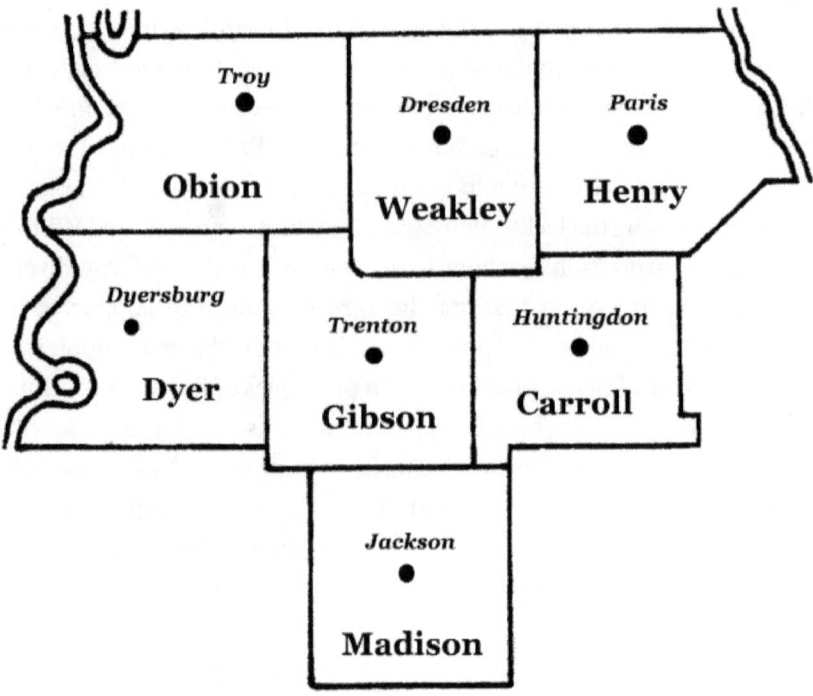

The 12th Congressional District

Huntsman had his own obstacles to overcome. Many voters looked upon lawyers with disdain, an attitude he handled with his usual self-deprecating wit. He claimed his choice of profession had been forced upon him owing to the debilitating loss of his leg. "I could not work, to beg I was ashamed, and I could not steal, because they would all know it was Huntsman by his track, and I was thus compelled to be a lawyer." The fact that he had fathered an illegitimate child may also have surfaced during the campaign, to which he answered that he would claim it only if it had a wooden leg like his own.[9]

---

9. Peter H. Burnett, *Recollections of an Old Pioneer* (New York: D. Appleton & Company, 1880): 45. Memucan Hunt Howard, "Recollections of Tennessee." <www.tngenweb.org/records/madison/history/misc/recolltn.htm> Accessed May 15, 2010. Williams, *Historic Madison*: 78. Unfortunately, Miss Williams does not cite her source for Huntsman's response to the paternity allegation, except to list "p. 65" in her notes. Emma Inman Williams Collection, Box 7, Tennessee Room, JMCPL.

As the candidates traveled the eight counties of the 12th District "speechifying the people," voters learned that both men shared similar backgrounds and campaign styles. They were born six months and six days apart (Huntsman being the older of the two); both had been Indian fighters, with Huntsman's peg leg serving as a visible reminder of the personal sacrifice he made. Crockett and Huntsman were both storytellers and frontier humorists who used their talents to entertain and enlighten their audiences. All things considered, one Western District newspaper concluded that the candidates were like *"tweedledum and tweedledee."*[10]

But differences were easily found in their political ideologies.[11] Crockett was a fervent anti-Jacksonian who supported a protective tariff, federal funding for internal improvements, and recharter of the Second Bank of the United States. Huntsman opposed each one, believing them to be "unconstitutional and inexpedient," and supported the policies of the Jackson administration. He laid out for the voters his own principles and attitudes on national affairs:

> I am in favor of a strict construction of the Constitution of the United States, and I particularly [favor] that article which says, that all powers which are not expressly given, shall be reserved to the States, or people, respectively. I am a State-rights man, but *never could see the benefits of the remedy of Nullification*. I have supported the main principles of Gen. Jackson's administration, and I expect to do so as long as it accords with the above principles; I shall support no administration upon any other.[12]

Crockett was known as a colorful stump speaker, but Huntsman had his supporters among the electorate as well. One Madison County voter believed Huntsman to be a better speaker than his opponent; Crockett

---

10. Manley F. Cobia Jr., *Journey into the Land of Trials: The Story of Davy Crockett's Expedition to the Alamo* (Franklin, TN: Hillsboro Press, 2003): 14. *Randolph Recorder*, April 17, 1835.

11. In his own words, Huntsman stated that he and Crockett "differ in politics toto coelo" (or "by the whole extent of the heavens"). Washington D.C. *Daily National Intelligencer*, September 23, 1835 (reprinted in *Nashville Union*, December 1, 1835).

12. *Nashville Union*, December 1, 1835

"was not a good speaker, but abounded in fun and anecdotes." Peter H. Burnett, who would later become the first governor of California, lived in Hardeman County at the time. He thought Huntsman was "fully equal to Crockett in native intellect, and much his superior in education and mental training."[13] In his speeches, Huntsman often quoted from the Bible. Crockett conceded that his rival "is a better scholar than I am. I have never read much scripture—not as much as I ought to." Not even Crockett's notoriety as a three-term congressman seemed to give him the upper hand. For the past twelve years, Huntsman had addressed courtrooms throughout the Western District, making him as well-known among voters as his opponent. He was also a champion of the recently revised 1835 state constitution and held the distinction of having never been beaten for elected office, a fact he made sure to remind voters.[14]

Crockett's bitter hostility toward Martin Van Buren—whom he branded as "the little Kinderhook intriguer"—was prevalent in his campaign. He vowed in December 1834 that if Van Buren was elected president, he would "leave the united states for I never will live under his kingdom." In his stump speeches, he often compared President Jackson's affinity for the red-haired Van Buren to a farmer on the Illinois prairie who instructed his young son to plow straight rows toward a red heifer in the field. When the father returned later in the day, he found the rows went in all directions and asked his son what happened. The boy said he plowed toward the heifer as he was told "and I have been ploughing after her all day.'" Crockett had followed the Old Hero on the battlefield and the political field, he explained, but "when the General began to plough after the red heifer of Kinderhook, that was grazing in every direction, I quit him on account of his crooked rows, for I was learned to plough by an old Quaker, whose directions were to plough straight rows, and go ahead."[15]

There was even a biography of Van Buren published during the campaign that claimed Crockett as its author. Although ghostwritten, *The Life of Martin Van Buren, the Heir-Apparent to the "Government," and*

---

13. Burnett, *Recollections*: 44-45. T.M. Gates, "Jesse Russell Sr." *Jackson* (TN) *Sun*, March 7, 1912.
14. Washington D.C. *United States Telegraph*, July 27, 1835. *Arkansas Advocate*, July 10, 1835.
15. Davis, *Three Roads*: 397. Washington D.C. *United States Telegraph*, July 27, 1835. Franklin (TN) *Western Weekly Review*, August 21, 1835.

Huntsman and Crockett "speechifying the people"
Illustration by Wade Dillon

the Appointed Successor to General Andrew Jackson was a highly critical and potentially libelous work inspired by Crockett. On the campaign trail, he claimed he would write a book that chronicled the "Second Fall of Adam." Huntsman playfully replied that he hated for him to waste his time on such a project, as Crockett would soon be "up a tree" and beaten before it could be completed.[16]

OUTWARDLY, CROCKETT WAS confident that he would prevail; for a time, he believed his popularity might even convince his competitor to drop out of the race. "[I]f he does not, I have no doubt of beating him with ease," he wrote. His morale never wavered over the summer months: "I have him bad plagued for he dont know as much as me about the Government [President Jackson] … I handle the Administration without gloves and I do believe I will double my competitor[.] Jacksonism is dying here faster than it sprung up[.]" Yet a congressional colleague later claimed that privately, Crockett may not have been as certain of his chances. "I do not know, my boy, that I shall ever return to this city," he reportedly said. "It is possible that old Adam Huntsman may best me. If he does, there will be an end to my public life."[17]

Not content with Huntsman alone, Crockett also quarreled with Governor William Carroll, who was running for reelection, and Judge Joshua Haskell, a candidate for Huntsman's old state senate seat. He claimed Haskell had told him that Van Buren offered Carroll an appointment as minister to Great Britain in exchange for his support. Crockett insisted the governor had been seen walking "hand and glove through the Capitol" with Van Buren in Washington and riding in the vice president's "fine English carriage, with his white drivers, with their gold and silver bands on their hats[.]" Carroll vehemently denied the charge as "a base and infamous falsehood." The accusation led to an exchange of letters between Crockett and Haskell in the Jackson *Truth Teller*. Crockett reiterated what he had been told, Haskell denied having ever said it, and the issue was never resolved.[18]

16. Davis, *Three Roads*: 397. *Arkansas Advocate*, July 10, 1835.
17. Davis, *Three Roads*: 403. Shackford, *Crockett*: 204. *Philadelphia Inquirer*, May 21, 1839.
18. Franklin *Western Weekly Review*, August 14, 1835

As the contest progressed, Huntsman kept Crockett on the defensive. He challenged his opponent's stand against the Indian Removal Act and his failure to pass his occupant land bill. Crockett made no apology for voting against removal, considering it to be "the brightest act of my life; I would do it again forty thousand times, and shall die contented with it."[19] Huntsman reminded voters that Crockett had abandoned his congressional seat while the House was still in session to embark on a much-publicized tour through the Northeast. Their congressman had dined at elegant banquets, made speeches, accepted gifts from Whig admirers, and hawked his autobiography while still collecting his salary. "Whatever may be the fashion of those who breathe the atmosphere about Washington," Huntsman scolded, "we of the West consider that no man should take a tour of pleasure for three weeks, *and then charge us eight dollars per day for it.*"[20]

The joint canvass afforded Crockett the opportunity for retribution—and a little late night mischief—at Huntsman's expense. While lodging at the home of a pro-Jackson farmer, he concocted a scheme to win the man's vote. The candidates shared a room at the back of the house that was connected by a porch to another room belonging to the farmer's daughter. As everyone slept, Crockett crept outside with a chair in hand and walked across the porch to the daughter's door. He tried opening the door, making enough noise that it sounded like an intruder, and the daughter screamed. Quickly he turned the chair backward, placed his foot on the bottom rung, hobbled back across the porch to his room, jumped into bed, and feinted sleep. The farmer burst into the room with every intention of killing Huntsman, who had no idea what was going on and pleaded his innocence. But his host was not convinced: "I know you too well and I heard that damned old peg-leg of yourn, too plain."[21]

On another overnight stay, Crockett supposedly placed a hot coal from the fireplace on Huntsman's peg leg to create a large scorched spot that Huntsman's trousers would not conceal. At their next speaking

---

19. Washington D.C. *United States Telegraph*, July 27, 1835

20. *Nashville Union*, December 1, 1835

21. J.M. Keating, *History of the City of Memphis and Shelby County, Tennessee* (Syracuse, NY: D. Mason & Company, 1888) 1:180

David Crockett bust
Gibson County Courthouse,
Trenton, Tennessee

Photograph by the author

engagement, Crockett told the crowd: "Now Huntsman has accused me of being a whiskey man. We stayed at the same man's house and I had a little whiskey just for my stomach's sake. Huntsman got hold of it, got drunk and fell in the fire, burning his leg. Don't you see the place?" Another story claimed that Crockett placed it on the campfire and watched it be consumed as Huntsman slept nearby.[22]

While political gamesmanship was evident on both sides, the campaign lacked the vindictiveness of the previous two congressional elections. It had been conducted with "perfect harmony and good humor," commented one newspaper, noting that it "had produced but little excitement." Yet family tradition among Huntsman's descendants insists that at one point, both Huntsman and Crockett came close to fighting a duel. A brace of pistols had even been purchased and affixed "with silver plates

---

22. "David Crockett, as I Knew Him, by Uncle Billy Ridgeway of Buford, Arkansas." *San Antonio* (TX) *Express*, 1912. <www.geocities.com/moedini2001/Crockett_WCdis.html?1006559449370>

which bore the names of the duelers." But calmer heads prevailed and the duel never took place.[23]

Still, the tone grew agitated a month before the election when Crockett's salary and mileage figures between his home in Weakley County and Washington were published in the Paris *West Tennessean* on July 8. The article also alleged that he had been reimbursed for too many miles traveled, a charge Crockett himself had made two years earlier against former representative William Fitzgerald.[24]

Crockett's allies were particularly upset about how the figures had been obtained. George W. Terrell, a Paris, Tennessee attorney who would later serve as secretary of war for the Republic of Texas, said they had been franked to him by Andrew Jackson Donelson, nephew and private secretary to the president. Franked copies of the *Washington Globe* also found their way to post offices in the Western District to bolster Huntsman's candidacy and garner support for Van Buren. These free postage mailings were proof, claimed Crockett's defenders, that the president "is not satisfied with using his name and office to make Van Buren his successor, but condescends to frank documents which he thinks will operate to the prejudice of any and particularly to Col. Crockett, who is opposed to Van Buren."[25]

---

23. "Paul Flowers' Greenhouse." Undated clipping from the *Memphis Commercial Appeal*, contained in Adam Huntsman folder, Tentative Box 4 (Individuals), Seale Johnson Collection (unprocessed collection), Tennessee Room, JMCPL. Patricia Grames Pollock to the author, January 9, 2010. No contemporary accounts could be found to indicate that the rivalry ever reached the point of violence between the two candidates. Patricia Grames Pollock, great-great granddaughter of Huntsman, told the author that according to family tradition, the pistols were with family members in Texas for many years, but their present whereabouts are unknown. Edith Grames Schay, Huntsman's great-granddaughter, believed Huntsman "had a fiery temper," though no eyewitness accounts during his lifetime mention such temperament. As for Crockett, one modern biographer believed he "was never a man quick to violence" and "more prone to ridicule dueling than to participate…" Davis, *Three Roads*: 125.

24. Cobia, *Journey*: 14. Paris *West Tennessean*, reprinted in the Franklin *Western Weekly Review*, August 14, 1835.

25. Franklin *Western Weekly Review*, August 14, 1835. Jon Meacham, *American Lion: Andrew Jackson in the White House* (New York: Random House, 2008): 309-312. After his defeat, Crockett claimed his mileage figures had been published "Just days before the election." In fact, they had appeared in the Paris *West Tennessean* as early as July 8, almost a month before the election on August 6. Shackford, *Crockett*: 205.

Huntsman took responsibility for securing the franked documents. Having learned of Crockett's New England tour in the fall of 1834, he sought proof that his opponent had accepted his congressional salary despite his absence. He tried unsuccessfully to obtain Crockett's payroll from members of the House of Representatives and even solicited a copy from Speaker John Bell, with whom he had served in the state senate eighteen years earlier. Without the evidence he sought and with the election approaching, he finally obtained it through President Jackson. Huntsman insisted that he never "used it directly, or indirectly" against Crockett, but the information was indeed used by his supporters during the final weeks of the campaign.[26]

At the same time, Huntsman defended the president franking documents into the 12th Congressional District that favored his administration. It was done to counter some twenty thousand anti-Jackson documents that were "full of vituperation, abuse, and slander" which Crockett had mailed under his own frank for the past two years. At the same time, Huntsman alleged that Crockett ignored requests from his constituents for documents that sided with Jackson. "If any man can tell me upon what principle the President of the United States is deprived of the same right to defend himself from slanders, abuse, and misrepresentation, that the most indignant man in society has, I shall like to know it."[27]

THE CAMPAIGN CONCLUDED the first week of August 1835. After their last scheduled engagement at Huntingdon, Crockett and Huntsman left for their respective homes to await the results. While traveling back to Madison County, Huntsman remembered that the Weakley County Court would be in session at Dresden. There would be a large crowd in town and Crockett could not resist making a final appeal for their votes. So Huntsman turned his horse around and pointed it toward Dresden, where his suspicion was confirmed. He hitched his horse and made his way through the crowd until he stood in front of his opponent. Crockett stopped his

---

26. *Nashville Union*, December 1, 1835
27. Ibid

speech and both men stared at each other. Finally, he exclaimed: "Adam Huntsman, I believe if I were to go to hell you'd follow me there."[28]

Hell was a consistent theme for Crockett in his speeches. The ultimatum he made to his constituents should they vote him out of office—"You can go to hell, but I am going to Texas"—apparently had different implications as the campaign progressed. He would either go to hell *or* to Texas, or Huntsman would go to hell and Crockett would go to Texas. At one point, Huntsman challenged his opponent's inconsistent message, but Crockett corrected him: "Now Huntsman, I didn't say that. I said 'you may go to Congress and I will go to Texas.'"[29]

Crockett was more prophetic than he realized. The election on August 6 was close, but Huntsman prevailed by 252 votes, 4,652 to 4,400. He carried majorities in five of the eight counties in the 12th District.[30] His victory gave Tennessee Democrats a rare moment for celebration in an otherwise disappointing election. Making full use of Hugh Lawson White's candidacy to divide the party, the anti-Jacksonians gained control of the governor's chair and both houses of the General Assembly, as well as a majority of the state's congressional delegation. Sixty percent of the electorate voted for pro-White candidates in races across the state, giving birth to the opposition Whig party and ending Andrew Jackson's dominance of Tennessee politics.[31]

But the success of the anti-Jackson movement was little consolation to David Crockett. His pride had been wounded by his defeat and he lashed out in a letter to the *National Intelligencer*. Giving no credit to his rival's successful campaign against him, Crockett attributed his loss instead to alleged voting fraud and the interference of President Jackson and his administration. He claimed managers of the Union Bank of Tennessee

---

28. *Jackson Sun*, March 7, 1912

29. Cobia, *Journey*: 14-15. "David Crockett as I Knew Him." *San Antonio Express*, 1912.

30. The only counties Crockett carried were his home counties of Gibson and Weakley, as well as Carroll. The tabulations were as follows: Madison (AH 969, DC 728); Gibson (DC 717, AH 623); Haywood (AH 606, DC 404); Carroll (DC 816, AH 650); Weakley (DC 493, AH 479); Obion (AH 293, DC 178); Henry (AH 847, DC 703); Dyer (AH 185, DC 161). 1835 Congressional Election (12th District) official tally sheet in David Crockett Vertical File of the Tennessee Room, JMCL.

31. Pro-White (or Whig) candidates across Tennessee received 53,255 votes out of 89,156 ballots cast in the 1835 elections. Bergeron, *Antebellum Politics*: 45. Sellers, *Polk: Jacksonian*: 283-284.

branch at Jackson had offered twenty-five dollars to every voter who cast his ballot for Huntsman and that the election officials were allied with his competitor. "I am astonished that I came as near beating him as I did," Crockett remarked. His congressional mileage figures and franked copies of the *Washington Globe* had been mailed throughout the district by President Jackson, who was "determined to expend every dollar of the Treasury, [to] make Van Buren his successor." Governor William Carroll had also exerted his influence against him. "I have no doubt that I was completely Raskeled out of my election. I do regret that duty to my Self & to my Country Compals me to expose Such viloney."[32]

Huntsman responded in a letter of his own published in the *National Intelligencer* on September 23, denying every charge Crockett leveled against his campaign. Those who had spread rumors about bribed voters were "unprincipled men" with "no character for truth or credibility." It was interesting that Crockett would raise the subject of buying votes, noted Huntsman, when Crockett himself was known to purchase whiskey in an effort to secure them on his own behalf. "I have never done so although I have been a candidate for one appointment of another, for upwards of twenty years," he wrote. "I have never solicited a man for his vote, or his interest, in my life." As for election officials being among his supporters, Huntsman believed they would have benefited him more casting their votes in the ballot box rather than supervising them. The election had been decided on the candidates' positions on national issues rather than alleged voting fraud and excessive franking. He concluded that the reason Crockett lost the election, put simply, "was because he did not get votes enough."[33]

HUNTSMAN'S VICTORY WAS APPLAUDED by Democrats throughout the Western District. A Carroll County supporter proudly proclaimed "that the great *Hunter* one Davy has been beaten by a *Huntsman*," and with his

---

32. Shackford, *Crockett*: 205-206. *New York Spectator*, September 7, 1835. The *Boston Reformer*, sympathetic to Crockett, reiterated his claim of voting fraud: "[W]hile honest Davy was grinning up a stamp by the roots in order to show his prowess, the more adroit Huntsman was grinning Davy's name from the ballots as they went into the box, and his own on." *Salem Gazette*, February 12, 1836.

33. *Nashville Union*, December 1, 1835

Tennesseans vying for House speaker: John Bell (left) and James K. Polk

Courtesy of the Library of Congress

election, "the District has to a certain extent redeemed herself." A Madison County Democrat had "great hopes Huntsman will do us credit."[34]

But it did not mean their nemesis Crockett had been replaced by a strict Jackson party man. Instead, the administration had exchanged an intolerable relationship for a precarious alliance. Like all newly-elected members of the Tennessee congressional delegation, Huntsman supported the presidential aspirations of Hugh Lawson White. The first vote he would cast in Congress would test his loyalty to the administration.

The election for House speaker would likely put James K. Polk, a political associate of Huntsman and President Jackson's choice, against the incumbent John Bell, who had helped initiate White's presidential aspirations. Over the next four months, Polk worked behind the scenes to determine whose support he could count on among the Tennessee delegation. He was uncertain where Huntsman's allegiance lay in the contest, though he believed him to be his political friend. During the campaign, Huntsman had said he would support Bell or any other candidate favored

---

34. Joel R. Smith to JKP, August 9, 1835. CJKP 3:261. William Armour to JKP, September 7, 1835. Ibid: 286.

by White's supporters. But Polk's brother-in-law had heard a rumor that after reading a letter written by Bell during the campaign that Democrats considered proof of Bell meddling in Polk's election, Huntsman "was not to be considered pledged" to Bell.[35] Polk confided to President Jackson that he had "some hope that he may go right though what I hear it is not positively certain, what his course would be." Senator Felix Grundy wrote Polk with disdain that when he visited the Western District after the election, he chose not to meet with Huntsman. Instead, he instructed Dr. William E. Butler, a fellow Democrat who was related by marriage to the president, "to hold the proper talk with him" regarding Polk's candidacy. By mid September, Polk had gained enough insight into the eccentric congressman-elect's mind-set to say with confidence that Huntsman would indeed vote for him.[36]

35. Referred to as the "Cassedy Letter" or the "Bedford Letter," it was written by John Bell on May 11, 1835, in response to a letter sent by Charles Cassedy, a freelance writer who lived in Bedford County, part of James K. Polk's congressional district. The *Nashville Union* acquired a copy and focused in particular on one statement made by Bell: "It would not do to ask Polk to vote for me against himself [for House speaker]; but he might be made to pledge himself for me against any other candidate." The partisan *Union* editor interpreted it as Bell suggesting to a voter in Polk's district that the congressman could be made to vote for Bell against any candidate for speaker other than himself. *Nashville Union*, June 26, 1835. CJPK 3:211fn.

36. JKP to AJ, August 14, 1835 CJPK 3:265. SHL to JKP, August 21, 1835 Ibid: 271. JKP to SHL, September 6, 1835 Ibid: 285. Felix Grundy to JKP, September 11, 1835 Ibid: 290. JKP to Andrew Jackson Donelson, September 22, 1835 Ibid: 304.

Chapter Seven

Spice of the West

1835–1836

The essence and quintessence of our republican institutions, require the representative to speak fully, and truly, the voice of his constituents. Whenever he fails to do that, he is a misrepresentative. He is a man whom republicans despise, and fools laugh at as an aristocrat in republican clothing.
—Adam Huntsman, April 4, 1836

There are many people in this world who have all sorts of sense but common sense, which is much the most useful to nine tenths of the human family.
—Adam Huntsman, April 18, 1836

THE FIRST WEEK OF NOVEMBER 1835, David Crockett and Adam Huntsman left the Western District for new opportunities in opposite directions. Crockett went to Texas to explore it for a possible move of his family. "I do believe Santa Ana's kingdom will be a paradise, compared with this [under Van Buren], in a few years," he wrote. Before leaving Tennessee, he reiterated the promise he had made during the election:

The U.S. Capitol Building and Washington D.C. in 1839. Huntsman's Dowson's Row boarding house likely resembled one of these buildings.

Courtesy of the Library of Congress

"Since you have chosen to elect a man with a timber toe to succeed me, you may all go to hell and I will go to Texas."[1]

Huntsman made his way to Washington City, a journey of 861 miles, where he would serve for the next two years as the representative for the 12th Congressional District. He reached Nashville on or about November 14, and stayed at least three days before continuing his trip east. The road took him through parts of the Mountain District where he first practiced law and began his political career over twenty-five years earlier, and to Knoxville where his interest in both fields began. He continued northeast through his native Virginia and reached the nation's capital in late November or early December.[2]

The first two things Huntsman would have done upon arriving in Washington were find a place to stay and claim his seat in the House of

---

1. Davis, *Three Roads*: 407-409. Shackford, *Crockett*: 212-213. Boylston and Wiener, *Crockett in Congress*: 122. Davis, *History of Memphis*: 143.

2. Robert M. McBride and Owen Meredith, eds. *Eastin Morris's Tennessee Gazetter 1834 and Matthew Rhea's Map of the State of Tennessee 1832* (Nashville: The Gazette Press, 1971): 181-182. *Nashville Union*, November 14, 1835. Samuel H. Laughlin to JKP, November 18, 1835, CJKP 3: 364.

Representatives chamber.[3] He found accommodations at Dowson's Row, a pair of adjacent three-story brick buildings on Capitol Hill that had exclusively lodged members of Congress since 1816. The proprietor was Alfred R. Dowson, a fifty-two year old clerk at the Treasury Department. One congressman found it to be "old and cracky—and the furniture in good keeping with it," but it was the closest boardinghouse to the Capitol Building.[4] Depending upon its size and location in the household, a room at a typical Washington boardinghouse with basic furnishings such as a bed, table, and wash stand rented for $8 to $12 a week. Boardinghouses served as both fraternity house and political club, bringing "together… kindred spirits engaged in the same pursuit." Boarders shared their meals together at a common mess table and socialized in the parlor, often playing cards, swapping stories, or engaging in political conversation. Because of living expenses in the capital and family obligations at home, it is unlikely that Elizabeth Huntsman accompanied her husband to Washington.[5]

Huntsman was among eight congressmen who messed at Dowson's No. 1 during the first session of the 24th Congress. For many years, the boardinghouse was considered a domain for Southern lawmakers; when Huntsman was a boarder, all but one of its residents were representatives of southern and western states. The exception was Franklin Pierce of New Hampshire, though he was considered sympathetic to Southern interests. (Pierce would later become fourteenth President of the United States.) Among Huntsman's messmates were fellow Tennessean William B. Carter, who had served with him at the Tennessee Constitutional Convention, and Thomas Hart Benton of Missouri, a former Tennessean who was

---

3. John Fairfield, a freshman representative from Maine, recalled that he and members of the New York delegation "ran up to the Capitol to secure seats" upon their arrival in Washington. Arthur G. Staples, ed. *The Letters of John Fairfield* (Lewistown, MA: Lewiston Journal Company, 1922): 23.

4. Dowson's Row was located on A Street between North Capitol Street and East First Street. Originally known as Mrs. Dowson's, it was operated by Elizabeth Dowson from 1809 until her death on 15 September 1816. Alfred R. Dowson took over in December 1816 and continued to house members of Congress until the late 1840s. Staples, ed. Fairfield: 24. Perry M. Goldman and James S. Young, eds. *The United States Congressional Directories 1789-1840* (New York: Columbia University Press, 1973): 291.

5. Robert V. Remini, *The House: The History of the House of Representatives* (New York: Smithsonian Books, 2006): 124, 304. Washington D.C. *Daily National Intelligencer*, October 18, 1826.

Boarders at Dowson's No. 1 during Huntsman's residence (left to right): Sen. Thomas Hart Benton of Missouri, Rep. James I. McKay of North Carolina, Rep. Francis Thomas of Maryland, and Rep. Franklin Pierce of New Hampshire.

Courtesy of the Library of Congress

beginning his fourteenth year in the Senate. With the exception of Carter, all the boarders were Jacksonian Democrats.[6]

HUNTSMAN WAS ALMOST FORTY-NINE YEARS OLD when he took his seat among the 242 members of the House of Representatives in December 1835. A Democrat from Maine named John Fairfield recorded his impressions of him in a letter to his wife: "He is short and rather fleshy, [with a] round face and bald head, one wooden leg, and one not wooden. He speaks rapidly, in a small, clear voice, but when very earnest[,] clips his words so that you cannot always understand him. He appears to be a man of good sense having a spice of the West in his composition." During his time in Washington, Huntsman sat for a graphite and charcoal sketch that showed him with side whiskers and what must have been a hairpiece.[7]

The Hall of the House of Representatives was one of the earliest examples of Greek Revival architecture in America. Located on the second floor of the south wing of the Capitol Building, it was a large semi-circular room designed like an ancient amphitheater, with separate galleries for ladies and gentlemen to listen to the deliberations. Each representative had his own small mahogany desk and armed easy chair on the marble tiled floor, which were arranged in a tiered semi-circular fashion and divided by aisles facing the elevated Speaker's Rostrum. The chamber was heated in the winter by two large fireplaces that flanked the Rostrum. Above their heads was a ninety-six foot high wood dome ceiling with a light-emitting cupola and a massive and ornate bronze gilt chandelier with 78

---

6. Goldman and Young, eds. *Congressional Directories*: 291. Biographical Directory of the United States Congress, 1774-present. <www.bioguide.congress.gov>. *Daily National Intelligencer*, October 18, 1826. James Sterling Young, *The Washington Community 1800-1828* (New York: Columbia University Press, 1966): 100. Nathan Sargent, *Public Men and Events from the Commencement of Mr. Monroe's Administration, in 1817, to the Close of Mr. Fillmore's Administration, in 1853* (Philadelphia: J.B. Lippincott & Company, 1875) 2:23-24. Other messmates during the first session were Edward A. Hannegan of Indiana; Thomas L. Hamer, Ohio; James I. McKay, North Carolina; and Francis Thomas, Maryland. Three fellow members of the Tennessee delegation—William C. Dunlap, Cave Johnson, and Ebenezer J. Shields—boarded next door at Dowson's No. 2. Goldman and Young, eds. *Congressional Directories*: 291.

7. Family tradition says the artist was an African-American woman who drew the sketch using her toes. "Paul Flowers' Greenhouse." Undated clipping in Adam Huntsman folder, Tentative Box 4 (Individuals), Seale Johnson Collection (unprocessed collection). Tennessee Room at JMCPL.

oil-burning lamps. The ceiling made acoustics in the chamber terrible, resulting in echoes that made it difficult for speakers to be heard by visitors in the galleries and even their own colleagues on the House floor.[8]

The first session of the 24th Congress officially convened at noon on Monday, December 7. The first order of business was the election of a new speaker. How he would be chosen became the subject of lengthy debate when one member suggested that it be done by voice vote rather than the customary paper ballot. Eventually, the motion was rejected and the vote proceeded as usual. The anticipated contest between incumbent speaker John Bell and fellow Tennessean James K. Polk, a showdown between the opposition and administration forces in the House, proved anticlimactic: Polk was elected on the first ballot with 132 votes to Bell's 84. Afterward, Walter S. Franklin was elected clerk for the House and Francis P. Blair and John C. Rives, publishers of the Jackson newspaper, the *Washington Globe*, were chosen as the official printers.[9]

The next two weeks were spent organizing the House. The remaining officers were elected, rules were adopted, and committee assignments were made. Huntsman was named to the Committee on Private Land Claims, which handled bills, petitions, and memorials related to individual claims on public lands. The normal course of business was interrupted when two members of Connecticut's congressional delegation and an Illinois senator all died within the same week. Both houses of Congress along with the president, vice president, and cabinet officials attended the

---

8. Young, *Washington Community*: 157. William Lee Miller, *Arguing about Slavery: The Great Battle in the United States Congress* (New York: Alfred A. Knopf, 1997): 45. Jonathan Elliot, *Historical Sketches of the Ten Miles Square Formed the District of Columbia; Etc.* (Washington D.C.: J. Elliot Jr., 1830): 110, 112. Remini, *Clay*: 379. Sellers, *Polk: Jacksonian*: 102. When the lamps were filled with whale oil to illuminate the chamber, the chandelier weighed over seven hundred pounds. It crashed to the floor four years after Huntsman left the House; fortunately, no one was hurt. Remini, *The House*: 157. The Hall of the House of Representatives during Huntsman's tenure is now known as Statuary Hall.

9. Congressional Globe, 24th Congress, 1st Session: 1-3. Six votes were cast for three additional candidates, including Massachusetts representative and former president John Quincy Adams. Three ballots were left blank. Ibid: 3.

The only known likeness of Adam Huntsman, this graphite and charcoal sketch shows him as a member of Congress circa 1836.

Courtesy of the East Tennessee Historical Society

funerals. Congressmen wore mourning crape on their left arms for thirty days in their memory.[10]

Huntsman soon settled into the routine of a congressman's life. The House met six days a week. On a typical day, committees met in the morning before members assembled for the legislative session, which began at ten o'clock or noon and adjourned late in the afternoon. They did not have the luxuries of a Capitol Hill office with staff members at the disposal. Their business was conducted at their desks on the House floor, where they read newspapers and correspondence, answered letters, or took occasional naps amid winded speeches and arguments going on around them. Huntsman found the sofas that lined the chamber to be especially comfortable. During debates, members fought to be recognized by the Speaker in order to address the House. Although much preparation went into them, their speeches were never read verbatim; those who did were ridiculed by their colleagues. If the House was not in session, Huntsman may have wandered into the gallery of the Senate chamber and listened to speeches made by such orators as Daniel Webster, Henry Clay, John C. Calhoun, and his fellow messmate Thomas Hart Benton.[11]

Lawmakers enjoyed the casual atmosphere of the House chamber. One freshman representative observed: "The members wear their hats, and talk and buzz while the business is going on so that much of the time it sounds like a town meeting, the Speaker only appearing to attend to the business of the House." While in session, they could leave their desks to take pinches of snuff from silver urns or quench their thirst with a mixed drink of spring water, ginger, molasses, and Jamaica rum called "Switchell." Members "who were not always good marksmen" would lean back in their chairs, with their feet propped on their desks, and spit tobacco juice into spittoons. One foreign visitor noted the unintended patterns on the

---

10. *Register of Debates*, 24th Congress, 1st session: 1948-1958. The congressmen who died were Senator Nathan Smith of Connecticut; Senator Elias Kane of Illinois; and Representative Zalmon Wildman of Connecticut. *Congressional Globe*, 24th Congress, 1st session: 11, 21, 22.

11. Miller, *Arguing about Slavery*: 45. Young, *Washington Community*: 96-97. Remini, *The House*: 112-113. One New England newspaper noted: "Adam Huntsman...stretched himself at full length on one of the sofas in the House of Representatives the other day, and falling fast asleep, snored like 'all natur.'" *Vermont State Paper*, March 15, 1836.

carpets resulting from their poor aim and advised visitors "not to look at the floor" or pick up items dropped onto it "with any ungloved hand."[12]

THE UNEXPECTED DEATHS of three colleagues were the first indications that the 24th Congress would be anything but routine. Over the next two years, Huntsman witnessed the beginning of a tumultuous debate on the House floor between Southern and Northern legislators over the divisive issue of slavery, one that would persist well after his tenure had ended. It was President Jackson who first addressed the subject in his Annual Message to Congress read to the House on December 8. Responding to the flood of "inflammatory" abolitionist pamphlets being mailed to Southern states by the American Anti-Slavery Society, he asked Congress to pass legislation that would prohibit the circulation through the federal postal system "of incendiary publications intended to instigate the slaves to insurrection."[13]

Another source of discontent among Southern legislators was antislavery petitions presented by their Northern counterparts. It was common practice on specific days for members to read petitions submitted by their constituents, after which the petitions were referred to the appropriate committees for further action. Since 1833, the American Anti-Slavery Society had utilized the right of petition to call for the abolition of the slave trade and slavery itself in the District of Columbia. The roll call customarily began with the New England states, forcing Southern representatives to listen to them. Typically, a motion was made that the offensive petition be laid on the table, essentially dismissing it and defusing the subject.[14]

This course of action worked as it had in past House sessions when two antislavery petitions were presented on December 16. But Southern lawmakers realized a disturbing trend two days later when William Jackson of Massachusetts presented a similar petition from his own constituents and asked that it be referred to a select committee. "It has precipitated, and brought on prematurely, a debate, which must sooner of later have

12. Staples, ed. *Letters of Fairfield*: 33. Remini, *The House*: 112. Charles Dickens, *American Notes for General Circulation* (London: Chapman and Hall, 1842) 1: 294-295.
13. Congressional Globe, 24th Congress, 1st Session: 10. Meacham, *American Lion*: 304-306.
14. Peter A. Wallner, *Franklin Pierce: New Hampshire's Favorite Son* (Concord, NH: Plaidswede Publishing, 2004): 58. Miller, *Arguing about Slavery*: 107-108, 199. Sean Wilentz, *The Rise of American Democracy: Jefferson to Lincoln* (New York: W.W. Norton, 2005): 451-452.

come," an observer for the *Boston Patriot* believed. "And I fear these Petitions will, if they continue to be sent, continue to keep alive, and even augment the heat and bitterness of the South; and have a bad effect on the mutual relations of the North and South."[15]

James Henry Hammond of South Carolina, a fellow member of the Private Land Claims Committee with Huntsman, believed the fate of such petitions had already been settled. But knowing that they would continue to be presented, he motioned for "a more decided seal of reprobation" against future petitions that would "peremptorily" reject them before they could be introduced on the House floor.[16] Hammond's motion sparked a contentious six-week debate that only intensified with the introduction of each new petition. ("Some members from the South go off like a rocket, the moment the word slavery is uttered in Congress," one New England correspondent noted.[17]) Members argued over the constitutional right of citizens to petition the government for a redress of grievances granted by the First Amendment and if Congress had the authority to abolish slavery in the District of Columbia, let alone the rest of the country.[18]

In February 1836, the troublesome petitions were sent to a select committee chaired by Henry Pinckney of South Carolina. A committee report was presented to the House on May 18 that denounced the abolitionists who were sending the petitions to their representatives and offered three resolutions to resolve the contentious debate. The first resolution declared that Congress had no authority to abolish slavery in the states, which was approved 182 to 9; the second that affirmed it would be "inexpedient" to do so in the District of Columbia passed as well, 132 to 45. But the third resolution proved to be the most controversial. It stated that petitions, memorials, and other forms of communication by members of the House concerning slavery should lie on the table without being printed or referred to a select committee. This resolution, which attempted to suppress all discussion of slavery, came to be known as the "gag rule." It passed on

---

15. Leonard L. Richards, *The Life and Times of Congressman John Quincy Adams* (New York: Oxford University Press, 1986): 115-116. *Norfolk* (VA) *Advertiser*, December 26, 1835.
16. Congressional Globe, 24th Congress, 1st Session: 27
17. *Norfolk Advertiser*, December 26, 1835
18. Richards, *Life and Times of Adams*: 116-117

Debate in the Hall of the House of Representatives over the "gag rule" in 1836.
Courtesy of istockphoto.com

May 26 by a 117-68 vote and became a standing rule of the House for the remainder of the session.[19]

Huntsman voted with the majority on all three resolutions. Although he did not participate in the heated exchanges over slavery, his position coincided with that of his fellow Southerners; his first recorded vote in Congress was to table two petitions seeking its abolition in the District of Columbia. Twenty years earlier, as a freshman state senator, he had advocated the reading of such petitions, even though he disagreed with them. He addressed the slavery issue indirectly when he chastised John Quincy Adams of Massachusetts for labeling the American Colonization Society (to which Huntsman belonged) as a group of abolitionists. He believed Adams's criticism was merely an attempt "to slide in a discussion on the subject of abolition."[20]

---

19. Miller, *Arguing about Slavery*: 139-145. Remini, *The House*: 128-129. Journal of the House of Representatives, 24th Congress, 1st Session: 876-877; 881-882; 884-885.

20. Congressional Globe, 24th Congress, 2nd Session: 161, 24. Huntsman also interjected himself in an attempt by John Quincy Adams on January 23, 1836, to introduce a petition that alluded to upholding the Declaration of Independence while not specifically calling for the aboli-

Huntsman was upset when he received in the mail an unsolicited copy of *The Friend of Man*, an abolitionist newspaper published by the New York State Anti-Slavery Society. He fired off a letter to its editor, William Goodell, berating him for abusing "the privilege of my frank to send me a paper that I did not desire, would not have subscribed for, and consequently you have defrauded the government out of its postage." Had he received the abolitionist paper in Tennessee rather than Washington, Huntsman claimed he would have violated a law enacted by the General Assembly in 1835 prohibiting antislavery materials in the state. Punishment was five to twenty years in the state penitentiary.[21] Assuming Goodell was unaware of the laws in Tennessee, Huntsman warned him that mailing his paper to its citizens would result in their imprisonment. "I cannot consent to discuss the propriety or impropriety of your doctrines," he added. "Tennessee will be prepared to meet any danger arising out of them, as she always has been prepared to meet danger in whatever form it presented itself."[22]

ON DECEMBER 31, 1835, Huntsman was appointed to a select committee charged with investigating banks in the District of Columbia that had applied for extensions to their charters.[23] Its chairman and Huntsman's messmate, Francis Thomas of Maryland, presented a bill two weeks later to extend the charters of seven banks to October 1, 1836, giving his committee sufficient time to investigate the financial condition of each institution. A few legislators, particularly members of the Committee on

---

tion of slavery in the District of Columbia. Register of Debates, 24th Congress, 2nd Session: 1431-1432. On the same day that Huntsman accused Adams of "attempting to slide in a discussion on the subject of abolition," Adams was censured by the House "for having attempted to present to this House the petition of slaves." Ibid: 162.

21. White, ed. *Messages* 3:101

22. Huntsman to William Goodell, January 6, 1837, published in the *Boston Liberator*, April 28, 1837. Goddell's lengthy response to Huntsman's letter is given in the *New York Emancipator and Republican*, March 9, 1837. In addition to serving as editor of *The Friend of Man*, Goodell also helped organize the American Anti-Slavery Society and was a founder of the anti-slavery Liberty party.

23. Other members of the select committee were Huntsman's fellow messmate Franklin Pierce of New Hampshire, John Reed of Massachusetts, William L. May of Illinois, Andrew Beaumont of Pennsylvania, James Garland of Virginia, and John F.H. Claiborne of Mississippi. Journal of the House, 24th Congress, 1st Session: 126. Goldman and Young, eds. *Congressional Directories*: 291.

the District of Columbia, objected to the length of the extension and the hastiness with which the chairman sought its passage. Questions were also raised why the select committee had not already begun its investigations. Was it not the reason the task had been taken from the Committee on the District of Columbia in the first place? Two representatives believed the matter should be returned to that committee, which "would have performed the business promptly, quickly, and with ability."[24]

Huntsman took this occasion to rise from his seat and give his maiden speech on January 15, 1836. He believed members of the Committee on the District of Columbia felt "robbed" they had not been allowed to investigate the banks themselves. Sarcastically, he conceded their committee must possess "more ability, and can transact this business in a style exquisitely genteel, systematic, nice, and scientific—more so than any committee in the House, or that ever was in it." He disagreed with one member's contention that the records of one bank could be investigated in three hours. It was this kind of hasty inquiry that had "enabled many of them to commit the deepest frauds, and to fatten upon the substance of the laboring classes of society."

Huntsman contended that the records of each District bank should be examined meticulously for as long as it took to determine its solvency. "It is true, sir, they may bring up the prettiest set of bank books, more neatly bound, and more handsomely gilt, with the finest writing; the t's crossed and the i's all dotted, which will exhibit a most splendid appearance, and which will answer all the purposes intended by a three hours' examination," he asserted. "But, sir, all things may not be so smooth, honest, and fair, when we get a peep behind the curtain; there may be something rotten in Denmark." Some banks seeking recharter had suspended specie payments and required particular scrutiny to determine why they had been forced to do so.

Extending the charters to the first of October 1836, Huntsman argued, would give the select committee sufficient time to conduct its examinations during the present congress and give those banks that would be denied their charters time to "wind up their business." "For myself, I

---

24. Register of Debates, 24th Congress, 1st Session: 2213-2215

The Capitol Building in Washington D.C. as it looked during Huntsman's term in the House. *Courtesy of the Library of Congress*

have not much favor for the banking system, much less for its abuses," he confessed. (He had voted for only one such institution during his political career—the Bank of the State of Tennessee—while serving in the state senate in 1820.) "In some instances it may be a necessary evil. When it is so, the charters should be so framed as to make that evil as light as possible."[25] The bill passed the House on its third reading, but it was superseded in June 1836 by a Senate version that extended the charters to July 4, 1838. One Northeastern newspaper correspondent remarked that he had "made a very sensible speech."[26]

Journalists who covered the House proceedings compared Huntsman to his predecessor and discovered him to be just as colorful and eccentric as David Crockett. He was jovial in conversation and drew a crowd around his desk on the House floor.[27] The facial expressions he made during his speeches were similar to those used by his former rival. "From the peculiar facility with which both these gentlemen distort their phizzes

---

25. Ibid: 2215-2216
26. Portland (ME) *Eastern Argus*, January 26, 1836
27. *Salem* (MA) *Gazette*, February 2, 1836. The newspaper added: "[T]he members more generally crowded round him [Huntsman] than they have ever been known to crowd around John Quincy Adams."

[faces]," observed one reporter, "we are inclined to think that to grin well must be the chief qualification of candidates in their district." But what set him apart from Crockett was the effective use of his wooden stump. When he spoke, Huntsman brought his "heavy hickory iron shod leg... down upon the floor in confirmation of a position," which "produced an astonishing effect." One correspondent cleverly noted that Huntsman was "a greater stump orator than Davy Crockett, who was unable in pugilistic strife to knock Huntsman off his pins."[28]

In mid April 1836, word reached Washington of the attack by Mexican forces against a fortified Spanish mission in Texas called the Alamo and the deaths of its defenders, including Crockett.[29] Huntsman did not record his thoughts at the time, but the news would have been cause for reflection on his past political battles with his former rival. The differences he had with Crockett were political—but never personal—in nature. The satires he wrote against him rankled Crockett, but none hinted at any personal malice or animosity. Being the man who had beaten him in his last political campaign, Huntsman found himself forever linked to Crockett by his contemporaries and future generations. Reporting on political affairs in the Western District, one correspondent referred to him simply as "Mr. Huntsman—of Crockett notoriety."[30]

HUNTSMAN'S FRESHMAN STATUS did not inhibit him from taking part in debates or confronting his esteemed colleagues on the House floor. He took particular delight in verbal jousts with former president John Quincy Adams, who at the time was among the most respected men in the

28. Ibid. The writer added: "Quintilian enumerates among the arts of rhetoricans the supplosio pedis [stamping of the foot], and percussio femoris, but he was a stranger to the modern 'mortal pestle pound ye.'" Ibid.

29. Shackford, *Crockett*: 235. As early as February 17, 1836, one Washington correspondent reported that "a member of Congress from Brownsville, Tennessee" had received a letter from home "that intelligence had been received there of the death of Col. David Crockett, in Texas, soon after his arrival in that country." Obviously it was a false rumor, coming almost three weeks before the attack on the Alamo on March 6. *New York Mercury*, February 23, 1836. There was no member of the Tennessee delegation who lived in Brownsville; the unnamed representative may have been William C. Dunlap of Bolivar.

30. David A. Street to John C. Calhoun, May 25, 1844. Clyde N. Wilson, ed. *The Papers of John C. Calhoun* (Columbia, SC: University of South Carolina Press, 1988) 18:619-620.

chamber. An editorial had been published in the *Washington Globe* on May 13, 1836, refuting a claim made by Adams a few days earlier. Adams had rejected a comment made by Waddy Thompson Jr. of South Carolina that essentially blamed him for the loss of Texas during negotiations to purchase Florida when Adams was secretary of state under President James Monroe. Adams claimed that Andrew Jackson (then a major general in the United States Army) had read a draft of the Adams-Onís Treaty before its ratification and advised Adams that the U.S. claim to Texas should be relinquished in order to obtain Florida. When asked about the former president's claim in the *Globe* article, President Jackson could not remember ever consulting Adams about the treaty, much less advising that Texas should be given up. (He had in fact done so.)[31]

That morning, the galleries of the House were filled with spectators, anticipating that Adams would have something to say about the offensive article. The Massachusetts representative did not disappoint. As the House began its legislative day, he asked that the rules be suspended to allow him the opportunity to respond to it. With the newspaper in hand, he meticulously read sections from the offensive article for thirty minutes while insisting that he had told the truth about Jackson's recommendation. He made sure his colleagues knew that his remarks were directed not toward Francis P. Blair, the editor of the *Globe* and Jackson's "ambassador," but toward the president himself.[32]

When he finished, Adams took his seat amidst "a very general and very pleasant uproar." Immediately, Huntsman rose and asked for suspension of the rules to offer a rebuttal. Objections were made but after a few minutes of parliamentary wrangling, he was permitted to speak.[33] He felt obligated as a member of the Tennessee delegation to respond to the former president's statement against the sitting chief executive that alleged—in Huntsman's interpretation—"*That General Jackson uses the editor of the Globe as an [a]mbassador to send abroad and propagate lies for him.*" He believed the charges had been made "under the influence

---

31. Congressional Globe, 24th Congress, 1st Session: 434. Robert V. Remini, *Andrew Jackson and the Course of American Empire* (New York: Harper & Row, 1977): 388-389.
32. Congressional Globe, 24th Congress, 1st Session: 455-456
33. Hartford *Connecticut Courier*, May 23, 1836

of deep excitement and without due reflection" and demeaned Adams's reputation and accomplishments. The disagreement had not been intentional or malicious, respectfully suggesting that the memories of both gentlemen might be imperfect.[34]

"It seems, Mr. Speaker," Huntsman said, "that the high and distinguished personages of this Government have their troubles as well as we who are of the smaller fry." He took exception that a fellow representative would waste time presenting his own personal grievances "in deep and doleful terms" on charges made against him in the press. Adams had unfolded a "tale of private griefs in more sympathetic streams than Jeremiah did in writing his longest chapter of [L]amentations." Huntsman suggested that the former president take his objections to the Executive Mansion rather than the House floor, where he could question his accuser face to face. "[T]hat is the manly mode of doing business in the West."

> To pour out his complaints and charges here, where the party charged can neither hear nor answer the charge, is not the sort of chivalry that I admire. Now, as these old gentlemen are about of equal age—both have filled many important stations in the Government—the one President, the other ex-President of the United States—let the gentleman from Massachusetts go and demand satisfaction from the President himself; I have no doubt the President will give him any sort of satisfaction; I will agree, crippled as I am, to underwrite for General Jackson.[35]

The thought of a fight "between the grey haired General and the bald headed Ex president created a universal laugh among the members," observed one journalist.[36]

---

34. Ibid: 456. Register of Debates, 24th Congress, 1st Session: 3707. Boston *Daily Courier*, May 19, 1836.
35. Congressional Globe, 24th Congress, 1st Session: 456
36. Hartford *Connecticut Courier*, May 23, 1836

Huntsman suggested that President Andrew Jackson (left) and former president John Quincy Adams—both almost 70 years old—should meet face-to-face and fight out their differences.

Courtesy of the Library of Congress

Not surprisingly, Adams would not back down from his statements, though he "seemed to enjoy Huntsman's exhibition amazingly." He confided to his diary that the Tennessean's speech "was a mixture of archness, buffoonery, and ignorance with spirit and good humor, as all his speeches are." One newspaper editor back home commended Huntsman for taking on the former president "in real backwoods style."[37]

Two weeks later, Adams wanted the House Journal corrected to reflect that two members had refused—rather than simply declined—to vote on the first of Henry Pinckney's slavery resolutions on May 26. Huntsman suggested that it was better that the Journal not contain exactly ev-

---

37. Charles Francis Adams, ed. *Memoirs of John Quincy Adams, Comprising Portions of His Diary from 1795 to 1848* (Philadelphia: J.B. Lippincott and Company, 1876): 280–281. Adams added: "His [Huntsman's] great annoyance was that I had charged the President with keeping the Globe to lie for him...But [John] Bell, of Tennessee, came afterwards to my table, and said that what I had spoken of the Globe was not one particle too strong. I told Bell that I had had thoughts of referring Huntsman to him, as he spoke for the Tennessee delegation. He said he wished I had; that he would have sustained my statement." Ibid: 281. *Memphis Enquirer*, June 8, 1836.

ery word uttered by members of Congress; such practice "might lead to the most inconceivable mischief." Members would expect an entire two-hour long speech to be recorded or "introduce a few chapters of Vattel" into the Journal. "There is a great deal said…which, for the sake of those concerned, had better never [to] be repeated."[38]

ON JUNE 8, 1836, the Democratic majority moved forward in its efforts to bring Arkansas and Michigan into the Union, the first time in thirty-one years that the statehood process had been initiated. Hoping to avoid a contentious debate over slavery, they tied the admissions of Arkansas and Michigan into a joint effort to maintain the balance between slave and free states that had been created by the Missouri Compromise. But debate was inevitable, owing to a provision in Arkansas' proposed constitution that prohibited its legislature from freeing slaves without their owners' consent. An unsettled and hostile dispute over Michigan's claim to a slice of land on its southern boundary with Ohio made its admission problematic as well.[39]

An eight-hour debate on June 8 preceded a continuous twenty-five hour session the next day that extended to almost midday on the 11th. Unlike many of his colleagues who had to be brought back to the chamber from nearby taverns or awakened from their beds, Huntsman was present for every roll call necessitated by the need for a quorum to thwart opposition efforts to adjourn. During the course of debate on the exhaustive evening of the 9th, he gave a few remarks that were recorded by the *Baltimore Patriot*:

> [Huntsman] said he had spoken a good deal this session, but he had always been short in his remarks. His claim upon the attention of the committee [the House assembled as a Committee of the Whole] being thus established, he went on to boast that he lived in a very large slave holding district,—that he viewed them as

---

38. Congressional Globe, 24th Congress, 1st Session: 507
39. Miller, *Arguing about Slavery*: 210-211. Remini, *Jackson and Course of American Democracy*: 375-376.

intellectual a people as any in America, and as being perfectly competent to manage their own Presidential matters for themselves,—that he had been the earliest prosecutor of [John A.] Murrel,[40] the land pirate,—that there were fanatics in all parts of the world, and "in every country that ever lived on the face of the earth,"—that he "should vote for the whole squad of bills now before the committee,"—and that he "was not" (he acknowledged himself aware) "the greatest man he ever see by a great sight."[41]

The Michigan bill was the first to pass on June 13, immediately followed by a third and final reading of the Arkansas bill. Huntsman moved the previous question to close debate, prevent further amendments, and bring it to a vote. The bill passed 143-50, making Arkansas the twenty-fifth state in the Union. Henry W. Conner of North Carolina thought "as the House had been delivered of twins" that "after the operation the House might adjourn," which it did.[42]

Huntsman and his colleagues endured many late-night sessions during the 24th Congress. One House clerk recalled there being a certain beauty to the chamber on such occasions, as if it were illuminated by "at least 1,000 candles...The beautifully painted roof, the vast pillars, the red drapery about the Speaker's chair & between the columns, all appear richer, if possible, by artificial light than by the light of day."[43] He described a typical late-night session as an "imposing spectacle." In its early hours, the galleries were filled with ladies and gentlemen of Washington society and senators from the adjacent chamber, when it was not

---

40. John A. Murrell was found guilty of slave stealing in the Madison County, Tennessee circuit court in 1834 and sentenced to the state penitentiary at Nashville. Huntsman was not the prosecutor of Murrell in this trial. Perhaps he refers to an earlier case between 1831 and 1834, when Murrell lived in Madison County. James Lal Penick Jr., *The Great Western Land Pirate: John A. Murrell in Legend and History* (Columbia: University of Missouri Press, 1981): 26

41. Indianapolis *Indiana Journal*, June 25, 1836, reprinted from the *Baltimore Patriot*. Huntsman's remarks were not published in either the Congressional Globe, Register of Debates, or Journal of the House of Representatives.

42. Journal of the House of Representatives, 24th Congress, 1st Session: 1001-1003

43. Donald B. Cole and John J. McDonough, eds. *Witness to the Young Republic: A Yankee's Journal, 1828-1870* (Hanover, NH: University Press of New England, 1989): 72

in session. But once the proceedings approached midnight and the spectators (and even some of the representatives) had filtered out, fatigue set in and tempers flared.

> [T]he debaters grow angry, motions are made to adjourn & negatived, noise & confusion frequently occurs, the Speaker calls "order—order" at the top of his voice, the members may be seen sleeping in their seats or stretched upon the sofas & chairs, & even upon the carpet in the esplanade, or back of the Speaker's chair. At 2 o'clock, or thereabout, someone will move a call of the House, &...by about 5 A.M. the Sergt. at arms begins to report members, who have been arrested by him, as...they come into the Hall wrapped in their cloaks or overcoats, with their toilets unattended to, looking as little like "the first gentlemen" in America as possible...By daybreak a quorum is in attendance, & after wasting a night, a little after sunrise the House in its wisdom adjourns! I have witnessed this farce many times & have seldom known any beneficial result from a night session.[44]

Although he had proposed no significant legislation of his own, Huntsman had been a vocal participant in debates on several important issues before the House. He chastised his colleagues for wasting time on insignificant matters and wasteful spending on unlimited volumes of a history of the American Revolution, a copy of which each member would receive at taxpayers' expense.[45] He had opposed an amendment for a schedule of postal rate increases for 1837 and insisted that increases be reduced "to the lowest rates possible." He had presented bills on behalf of the Private Land Claims Committee and sought a new postal route "from the town

44. Ibid: 71-72
45. This multivolume endeavor funded by Congress was published as *American archives; consisting of a collection of authentick records, state papers, debates, and letters and other notices of the origin and process of North American colonies; of the causes and accomplishments of the American revolution; and of the Constitution of government for the United States, to the final ratification thereof* (Washington D.C.: Peter Force, 1837-1853).

of Jackson…by Trenton, Gibson County, to Troy in Obion County…and to Mills' Point in Kentucky." He tried unsuccessfully to establish a federal court for the Western District at Jackson and allocate $15,000 in the 1836 appropriations bill for a marine hospital at Memphis. But he did manage on a few occasions to agitate John Quincy Adams, which surely won the approval of those constituents who still remembered the disputed presidential election of 1824.[46]

46. Mooney, "Huntsman": 118. Congressional Globe, 24th Congress, 1st Session: 118, 369. Washington D.C. *Daily National Intelligencer*, February 3, 1836.

Chapter Eight

A White Man

1836–1837

Adam Huntsman, the Tennessee Congressman and successful rival of the lamented Crockett, sustains the independent character of his predecessor. He writes his friends ... that to remove all surmises about him, he shall, should the election of President come to the House, 'vote for White as long as he had a flag flying," as it is his duty & inclination, and a part of his contract.
—Raleigh Register & North Carolina Gazetter, July 12, 1836

For our next President. Give us a man White by name, White by nature, and who will prove to be a White man in all the acts of his Administration.
—Adam Huntsman, 1836

The first session of the 24th Congress adjourned on the Fourth of July 1836. Huntsman returned home to his wife Elizabeth and their children, whom he had not seen in eight months. But there was little time for rest: his law practice that had been neglected during his absence required his attention, which meant attending to clients and traveling to courts across the Western District. There were constituents who sought his attention about matters in Washington and party leaders who sent invitations for him to attend political meetings and dinners.[1]

---

1. *National Banner and Nashville Whig*, October 10, 1836. *Knoxville Register*, October 19, 1836.

Vice President Martin Van Buren, the choice of Pres. Jackson to succeed him in the 1836 election. Huntsman—as most Tennesseans—instead sided with Hugh Lawson White.

Courtesy of the Library of Congress

But the most important political event was the 1836 presidential election, in which Huntsman held a personal interest in the candidacy of Hugh Lawson White. He had known White for thirty years as far back as his residence in Knoxville. He had studied law under White's brother-in-law, John Williams, and as a practicing attorney had argued cases before the Tennessee Supreme Court when White was a judge. The first vote Huntsman ever cast in an election was for White in the 1807 state senate contest; as a politician, he had served with him in the senate and attended dinners held in his honor. "I think I have had a thorough opportunity of forming an accurate opinion of his talents, integrity and business habits," he wrote. "I consider him pre-eminently qualified to fill the Presidential chair with honor to himself and usefulness to his country."[2]

Like other White supporters in Tennessee, Huntsman separated his loyalty to Andrew Jackson from his objection to the successor he had chosen, Martin Van Buren. He believed White was an honest man who stood for the same republican principles as Jackson, despite charges from the president's followers that White had abandoned them and allied himself with elements of the old Federalist party. Huntsman's friendship and loyalty to White led Jackson's enemies to seek his company. He was invited to an honorary dinner for John Bell in Lebanon, Tennessee and praised by fellow congressman Balie Peyton as one of the "jewels" of the state's congressional delegation.[3]

While reaffirming his support of the administration itself, Huntsman let both Jackson and Van Buren know decidedly who his choice would be in the presidential contest. "I am now, and have always been a supporter of the main principles of this Administration. I expect to continue so—

---

2. *Knoxville Register*, October 19, 1836

3. Ibid. Gresham, "White": 313. Holt, *Whig Party*: 43-44. *National Banner and Nashville Whig*, September 9, 1836. All members of the Tennessee House delegation except James K. Polk and Cave Johnson were invited to the Lebanon dinner held on September 6. Among the toasts Peyton gave at the dinner was the following: "[Luke] Lea and Huntsman, [William B.] Carter, [Samuel] Bunch, and [James I.] Standifer—Other of our Representatives—Tennessee may well be proud of them and their public acts; and exultingly exclaim with the Roman mother, 'these are my jewels.' 3 cheers." Ibid.

U.S. Senator Hugh Lawson White was a brother-in-law of Huntsman's legal mentor, John Williams, and had known Huntsman for 30 years. Huntsman did not hide his support for his friend's presidential aspirations in 1836, even though Martin Van Buren was President Jackson's hand-picked successor.

Sketches of the Bench and Bar of Tennessee

my constituents expect it of me."[4] Yet when the *United States Telegraph* mistakenly labeled him among the "admitted partisans of Mr. Van Buren" in the House, Huntsman was quick to correct its assessment: He was "the partizan of no man" and insisted he "never intended to be so." The votes he cast in Congress were not influenced by his preference or opposition to a particular candidate. "The people whom I have the honor to represent, sent me here to attend to other business; and reserved the right to make a President themselves." As for himself, he would "vote for Judge White, if he gets no other upon earth." But should the election be decided in the House of Representatives (as it had been in the 1824 election between John Quincy Adams, Andrew Jackson, and William Crawford), he would concede his personal choice for that of the majority of his constituents.[5]

Explaining his commitment to vote for the choice of his constituents, Huntsman articulated the principles that guided him throughout his public career.

> These great and fundamental principles of American liberty were inculcated upon my mind when I went to school in the old fields of Virginia in my boyhood, in the forests of the far west they have grown to maturity. I am pertinaciously in favor of the holy and sanctified right of instruction. *No twisting, no dodging*—and I shall obey the wish of a majority of my constituents in this instance, *or resign.* I consider it not only the corner stone, but pillar also, of our political edifice. The essence and quintessence of our republican institutions, require the representative to speak fully, and truly, the voice of his constituents. Whenever he fails to do that, he is a misrepresentative.

---

4. *National Banner and Nashville Whig*, April 4, 1836. Huntsman wrote: "I had proclaimed my preference for Judge White not only in public speeches throughout the [Western] District, but also in private conversations, here and at Washington City, and particularly to Gen. Jackson and Mr. Van Buren both." Ibid.

5. *Randolph Recorder*, May 6, 1836. In a letter published in the *Paris West Tennessean* on May 4, 1836, Huntsman stated that he would "vote for White as long as he had a flag flying." *Raleigh Register and North Carolina Gazette*, July 12, 1836.

POLITICAL RACE COURSE - UNION TRACK - FALL RACES 1836

The "political horse race" that was the 1836 presidential campaign, with four candidates in the running. (Left to right) William Henry Harrison, Martin Van Buren (ridden by Andrew Jackson), Daniel Webster, and Hugh Lawson White.

Courtesy of the Library of Congress

> He is a man whom republicans despise, and fools laugh at as an aristocrat in republican clothing.[6]

During the campaign, President Jackson criticized several members of the Tennessee congressional delegation—including Huntsman—for their endorsement of White. He was allegedly overheard at a reception in Jonesborough, Tennessee, saying that he believed Huntsman was "hanging on the fence, and it was doubtful which side he would fall." White brought up the statement during a speech he gave in Knoxville on August 30.

> In justice to that gentleman [Huntsman] I must be permitted to state, if there be any sincerity in man, he is as much on the Tennessee side of the fence, as any of his colleagues. I have thought it right on this occasion to bring this point plainly and distinctly to your view that you

---

6. *National Banner and Nashville Whig*, April 25, 1836

might every one see the reason why I and my friends are denounced as Federalists, opposed to the Administration and the Antipodes of our esteemed and venerable Chief Magistrate.[7]

Before leaving for Washington to attend the second session of Congress, Huntsman accepted an invitation to a barbecue held in White's honor that the presidential candidate attended near Jackson, Tennessee on September 29.[8] After making a speech, the guest of honor gave a toast reaffirming that his friend Huntsman stood "on the Tennessee side of the fence," to which those in attendance responded with loud cheers. Huntsman stood and reassured them of his position and in "pungent and severe" fashion, he chastised the person whom he suspected of initiating the fence remark. Then he raised his glass and offered a reciprocal toast: "For our next President. Give us a man White by name, White by nature, and who will prove to be a White man in all the acts of his Administration."[9]

Despite widespread support in Tennessee, the fledgling Whig party could not unite behind Hugh Lawson White or any other single candidate. Instead it fielded three regional candidates, hoping Van Buren would be deprived of enough electoral votes that the election would be decided by the House. The scheme failed: Jackson's chosen successor triumphed over his Whig opponents with 170 electoral votes to 124 divided between White, Daniel Webster, and William Henry Harrison. White carried Georgia and, much to Jackson's chagrin, took from Van Buren the honor of winning the president's home state. In the Western District, White won majorities in all but three counties.[10]

Although loyal to White, Huntsman nonetheless refused to lead a "crusade" against Van Buren during the campaign or follow "the beaten track of abusing others who were likely to come in competition" with

7. (Salisbury NC) *Carolina Watchman*, November 5, 1836
8. *Knoxville Register*, October 19, 1836
9. *National Banner and Nashville Whig*, October 17, 1836. *Raleigh Register and North Carolina Gazette*, November 8, 1836. The newspaper articles do not reveal who Huntsman believed to be the instigator of the fence statement.
10. Atkins, *Parties*: 51-52

Huntsman confronted President Jackson about a remark attributed to him that Huntsman was "on the fence" between supporting Hugh Lawson White or Martin Van Buren during the 1836 presidential election

Courtesy of the Library of Congress

him. He had supported Van Buren for vice president in 1832 and did not want to be charged with "inconsistency" for campaigning against him four years later.[11] This position was criticized after the election by an anonymous White supporter (believed to be John Bell), who charged that Huntsman and three fellow Tennessee congressmen failed to defend White; he suspected that they might even be "secretly the friends of V. Buren." Such lackluster support by White's "pretended friends" had done more harm than good to his candidacy. "[T]heir true feelings [were] well known to many here last winter," the anonymous writer claimed, "but it was thought best, as they all had warm friends at home, not to denounce them for their defection and treachery."[12]

The *Washington Globe* came to the congressmen's defense, pointing out that White had garnered more votes from their districts than those of Bell and Balie Peyton. Huntsman's district alone had given White one-fourth of his total popular vote in Tennessee. If loyalty was measured in votes, as the anonymous critic suggested, "Mr. Huntsman was 217 votes more faithful and zealous in Judge White's cause, than Bell and Peyton put together." The *Globe* contended that it was because Huntsman and his colleagues refused to attack Jackson and Van Buren that White received as many votes as he did, whereas Bell and Peyton "delivered an innumerable volley of stump speeches of the most bitter and vindictive character, against Gen. Jackson and his Administration" and White did not carry their districts in Middle Tennessee.[13]

HUNTSMAN RETURNED TO WASHINGTON for the second session of Congress in November 1836. Once again he lodged at the Dowson's No. 1 boardinghouse, where his fellow messmates were Thomas Hart Benton and

---

11. *Knoxville Register*, October 19, 1836. *Randolph Recorder*, May 6, 1836.
12. *Washington Globe*, March 18, 1837. The other congressmen were John B. Forrester, representing the 5th District; Ebenezer J. Shields of the 10th District; and William C. Dunlap of the 13th District.
13. Ibid

Francis Thomas.[14] The 24th Congress reconvened at noon on December 5, 1836, and the next day it received the president's last Annual Message to Congress. The House recognized the deaths of two colleagues from Georgia and Indiana as well as a former representative from Mississippi that occurred during the recess. Once again, members began the first thirty days of the session wearing mourning crape on their left arms.[15]

On New Year's Day 1837, Huntsman wrote to President Jackson, respectfully asking if he had made the fence statement attributed to him during the campaign. White told Huntsman that the president had been overheard making the remark at the Jonesborough reception by "a respectable man" named John O'Brien. Huntsman doubted its credibility, but still felt compelled to ask Jackson for the truth. "I hope you will not deem it disrespectful in me to ask from you a reflection or a confirmation of it," he wrote. "As I do not Consider that I occupied the doubtful position assigned me, and having no reason to believe you would knowingly do me the least injury…or injustice I ask with the same confidence, your answer, as early as it may be convenient."[16]

Jackson denied making the statement and claimed he would have remembered such a conversation with "a perfect stranger."[17] If he were asked what he thought of Huntsman, he wrote, "I [w]ould have said to him that I esteemed you from your votes & course in congress, as a friend to the Administration." Jackson knew Huntsman was "an avowed friend" of White, but he believed the remark had been conceived by White "and

14. Goldman and Young, eds. *Congressional Directories*: 304. Congressional Globe, 24th Congress, 2nd Session: 1. Two of Huntsman's messmates during the first session—James I. McKay of North Carolina and Edward A. Hannegan of Indiana—moved next door to Dowson's No. 2. Three members of the Tennessee delegation—William C. Dunlap, Cave Johnson, and Ebenezer J. Shields—were now borders at No. 2 as well.

15. Register of Debates, 24th Congress, 2nd Session: 1043, 1045-1048. The representatives who died were John Coffee of Georgia, George L. Kinnard of Indiana, and David Dickson of Mississippi. Coffee and Kinnard had both served with Huntsman in the first session.

16. AH to AJ, January 1, 1837. PAJ TSLA. Huntsman mistakenly wrote to Jackson that White's speech had been delivered at Jonesboro, when in fact it was given at Knoxville.

17. AJ to AH, January 2, 1837. PAJ TSLA. In his response, Jackson confused O'Brien as being the person to whom he had made the alleged fence statement. According to O'Brien's account, he overheard the conversation Jackson had "with some gentleman in the room" and "could distinctly hear every word he [Jackson] said." John O'Brien to William B. Carter, January 19, 1837, published in Scott, ed. *White*: 308.

his speechmakers" to use against him. "This, and many recent developments of character, show that Judge White, under strong temptation, has a lax code of morals for himself."[18]

White believed the president's forgetfulness might be attributed to imperfect memory: "[T]he best of us cannot always recollect what we have said." He regretted what he perceived to be "the temper" with which Jackson's response had been written and declared the president's accusations against him to be "unfounded and unjust." White asked that Huntsman allow him to use the two letters publicly in his defense.[19]

The "fence" controversy surfaced on the House floor during a speech by Henry A. Wise of Virginia, seeking to investigate impropriety and corruption by the executive departments in Jackson's administration.[20] White appeared before the Wise Committee and testified to the president's remarks made against members of the Tennessee delegation who had supported his presidential candidacy, including Huntsman. He presented Huntsman's correspondence with Jackson and himself as well as a letter written by John O'Brien and a certificate by Christian E. Carringer that corroborated the claim that Jackson had indeed made the statement.[21] The president offered letters of his own from witnesses that contradicted them, including one written by the owner of the house where the remark was allegedly spoken. The owner, Nathan Gammon, wrote that "at times [Jackson] spoke very indistinctly," but he could not recall ever hearing Huntsman's name mentioned by the president while he was there.[22]

The issue was never satisfactorily resolved; of Huntsman himself, who was at the center of the controversy, one reporter curtly remarked: "[N]o one cared where he was, on the fence or off—he was a 'small potato'" in national politics.[23]

---

18. AJ to AH, January 2, 1837, PAJ TSLA. "Administration of the Executive Departments" Report No. 194. 24th Congress, 2nd Session. House of Representatives: 118.
19. Hugh Lawson White to AH, January 4, 1837, published in Scott, ed. *White*: 307.
20. Resister of Debates, 24th Congress, 2nd Session: 1063
21. Scott, *White*: 305-308
22. *Niles Weekly Register*, July 8, 1837: 296-297. "Administration of the Executive Departments": 117-120.
23. *Wisconsin Territorial Gazette and Burlington Advertiser*, August 24, 1837

AS PART OF ITS INVESTIGATION into the executive departments, the Wise Committee also scrutinized the conduct of the Treasury Department. Among the first witnesses it called was one Reuben M. Whitney, a former director of the Second Bank of the United States who had allied himself with the Jackson administration and served as a consultant to the president during his war to destroy the Bank. Later, Whitney became an agent on behalf of several state banks that received federal deposits removed from the Bank. Jackson's opponents in the House suspected that Whitney had used his connection to the president to secure deposits for banks he represented and was compensated by them for his influence.[24]

Whitney refused to answer the summons to testify before the Wise Committee because of a previous confrontation he had with Wise and Balie Peyton while being questioned by another committee. He was charged with contempt of the House of Representatives and placed under arrest. When brought to the House chamber on February 13, 1837, Whitney gave a written statement that he intended no disrespect toward the House, but he believed he did not have to obey the summons. He had declined to testify for fear that he would exposed to "insult and violence" from chairman Wise. Whitney offered to testify either before a magistrate or the Wise Committee, but only if the committee assured him that no "secret and deadly weapons" would be brought into the room during his examination. A resolution was proposed by Samuel J. Gholson of Mississippi that another committee be formed to determine the validity of Whitney's reasons for not testifying.[25]

Before the resolution was voted upon, Huntsman believed the House should first determine whether it found Whitney's proposal acceptable or not. If it agreed that he could answer questions from either a magistrate or the Wise Committee, the second committee was unnecessary and "much valuable time [and] much expense, will be saved, that can be bestowed upon much more valuables subjects than any contest we can have with Reuben M. Whitney." The House had more important business on its agenda—including the long-delayed Tennessee land bill—and less than

---

24. Walter T. Durham, *Balie Peyton of Tennessee* (Franklin, TN: Hillsboro Press, 2004): 46. Cincinnati Daily Gazette, March 1, 1837.

25. Durham, *Peyton*: 46-50. Register of Debates, 24th Congress, 2nd Session: 1739-1740.

three weeks before the session adjourned. If it pursued the case against Whitney and found him guilty of contempt, the only punishment it could impose was "an exquisitely nice-worded reprimand from the Speaker."[26]

Notwithstanding the logic of Huntsman and several of his colleagues, the House approved the resolution to create a five-man committee of examination. Witnesses were questioned by both the committee and Whitney's attorney. Members of the House served as jury for what became a trial, not of Whitney, but the actions of Wise and Peyton against him. The proceedings came to an abrupt end on February 20, when a resolution was approved that it was "inexpedient" to continue and Whitney should be released from custody. Huntsman voted with the minority against his release, despite his earlier objection to wasting time and money holding the inquiry in the first place.[27]

A MORE IMPORTANT TOPIC to Huntsman in the spring of 1837 was recognition of Texas independence from Mexico. His interest mirrored that of his constituents back in the Western District, who held public meetings the previous year to raise volunteers and money for its cause. In late 1835, he had corresponded with President Jackson on the subject and learned that Anthony Butler, U.S. chargé d'affaires to Mexico, was negotiating with the Mexican government for its purchase.[28] Huntsman introduced a joint resolution on April 29, 1836, that the secretary of war be authorized to give rations to refugees fleeing across the Texas border into the United States during the Texas Revolution. His request for suspension of the rules that it be laid on the table and printed was rejected.[29]

---

26. Register of Debates, 24th Congress, 2nd Session: 1742-1743, 1752. This is the only recorded instance during his term that Huntsman ever mentioned the Tennessee land bill.

27. Ibid: 1743, 1878-1879

28. Z.N. Morrell, *Flowers and Fruits in the Wilderness: Forty-Six Years in Texas and Two Winters in Honduras* (St. Louis: Commercial Printing Company, 1882): 26-28. Morrell refers to a letter Dr. William E. Butler, Robert I. Chester, and other Tennessee friends who were visiting him in Yallabusha County, Mississippi "had just seen" that had been sent to Huntsman by Andrew Jackson. This visit occurred in early December 1835, so the letter must have been written before Huntsman left for Washington to begin his congressional term. No letters between Huntsman and Jackson prior to 1836 survive; this is the only reference to this particular exchange between them concerning Texas.

29. Register of Debates, 24th Congress, 1st Session: 3460

On May 24, he commented on two resolutions related to Texas that had been presented by John Quincy Adams. He had no objection to the first resolution, which asked the president for information on overtures made to the Mexican government since 1829 for the acquisition of Texas and correspondence related to the shared boundary between the U.S. and Texas. But he opposed the second resolution that wanted information Jackson might have pertaining to the abolition of slavery in Mexico and its territories. Adams modified his motion to appease Huntsman, seeking to suspend the rule for the first resolution but not the second. Still, the motion failed to gain the necessary two thirds vote from the House. That evening, a meeting of citizens seeking the recognition of Texas independence was held in Washington. Copies of the proceedings were given to Huntsman, Dixon H. Lewis of Alabama, and Senator William C. Preston of South Carolina.[30]

Huntsman's most passionate defense of Texas came on February 27, 1837. When the annual civil and diplomatic appropriations bill was taken up, Waddy Thompson of South Carolina offered two amendments calling for a diplomat to the Republic of Texas and expenses for a survey of its shared boundary with the United States.[31] Sometime past ten o'clock at night, Huntsman rose from his chair and "with much animation" gave his longest congressional speech, one that fellow Democrat and messmate Thomas L. Hamer of Ohio described as "one of the best speeches he had ever heard upon that floor."[32] Huntsman believed himself more qualified to address the controversial subject of the recognition of Texas independence than most of his colleagues. Many of his friends and former constituents had settled in Texas and sent news to the Western District about

---

30. Ibid: 3902-3903. "Proceedings of a Meeting of the Citizens of Washington in Favor of Recognizing the Independence of Texas, &c." U.S. Congress, Senate Serial Set Vol. 283, Session Vol. No. 5, 24th Congress, 1st Session, S. Doc. 384. A copy of the proceedings and resolutions from the Texas meeting was submitted to the Senate Foreign Relations Committee by Senator Preston on 26 May 1836. Congressional Globe, 24th Congress, 1st Session: 500.
31. Register of Debates, 24th Congress, 2nd Session: 2010-2011
32. Mooney, "Huntsman": 120. Register of Debates, 24th Congress, 2nd Session: 2062.

the conditions there. Men from Tennessee had fought for its independence; some like "the brave and gallant Crockett" had given their lives for it.³³

First he acknowledged his inferiority compared to the "talents and intelligence" of Samson Mason of Ohio and Samuel Hoar of Massachusetts, both of whom had been critical of the amendments. Nevertheless, he pressed forward with

> the sword of Truth in one hand, and the eternal principles of Justice in the other. With these I will go forth ... and I will not only promise the gentlemen themselves, but all mankind, and as many of the ladies as are here to listen to me, that they have been misinformed, deluded, and wholly mistaken, in the history and facts appertaining to the connexion and final separation of Texas and Mexico.³⁴

Huntsman believed Mason and Hoar were misinformed about the integrity of the men of Texas. They were not outlaws, bandits, or degenerates; many of them were "equal, in points of talents, respectability, and high-souled patriotism, to any gentleman on this floor." They were not "mere transient visitors" or "self-styled Texians" as Hoar claimed. He reminded his colleague from Massachusetts that Mexico had sought American volunteers during its struggle with Spain and encouraged settlers to purchase land in Texas and fight the Comanches and other Native American tribes on its frontier. Texas "is a country where a man of industry can better his condition. [T]hese settlers and grantees went there by express contract with the Mexican Government, and not as usurpers in any respect whatsoever."³⁵

He gave a detailed history of Mexico's struggle for independence from Spain and republican government. But Mexican president and military hero General Antonio López de Santa Anna repudiated the constitution of 1824 and "started to rivet the chains of despotism" with the

---

33. Register of Debates, 24th Congress, 2nd Session: 2050. Milledgeville (GA) *Southern Record*, March 14, 1837. Memphis Enquirer, May 4, 1836.
34. Register of Debates, 24th Congress, 2nd Session: 2050
35. Ibid: 2026, 2050

establishment of a military dictatorship. The Texans rebelled; Santa Anna led an army to put down the uprising, resulting in the battles at Goliad and the Alamo before the revolution was won at San Jacinto.[36]

Huntsman dismissed Mason and Hoar's argument that Texas was not truly an independent and sovereign nation because its government was not financially or militarily strong enough without aid from the United States (in violation of the official U.S. neutrality stance). He also contended that Mexico did not need advance notice that the U.S. might acknowledge its independence. "This is certainly a new theory," he marveled. "There is no precedent upon earth for it." It had recognized Mexico's independence despite the fact that Spain occupied several of its forts. "I assert, sir, there is not now a Mexican foot that can tread upon the Texian soil. Texas, at this day, is more free than Mexico was when she received our acknowledgment, or than we were when we received that of France, Spain, and Holland."[37]

Both Mason and Hoar claimed that the size of the Texas army (which Hoar estimated at merely three hundred men) was inadequate to defend itself without help from the United States. Huntsman argued that the Texans' military capability should be measured by a force stronger than mere numbers.

> I lay it down, as a position that is incontrovertible, and which has been demonstrated by all history, that it does not depend so much the number of men to defend their rights, as it does upon that intellectual and moral force, and indomitable spirit, which determines that it will not

---

36. Ibid: 2051-2054. Of the Alamo's defenders, Huntsman said: "[A]lthough they fell, they fell like the strong men of old; they pulled down the pillars of Santa Anna's strength with them; for that immortal little band destroyed fourteen hundred of the enemies of liberty, and shed a lustre of immortality around their names which will secure them the brightest page in history. Their heroic deeds will be told in poetry and song to generations yet unborn, and the blood that was shed at the Alamo will generate millions of men, to fight the battles of freedom throughout the world." Ibid: 2053.

37. Ibid: 2018-2019, 2023, 2026, 2054

submit to oppression and tyranny. Three hundred men, imbued with this spirit, are equal to a host.[38]

He facetiously proposed that he would lead the three hundred Texan soldiers into combat against Hoar and "the eleven thousand Massachusetts militia who marched all around their capital during the last war, and would not fight at all."[39] As Hoar and his militia wasted time "philosophizing upon constitutional scruples and boundary lines," quipped Huntsman, "my men could play the game of decapitation to such an extent as to solve all constitutional scruples upon the subject. I would learn him not to despise numbers; for we are taught that the battle is not always to the strong, nor the race to the swift, but that the Lord of hosts has some direction in these events, and, so far as human eyes can see, there has been a most signal manifestation of it in favor of Texas."[40]

The time had come, he believed, for the House to make a decision on the recognition of Texas independence. He knew it would be opposed by representatives who were "aristocratical by nature" and held "no good will for republican forms of government anyhow." He knew some members from the North worried that recognition would lead to annexation and eventual statehood, shifting the balance of power to the South; others feared it would become another outlet for slavery. "We may as well meet the question at once; it has to be met, and that shortly," he concluded. The amendment was voted down 40 to 82. It was discussed again the next day and with slight changes, a U.S. diplomat to the Republic of Texas—and thus its recognition by the United States—was approved 121 to 76.[41]

THE HOUSE RUSHED to complete its work by March 3. Yet another late-night session that did not adjourn until two o'clock on the morning of the 4th was required, even though the members' terms of office had

---

38. Ibid: 2055
39. Huntsman refers to the refusal of Massachusetts Governor Caleb Strong to allow his state's militia to fight during the War of 1812, despite orders from President James Madison.
40. Ibid: 2056
41. Ibid: 2056, 2060-2064

officially expired at midnight.[42] It drew to a close the contentious 24th Congress, whose overall conduct was criticized in the Whig press. A New England paper believed it had "been characterized in its proceedings by the expression of as great bitterness of party feeling, by as many private feuds, and as much political mismanagement, as at any previous one." The opposition newspaper in Washington, the *National Intelligencer*, was certainly not impressed by its achievements: "[I]t may be safely said that it has left more business unfinished than any Congress which preceded it." One Philadelphia reporter concluded that "a Virginia cock fight or a Long Island horse race ... is the excess of sobriety, civilization and refinement" compared to the partisan bickering that prevailed in "the House of Representatives of this great republic."[43]

Washington was filled with citizens from across the country to witness the presidential inauguration. The weather was sunny and bright on the morning of March 4 as dignitaries and spectators gathered at the east portico of the Capitol Building. After delivering his Inaugural Address, Martin Van Buren was sworn in by Chief Justice Roger B. Taney as the eighth President of the United States. Huntsman likely wit-

---

42. Hartford (CT) *Patriot and Eagle*, March 11, 1837. During the March 3 session, members on the House floor were inundated by "a mob of brilliant, beautiful ladies." With no room left in the gallery to watch the proceedings, about 200 women "rushed into the Hall and pressed into the aisles and the very seats of the members, until…there were ladies occupying half the seats, and the members standing in the passage-ways and outside the bar." Confusion prevailed as members could not hear bills being read or were pleasantly distracted by the female company ("[W]hat did the members care for the Choctaw bill when a lovely woman was a much more agreeable subject of discussion?"). Needless to say, all legislative business came to a halt. "The ladies were buzzing with nods and wreathed smiles," the Washington *Daily National Intelligencer* reported, "as if the Hall had been converted into a drawing room; and they were evidently electioneering at a great rate with every member who had the felicity to sun himself in their smiles." Most of them left their seats when Speaker James K. Polk asked that the Hall be cleared, though many still remained past midnight. "The business of the nation," noted the Intelligencer, "is sometimes paramount even to politeness to the ladies." Washington *Daily National Intelligencer*, March 15, 1837.

43. Amherst (NH) *Farmer's Cabinet*, March 3, 1837. Washington *Daily National Intelligencer*, March 4, 1837. Philadelphia *Public Ledger*, March 15, 1837. That the second session of the 24th Congress had accomplished little was also expressed in the Bennington *Vermont Gazette*: "Very few if any public laws of importance have been passed. Their time has chiefly been spent in discussing an 'infinite deal of nothing.'" Bennington *Vermont Gazette*, March 7, 1837.

nessed the ceremony while seated among other members of the House of Representatives.[44]

AFTER RETURNING HOME in April 1837, he announced that he would not seek a second term in Congress.[45] He believed he could have won reelection despite the fact that two Whig candidates—John Wesley Crockett and Archelaus M. Hughes—had already announced their intentions to oppose him. To his fellow Democrats, he attributed his decision to the party's inability to thwart an upstart opposition newspaper, the *District Telegraph and State Sentinel*, that challenged the Democratic-leaning *Truth Teller* in Jackson. "[I]t would have been like [a] Pyrrhus victory"[46] had he chosen to run again, he told Polk. "The [Whig] party had so arranged their slanders purchased Presses told lies and nobody here to contradict them that in two years more they would have lied my friends and self into the Pacific Ocean." He believed it best that he "stay at home and attend to them for a while."[47]

Other factors likely influenced Huntsman's decision as well. His service to the people of the 12th District no doubt had been detrimental to his law practice. The congressional recesses left him little time to catch up on business and represent his clients in courts across the Western District.

There was also the prospect of losing to the son of his former rival David Crockett, the sentimental choice to reclaim his father's former seat. Huntsman knew John Wesley Crockett as a fellow attorney and believed he held generally "sound republican principles," opposing the recharter of the Second Bank of the United States, internal improvements funded by the federal government, and a protective tariff. Crockett would have his support "against any man *possessing contrary doctrines in these particulars.*" If it be said that he withdrew because Crockett "might have

---

44. Register of Debates, 24th Congress, 2nd Session: 2158. *Salem* (MA) *Gazette*, March 7, 1837. *Boston Daily Courier*, March 9, 1837. New York Spectator, March 10, 1837. Keene *New Hampshire Sentinel*, March 16, 1837.

45. *Nashville Republican*, April 25, May 2, 1837. The *Republican* reprinted an excerpt of Huntsman's letter to the *Jackson Truth Teller*.

46. The phrase "Pyrrhus victory" is taken from the battle between King Pyrrhus of Epirus and the Romans in 279 B.C. Pyrrhus won the battle, but at the cost of most of his men.

47. AH to JKP, January 1, 1838. CJKP 4: 310

beat me," Huntsman cited past incumbents who chose not to run for reelection for similar reasons. "Now, if such great men as these declined from an apprehension of being beat, I may be pardoned for following their example, even if that is the true grounds upon which I act. Be my motives what they may I have formed my determination and intend to act upon it with vigor."[48]

With the election only four months away, his decision not to run left Democrats with no candidate in the race. Neither Crockett nor Hughes would stand down, resulting in a contest between two Whigs. For Democrats, Crockett represented the lesser of two evils—Hughes being regarded as "the most violent and foul mouthed opposition man you ever heard"—and they threw their support behind his victory.[49]

Huntsman's single term in Congress would be the last elected office he would seek or hold. He went to Washington with no agenda to pursue or pet project to enact, but wanted only to represent the interests of his constituents. He spoke out on several issues that confronted the House, perhaps more than the typical freshman legislator would have. That he was relieved to be free from the yoke of political servitude was expressed to Polk about the prospects of the next Congress. He foresaw little change from what he had already endured. "I expect the session is to be exhausted without any profit to the people, in useless, irritating debate."[50]

---

48. *Nashville Republican,* May 2, 1837. *Memphis Enquirer,* May 13, 1836. Crockett had announced his intention to run for his father's congressional seat as early as mid February 1837. *Nashville Union,* February 18, 1837.

49. Joseph H. Talbot to JKP, April 21, 1837. CJKP 4: 94-95

50. AH to JKP, January 1, 1838. CJKP 4: 309

Chapter Nine

Log Cabins and Flummery

1837–1840

I now am ready to do battle for the cause of democracy any where the party may think it advisable for me to fight [either at] the head of a division or in the private ranks.

—Adam Huntsman, January 26, 1840

Tell your friends in Nashville that the Western District stands "fast anchored by her ancient principles." Put down her vote for Tip and Tyler at from 3 to 4000—not a vote less. An excitement unparalled in our political history is springing up here...The people are up. Every man here is a politician...

—Nashville Whig, August 7, 1840

Huntsman returned home in the summer of 1837 and turned his attention to his neglected law practice. But no matter how much time he spent in the courtrooms of the Western District, his thoughts never strayed far from politics. A few weeks into President Van Buren's new administration, the nation was gripped by a financial crisis that evoked painful memories of the Panic of 1819. Naturally, Whigs blamed the downturn on the economic policies of Andrew Jackson, particularly his Specie Circular that required the purchase of public lands in gold or silver rather than paper money.[1]

Huntsman wrote to Polk and kept him informed about political developments in the District. He reported that the recent defection of Senator John C. Calhoun from the Whig party had left his supporters more inclined to back Van Buren and more hostile towards the Whigs. "There has been some glorious fun here," Huntsman gleefully wrote on New Year's Day 1838. Pleasant M. Miller, a prominent Whig attorney, and his son William B. Miller were quarreling in the press with a colleague, Andrew L. Martin, who was a Calhoun partisan. The disagreement had turned into a small political war between the two factions. "There never was such a time since Judge White has been defeated for Van's friends to organize a powerful and energetic party and such as would beat Clay and Webster easily," he said.[2]

A mutual friend advised Polk that "a little attention at Washington" toward Huntsman "would make him think charitably of the administration." Regardless, Huntsman seemed to have a change of heart about the new president. He liked what he heard in Van Buren's inaugural address, especially his strong opposition to congressional efforts to interfere with slavery and his belief in "a strict adherence to the letter and the spirit of the Constitution as it was designed by those who framed it." Given the choice between Van Buren and the Whig duo of Clay and Webster, he wrote, "I am resolved to go with Kinderhook even to mounting the stumps."[3]

To help Van Buren, Huntsman wrote a series of articles in the summer of 1838 that were published in the Jackson *District Telegraph and State Sentinel*. Using the name of "A Subscriber," each one was directed against Clay, whom many considered to be the probable Whig nominee for president in 1840. The articles scrutinized his positions against the occupant settlers and in favor of the abolition of slavery. Using congressional journals secured through Polk, Huntsman recited derogatory comments made by the Kentucky senator against the occupants, whom Clay had labeled as "a *lawless banditti of land robbers grasping at the public treasure.*" He

---

1. Sellers, *Polk: Jacksonian*: 318
2. AH to JKP, January 1, 1838. CJKP 4: 310. AH to JKP, December 16, 1838. Ibid: 652.
3. Ibid. Joseph H. Talbot to JKP, April 21, 1837. CJKP 4: 95.

James K. Polk was a 23-year-old clerk for the Tennessee state senate when Huntsman first met him in 1819. He went on to serve in the U.S. House of Representatives, as Speaker of the House, governor of Tennessee, and ninth President of the United States.

Courtesy of the Tennessee State Library and Archives

also criticized Clay for presenting petitions for slave emancipation while representing a state that supported slavery. "These numbers [have] good effect here," Huntsman boasted to Polk. He forwarded the articles to him to be reprinted in Democratic papers such as the *Washington Globe* and the *Richmond Enquirer*. He also promised in the future to write a Book of Chronicles that featured Van Buren.[4]

Despite his recent support of the president, Huntsman maintained his allegiance to Hugh Lawson White and still considered himself among the "White Gentry" in the Democratic party. The fact that White had left its ranks and joined the Whigs did not seem to deter him. He assured Polk that he and other White loyalists in the Western District would not allow themselves "to be transferd by Mr [John] Bell to the Federalist[s]."[5] Democrats like Huntsman, Polk, and Jackson often referred to the Whigs as "Federalists," claiming the opposition party was merely a resurgence of the extinct Federalist party. The majority of Tennesseans since statehood had been Jeffersonian Republicans. Huntsman and Andrew L. Martin accepted invitations to Democratic dinners in the fall of 1838 to "explain our positions as White men and now we go on without embarrassment." Some Democrats felt Polk's confidence in Huntsman was undeserved. He and Martin's "folly" had prevented agreement within the party a year later on a candidate for the state house of representatives.[6]

Polk, now considered the leader of the Democratic party in Tennessee, left a successful thirteen-year congressional career and the House speakership to run for governor in 1839. Upon his shoulders were placed the hopes of the party faithful that the state could be "redeemed" from Whig domination that had been in place for the past four years in the governor's chair, the General Assembly, and the state congressional delegation.

---

4. AH to JKP, May 26, 1838. CJKP 4: 463-464. Jackson (TN) *District Telegraph and State Sentinel*, March 23, 1838, June 1, 1838. It is likely Huntsman wrote many other articles using pen names during his political career. Unfortunately, this is the only instance when it can be verified. AH to JKP, May 26, 1838. It appears Huntsman did not write a Book of Chronicles about Van Buren after all.

5. Democrats like Huntsman, Polk, and Jackson often referred to the Whigs as "Federalists," claiming the opposition party was merely a resurgence of the extinct Federalist party. The majority of Tennesseans since statehood had been Jeffersonian Republicans.

6. Daniel Graham to JKP, July 19, 1837. CJKP 4: 186. AH to JKP, July 30, 1838. Ibid: 515-516. Joseph H. Talbot to JKP, April 1, 1839. CJKP 5: 107. Daniel Graham to JKP, July 19, 1837.

His campaign against incumbent Newton Cannon emphasized national rather than state issues, among them Van Buren's proposed independent treasury system, the Whigs' insistence on a national bank, and federally funded internal improvements. Polk defended the policies of former president Andrew Jackson and charged Cannon, John Bell, and Ephraim H. Foster with maneuvering the state into the fold of Henry Clay.[7]

Both parties recognized how crucial the race in Tennessee was and that the results would impact the 1840 presidential election. Polk canvassed the state as no other candidate had done before, a rigorous schedule of speaking engagements that attracted large crowds throughout the three grand divisions. His itinerary lasted four months and gave him only two days' rest. In the Western District, he hoped to take from Cannon the votes of many disgruntled state's rights Whigs and made several speeches throughout the region in October.[8]

Huntsman promised Polk upon his arrival that he would arrange "dinners upon a large scale" and enough appointments to "draw out the democracy fully. I would not take less than $500 for my share of the fun." Suggestions made in the press that Huntsman might oppose John W. Crockett for his old congressional seat never materialized.[9] Instead, he seemed content to promote Polk's candidacy. Even if he lost, he promised, "I will have fun sufficient to pay me for the defeat."[10]

It was a close election, but Polk prevailed with 51 percent of the vote to beat Cannon. Overall, the Democratic party regained control of the General Assembly and won six congressional seats. Gains were made in the Western District, though Polk lost the region by 1,926 votes. Still, Huntsman was pleased with the results. "We fought a hard battle to make people understand the nature of the contest," he wrote. "In many places

---

7. Sellers, *Polk: Jacksonian*: 361
8. Ibid: 356-357
9. Stephen C. Pavatt, a lawyer and former state legislator from Huntingdon, Tennessee challenged John W. Crockett for the 12th Congressional seat, but the incumbent won reelection. McBride and Robison, eds. *Biographical Directory* 1: 574-575. AH to JKP, July 30, 1838. CJKP 4: 516.
10. Ibid: 356-357. AH to JKP, July 30, 1838. CJKP 4: 516.

in the State the Whig Electors hoisted the Clay Flag most incautiously—
The moment that was done our success became certain."[11]

TENNESSEE HAD BEEN RESTORED to the Democratic fold, and party leaders were confident that their success would carry over into the upcoming presidential election. Their overconfidence led them to delay preparations for the campaign until February 1840, while the Whigs began organizing local committees in each county a few weeks after their defeat. The Democrats' lack of initiative would affect the course of the campaign and the outcome of the election itself in the state.[12]

In December 1839, Tennessee Whigs were stunned when William Henry Harrison—and not Henry Clay—was chosen at the national convention to be their presidential candidate. Harrison had been chosen four years earlier along with Hugh Lawson White and Daniel Webster when the party offered a regionally fractured ticket in the 1836 contest. To appease its northern and southern factions, the convention intentionally drafted no party platform but instead touted Harrison's military record. To offer a Southern balance to the ticket, Senator John Tyler of Virginia, a former Jacksonian Democrat, was selected for vice president. The result was the first presidential campaign slogan: "Tippecanoe and Tyler Too."[13]

Disheartened at first by Harrison's nomination, the party faithful soon rallied behind his candidacy. A month later, Hugh Lawson White and Ephraim Hubbard Foster—Tennessee's U.S. senators who had resigned rather than follow the instructions of the new Democratic majority in the General Assembly—were selected as state electors-at-large. Foster boldly

---

11. CJKP 5: xii. Sellers, *Polk: Jacksonian*: 373. AH to Aaron Vanderpoel, August 26, 1839. Vanderpoel Family Papers, 1815-1839. Special Collection 14626, Box 1, Folder 1. New York State Library.

12. Eugene Irving McCormac, *James K. Polk: A Political Biography* (New York: Russell and Russell, 1965): 151. James Phelan, *History of Tennessee: The Making of a State* (Boston: Houghton, Mifflin and Company, 1888): 383-384.

13. Glyndon G. Van Deusen, *The Jacksonian Era, 1828-1848* (New York: Harper & Row, 1963): 143-144. Robert Gray Gunderson, *The Log-Cabin Campaign* (Lexington, KY: University of Kentucky Press, 1957): 63-64. Henry Clay, who had been displaced by Harrison's nomination, remarked: "I am the most unfortunate man in the history of parties: always run by my friends when sure to be defeated, and now betrayed when I, or any one, would be sure of election." Marquis James, *The Life of Andrew Jackson Complete in One Volume* (Indianapolis, IN: The Bobbs-Merrill Company, 1937): 738. AH to JKP, January 26, 1840. CJKP 5: 374

Illusion over reality: William Henry Harrison's depiction as a humble farmer and war veteran living in a rustic log cabin with an ample supply of hard cider.

Courtesy of Cornell University Library

took the reins of leadership from party stalwart John Bell and became the Whigs' chief campaigner. Taking a page from Polk's successful gubernatorial canvass, he toured the entire state to rally support and gain new followers for Tippecanoe and Tyler Too. Huntsman was encouraged by the turn of events among the opposition. "The Harrison nomination has completely enabled us to beat them in the District handsomely," he boasted to Polk.[14]

But the Whig ticket proved to be more problematic than Huntsman anticipated. Throughout the election, Democrats in Tennessee and across the country were perplexed over how to thwart it. Practically every criticism and mockery they made against Harrison, the Whigs turned to their advantage. A Baltimore newspaper editor thought he would forgo becoming president if given "a barrel of hard cider, and settle a pension of two thousand a year on him, and my word for it, he will sit the remainder of his days in his log cabin by the side of a 'sea coal' fire, and study moral philosophy." The condescending remark was turned into their campaign theme. They touted Harrison as a simple Ohio farmer and war hero who lived in a log cabin and drank hard cider—in stark contrast to Van Buren, whom they portrayed as an aristocrat with luxurious tastes and effeminate traits. The fact that Harrison was from a distinguished Virginia

---

14. McCormac, *Polk*: 173. Phelan, *Tennessee*: 387. After Hugh Lawson White's death on April 10, 1840, Spencer Jarnagin replaced him as state elector-at-large. *Columbia* (TN) *Observer*, 25 June 1840.

family and owned a twenty-two room clapboard home at North Bend, Ohio, while Van Buren was born in a tavern in Kinderhook, New York and was a self-made man, did not deter their efforts to promote Harrison as one of the "common man."[15]

The result was the most exciting and enthusiastic presidential campaign the nation had ever seen. In Tennessee, Nashville Whigs formed clubs such as the Harrison Guards, the Tippecanoe Club, and the Log Cabin Boys, who took part in grand parades with rolling log cabins on wheels and Tippecanoe songbooks and hard cider liberally distributed to spectators. The phrase "Keep the ball rolling" originated with the Harrison campaign as energetic supporters rolled large paper balls with printed slogans through the streets. Tippecanoe Liberty Poles flying Harrison and Tyler flags were hoisted in many towns of the Western District. The Whigs blamed Van Buren for the hard times and taunted him as "Martin Van Ruin" and "Sweet Sandy Whiskers" for perfuming his facial hair. "An excitement unparalleled in our political history is springing up here," wrote an enthusiastic Whig in Huntingdon. "The people are up. Every man here is a politician, and the excitement and the impending crisis is swallowing up everything in it."[16]

In late January 1840, Huntsman was recruited to serve as one of the state Democratic party's electors-at-large for the Van Buren ticket. Having overcome personal financial difficulties of late, he told Polk: "I am now ready to do battle for the cause of democracy anywhere the party may think it adviseable for me to fight, either at the head of a division or in the private ranks." He agreed to serve with the understanding that the responsibilities of his law practice prevented him from campaigning outside the Western District. As for Democratic electors in each of the thirteen congressional district, he felt they should be men who were "able capable and willing to present and discuss the principles of democracy upon a Stump and do it if needful."[17]

The party's state convention was held in Nashville on Huntsman's fifty-fourth birthday, February 11. As expected, he received the nomina-

---

15. Gunderson, *Log-Cabin Campaign*: 74-75, 126
16. *Nashville Whig*, July 1, 2, 6, 13, 1840; August 7, 1840. Van Deusen, *Jacksonian Era*: 147
17. AH to JKP, January 26, 1840 CJKP 5: 374

tion for one of the elector-at-large positions. The other went to a thirty-two year old state legislator named Andrew Johnson of Greene County, who twenty-five years later would become seventeenth President of the United States.[18]

In early April, Polk traveled to the Western District and met with Huntsman and other Democratic leaders. He found Huntsman enthusiastic and "more excited that I have ever seen him, and he will do his duty." Andrew Jackson, living his final years in retirement at the Hermitage outside Nashville, was equally pleased. "It gives me great pleasure to hear that Huntsman has taken the field & that you will give the Whigs a sure defeat this fall—let it be so."[19]

But a month later, there was grumbling among lieutenants in the District that he had not begun campaigning and failed to make speeches on court days in Madison County. One Democrat believed Huntsman "could not face up against a majority." A month later, Samuel H. Laughlin thought party leaders should write to Huntsman to "spur him up." But Huntsman was equally unhappy with the efforts of his associates. He critiqued in particular the speaking style of Levin Hudson Coe, elector for the 13th Congressional District, who he felt lacked "a sufficient quality of *life* and *enthusiasm*." A rumor attributed Huntsman's indifference to his displeasure with Polk that Huntsman's law partner and future son-in-law, Timothy P. Scurlock, had not been appointed to a state office. A few

---

18. *Nashville Union*, February 12, 1840. The *New Orleans Bee* noted: "The electors for the State at large [in Tennessee] are Messrs. Huntsman and Greene, two very important personages, no doubt though they are somewhat unknown to fame." ("Greene" was actually Andrew Johnson, who was from Greene County, Tennessee.) *Augusta (GA) Chronicle*, March 4, 1840. The *Nashville Whig* believed the Democratic electors was "by no means, a strong ticket. To say the least, the Whig nomination will not suffer by a comparison of the weight of personal influence." *Nashville Whig*, February 12, 1840.

19. JKP to Arthur R. Crozier, April 6, 1840 CJKP 5: 420. AJ to Robert I. Chester, April 9, 1840. Tennessee Historical Society Miscellaneous Files, Box 8, Folder J-63 TSLA. John Spencer Bassett, ed. *Correspondence of Andrew Jackson* (Washington D.C.: Carnegie Institution, 1933) 6: 416. Jackson made a notation on the letter: "Mr. Huntsman. The people [are] returning to their former respective opinions. This is what I allways expected so soon as they were convinced of their delusion brought over them by Bell and Co., hypocracy, yielded to and encouraged by judge Whites ambition."

Former U.S. Senator Ephraim H. Foster championed the Whig cause in Tennessee and canvassed throughout the state on behalf of William Henry Harrison's candidacy in the 1840 election.

Courtesy of the Tennessee State Library and Archives

Democrats privately confided to Polk that Huntsman should resign, but Huntsman blamed such talk instead on "the rascally Whigs."[20]

When he learned that Foster intended to campaign in the Western District, Huntsman related to Polk "in his humorous way, that if brother Ephm. crosses the Tennessee River, and attempts to 'poach on his dominions,' that he will collar him as he puts his feet on the Western bank, and gallant him through the District." Uncharacteristic of his normal speaking style, Foster had begun mixing amusing stories into his stump speeches. Huntsman looked forward to hearing the one "about a *Bull calf*, and that it is *funny*." In a letter to the Whig elector on June 28, he proposed a "mutual and friendly canvass" between them. He had read accounts about fellow elector Andrew Johnson facing Foster in East Tennessee, where his Whig opponent would ask to speak first and then proceed to speak for several hours or "long enough to tire out the audience."[21] Huntsman would not stand for such a game and suggested to Foster that each speak for two and a half or three hours—"I never did or could make a longer one and talk sense," he later wrote. But Foster declined the invitation; according to one newspaper account, he was unwilling to limit his time or make concessions "whereby a Democratic Elector could have an opportunity to address the public on the same day as him." Huntsman vowed that if Foster spoke in the Western District on his own, he would follow him "in his rear and on both of his Flanks" and show the voters the challenge he had made to Foster "proposing a manly discussion."[22]

20. JKP to Arthur R. Crozier, April 6, 1840 CJKP 5: 420. West H. Humphreys to JKP, May 17, 1840 Ibid: 456. Humphreys to JKP, May 23, 1840 Ibid: 459. AH to JKP, May 25, 1840 Ibid: 463-464. Samuel H. Laughlin to JKP, June 21, 1840 Ibid: 501.

21. AH to JKP, May 25, 1840 Ibid: 513-514. Foster reportedly did it on several occasions against Andrew Johnson in East Tennessee. "After he has finished," wrote the *Nashville Union*, "he tells the people he is very much exhausted and worn out...saying to the people he would be very glad they would stay and hear Col. Johnson." This was done "to break up the meeting and prevent Col. Johnson from being heard." *Nashville Union*, June 18, 1840. (Another instance was reported in the Union on 11 June 1840.) The *Nashville Whig* refuted the allegation, claiming that Foster later asked Johnson if "he had been cut off from speaking," and Johnson "had the manliness then to acknowledge...that the time allowed him at Pikeville was abundant." *Nashville Whig*, June 19, 1840.

22. JKP to Arthur R. Crozier, April 6, 1840 CJKP 5: 420. AH to JKP, May 25, 1840 Ibid: 513-514. *Nashville Union*, September 14, 1840. The *Union* (quoting from the *Bolivar, TN Sentinel*) stated that Foster thought such an arrangement with Huntsman "would be particularly embarrassing and objectionable." Ibid.

In late July, Coe suggested to Polk that Huntsman might be more effective campaigning in the Mountain District where he remained popular among his former friends and constituents. "The impression of many of our friends is that neither T[otten] or H[untsman] are producing much effect where they go," he wrote. Such a strategy would enable Laughlin to shift his efforts from the mountains to the Western District in Huntsman's place. It was an arrangement that had already crossed Polk's mind: that same day, he wrote Huntsman and asked if he would be willing to canvass in his old district. Whether Huntsman knew lieutenants in his home district were berating him to Polk is uncertain. But unselfishly, he backed down from his intention not to campaign far from home and told the governor he was "willing to fight upon any ground that may be chosen for me by my friends." His primary concern was to prepare for Foster's arrival; having obtained Foster's itinerary in advance, he made preparations for Totten to pursue him through the northern counties and Coe in the southern counties of the District.[23]

Huntsman reached his old stomping ground in the Mountain District on August 31 and spent about two weeks on the campaign trail, accompanied by Congressman Hopkins L. Turney. Handbills were circulated to promote his appearances, which included twelve appointments in Jackson, Overton, White, DeKalb, and Cannon counties.[24] An old friend approached him during his visit and asked if he remembered him. Huntsman looked him over and replied, "I think I used to know an old sinner about your size."[25] At one of his first appointments at Celina in Jackson County on September 1, Thomas L. Bransford, the local Whig elector, invited himself to join Huntsman and Turney on the platform built by local Democrats for the event. At one point, Turney's speech was interrupted by a Whig partisan who invited the crowd to move over to *his* party's platform and listen to Bransford speak instead. Such tactics

---

23. Samuel H. Laughlin to JKP, July 26, 1840 CJKP 5: 517. AH to JKP, August 4, 1840 Ibid: 530-531.

24. JKP to Samuel H. Laughlin, August 15, 1840 CJKP 5: 539-540. *Nashville Union*, September 10, 17, 1840. "Huntsman and Turney are dissipating the Federal slanders that have been sent into the Mountain District," noted the Union on September 10. Also included was the following notice: "We are authorized to state that Messrs Huntsman and Turney will address the people at Cedar Fork (Cannon county) Tittle's Old School House, on Monday the 14th September."

25. A.V. and W.H. Goodpasture, *Life of Goodpasture*: 35-36

"are the most efficient weapons of Whiggery in the Mountain District," wrote one disgusted Democrat. But Huntsman stoically pressed forward with his own speech, which drew praise from one former constituent. "Mr. Huntsman is a tower of strength.—He made old Federalism look blue; for I do assure you, we can point to changes in our favor. He put to flight all the little contemptible charges against Mr. Van Buren, by which the Whigs attempt to divert the 'public eye' from the deformity of their odious principles."[26]

With his appointments in the Mountain District completed, Huntsman made his way home to deal with Ephraim Foster, who had arrived in the Western District a few weeks earlier. In his absence, Laughlin and former governor William Carroll had canvassed the District, both together and separately, and Polk had made an appearance at Paris.[27] Huntsman passed through Nashville and met with Jeremiah George Harris, editor of the *Nashville Union*. "After he shall have crossed the Tennessee River, the public will hear from him often," Harris predicted. "As a popular speaker, he is a host within himself—always using up his opponent."[28]

During the contentious campaign, ideological political battles sometimes degenerated into physical violence. Huntsman's temperament toward his "Brother Whigs" was more humorous than hostile, but the same could not be said for a few of his party associates. Partisan newspaper editors like Harris of the *Union* who inflamed the opposition sometimes found themselves in the news. At one point he engaged in a fist fight with a Whig critic who branded him a liar. A year later, he was shot by the son of Ephraim Foster but recovered. On August 3, Levin H. Coe shot a Whig rival, Phineas T. Scruggs, who had tried to smash a chair over his head after insults were exchanged between them.[29]

IN SEPTEMBER, Andrew Jackson was asked to bolster Democratic efforts in the Western District. Huntsman traveled to the Hermitage and

---

26. *Nashville Union*, September 17, 1840
27. JKP to Robert M. Burton, August 20, 1840 CJKP 5: 545
28. *Nashville Union*, September 17, 1840
29. McCormac, *Polk*: 176. Sellers, *Polk: Jacksonian*: 423, 429. Levin H. Coe to JKP, August 4, 1840 CJKP 5: 527-529.

presented him with an invitation to attend a barbecue dinner in his honor at Jackson on October 8. The Old Hero felt it was important for him to be there. Should the party lose the region, "it might be said, that it was owing to my not going to this great meeting at Jackson."[30] Whigs labeled it a sad ploy that would diminish the former president's reputation and berated Democratic leaders for drawing him into the political fray. There was no "more intelligent, high-spirited, independent population than that of the Western District of Tennessee," the *Nashville Republican Banner* insisted. "General Jackson's visit there will be productive of injury to no one but himself and the party leaders for whose benefit he has been induced to undertake the journey."[31]

The "great meeting at Jackson" was held on October 8 in a shaded grove a few miles south of the Madison County Courthouse. An estimated crowd of between 8,000 and 10,000 gathered for the free barbecue, squirrel stew, and politicking. Huntsman no doubt was present at such an important Democratic event.[32] The former president was welcomed in an address by local attorney and educator Samuel McClanahan. But the seventy-three year old Jackson, fatigued from the journey and a recent surgical procedure, could not deliver a reply and Polk read it on his behalf.[33]

"It affords me unspeakable pleasure to be able to meet you on this occasion," he wrote. "It is probably the last time that I shall have it in my

30. Williams, *Beginnings of West Tennessee*: 274. AJ to Andrew Hutchings, September 7, 1840 quoted in Williams, *Historic Madison*: 7.
31. *Nashville Daily Republican Banner*, October 12, 1840
32. Williams, *Historic Madison*: 7-8. JKP to Samuel H. Laughlin, October 2, 1840 CJKP 5: 562. Polk stated in his letter to Laughlin that Andrew Jackson, Felix Grundy, Cave Johnson, and Aaron V. Brown would be at the Jackson dinner. Newspaper accounts mention Jackson, Polk, and Grundy, but whether Johnson, Brown, or Huntsman actually attended is not certain. It would be hard to imagine Huntsman not being at such an important Democratic event in his own hometown.
33. Andrew Jackson arrived in Jackson, Tennessee on the night of October 4, after a two-day journey through continuous rain over "rough roads." A few days earlier, he had endured minor surgery "in my ribs," which left him tired and aching. AJ to Andrew Jackson Jr. and Sarah Yorke Jackson, October 5, 1840. PAJ Reel 35, Microfilm Account No. 30a, TSLA. Remini, *Jackson and Course of American Democracy*: 468-469 describes Jackson giving the speech himself, but contemporary accounts indicate that Polk gave the speech for him. *Nashville Union*, October 15, 1840. Williams, *Beginnings*: 276. Jackson does not mention having spoken at the event in a letter he wrote later that day: "We had a large meeting to day Polk & Grundy both spoke…and all things look well in this District." AJ to Andrew Jackson Donelson, November 8, 1840. PAJ, TSLA. Though assisted by Donelson, the speech itself was written in Jackson's handwriting. Ibid.

Andrew Jackson (center) arrives at the "great meeting" held in his honor in Jackson, Tennessee on October 8, 1840. To Jackson's left is Gov. James K. Polk; to his right are U.S. Senator Felix Grundy and Adam Huntsman.

Illustration by Wade Dillon

Historical marker on South Royal Street in Jackson, Tennessee commemorating Andrew Jackson's last visit there on October 8, 1840.

Photograph by the author

power to exchange salutations with you—the last opportunity that I shall have to thank you personally for the many proofs you have given me of your respect for my character and services." The country need not fear for its security from foreign powers, he contended, but from sectional strife agitated by Northern abolitionists and the Whigs' desire to resurrect the extinct Federalist party. The Old Hero was disheartened that his fellow Tennesseans would allow their political divisions to bolster the efforts of the Whigs and give credence to their Federalist doctrines, which he believed were "dangerous to the public prosperity." He knew they would labeled him a "dictator," yet he felt compelled to warn voters of the dire consequences involved in the presidential election.

> This, my fellow citizens, is a great and momentous crisis in our national affairs in which our dearest rights as freemen are deeply concerned. The Presidential Election is near at hand, which will decide the fate of our Republican system: whether it will be perpetuated on the great principle laid down in our written constitution, or changed to a great consolidated Government in which the rights of the States will be destroyed, the confederation trodden under foot, the glorious Union burst assunder, and your constitutional liberty lost forever.[34]

Having read Jackson's address Polk gave his own speech for several hours, discussing Harrison's principles and efforts by the Whigs to keep him "a mum candidate." He also mentioned a recent abolitionist convention held in London, England, the proceedings of which were "too dangerous to be made known to the numerous slaves within hearing of the speaker's voice." The last speaker was Felix Grundy, who refuted the exaggerated claims perpetuated by the Whigs that Van Buren lived an opulent lifestyle in the Executive Mansion. To learn the principles of the opposition, he claimed, voters had to decipher them from their campaign banners and paraphernalia: "the coon, the log cabin, the canoe, the cider

---

34. *Nashville Union*, October 15, 1840

barrel, the gourd." Grundy spoke against a national bank and insisted that on the issues, Democrats "are where we have always been, and ever mean to be." When the speeches concluded, the gathering made their way to the tables to partake of the free food. It was a festive day, concluded one local partisan, despite the interruption by a few boys in the crowd "to raise a shout for 'Tip and Ty.'"[35]

The next morning Huntsman accompanied Jackson and Polk twenty-eight miles east of town to Lexington, where he had scheduled a speaking engagement for he and Polk. Originally it was to have been held at Harmon's Mills outside town, but the inclusion of the former president led Huntsman to hold it at the Henderson County seat. A Whig correspondent attributed the decision instead to the fact that it would be "disrespectful to carry [Jackson] to a Mill in the swamps of the Western District, near which there is a good *bald-faced still house.*"[36] Lodging overnight at a local hotel, the group awakened the next morning to find that a "liberty pole" had been raised nearby with a "Harrison and Tyler" flag flying atop it. Jackson declared it the work of abolitionists and that Harrison himself was an abolitionist and "no Military Man." His remarks offended the men who had raised the pole, who included former supporters and veterans who had served under Old Hickory.[37]

The Whigs criticized Jackson for politicking in the Western District. One newspaper editor in Jackson professed disappointment that the esteemed former chief executive would lower himself to partisan politics "for the benefit of such tools and minions as Polk and Grundy. The whole of his visit was devoted to a most undignified depreciation of the merits of General Harrison." Another Whig paper lampooned desperate Democrats for the tactic. "It has been whispered about for some time that the Locofocos had a strong card to play just before the election, and now we see what it is," the *Nashville Daily Republican Banner* wrote. "They

---

35. Ibid
36. *Nashville Whig*, October 21, 1840
37. Ibid. Phelan, *Tennessee*: 386-387.

have played it, and lo and behold, it is a speech which General Jackson was dragged all the way to Jackson...to make, or rather to read."[38]

Jackson's appearance did nothing to change the outcome of the election in the Western District. Harrison won in all but five counties with 12,677 votes to Van Buren's 8,334, and carried the state, 60,391 to 48,289. Even Huntsman's home county of Madison fell to the opposition, 1,312 to 537. Afterward, one disappointed partisan expressed what most Democrats thought: "The fact is the people like coonery and foolery better than good argument." Some party stalwarts believed the Whigs simply liked their candidate better than the Democrats did their own. One modern historian concluded that the election was "the triumph of illusion over reality."[39]

THE YEAR ENDED on a brighter note in Huntsman's personal life when his daughter Ann married his law partner Timothy P. Scurlock on December 22. She had lived with her grandmother Ann Quarles in Overton County since her mother's death and may have returned to Cotton Grove in the spring of 1839.[40] Scurlock, who was eleven years older than his seventeen-year-old bride, had been co-editor of the Jackson *Southern Statesman* newspaper which originally published the "Chronicles" during the 1831 congressional campaign. Huntsman did his best to promote his son-in-law's career over the next nine years, and Scurlock took care of legal business for his father-in-law's family after his death.[41]

---

38. *Jackson District Intelligencer*, quoted in *Nashville Daily Banner*, October 26, 1840. Ibid, October 17, 1840.

39. Issac Goladay to JKP, November 9, 1840, quoted in Sellers, *Polk: Jacksonian*: 427. Samuel P. Walker to JKP, November 4, 1840, quoted in McCormac, *Polk*: 173-174. David S. Reynolds, *Waking Giant: America in the Age of Jackson* (New York: HarperCollins, 2008): 323.

40. Madison County, Tennessee Marriage Licenses 1838-1847: 14. 1840, 1850, 1860 U.S. Census for Madison County, Tennessee. Jonathan K.T. Smith, *Reported Council Minutes of the City of Jackson, Tennessee, 1871-1878* (Jackson, TN: Self-published, 1993): 264-265. Scurlock family history provided to the author by Mary Dorris Hanna. In AH to JKP, June 12, 1839 AH Papers TSLA, Huntsman writes from Nashville: "I am on my way to Sparta [in White County] to Settle some private business and to carry my Daughter to the [Western] District." Perhaps this is when Huntsman brought his daughter Ann back home to Madison County after being raised by her maternal grandmother Ann Quarles at White Plains in Overton County.

41. Regarding efforts made by Huntsman on his son-in-law's behalf, refer to Appendix A. Scurlock was executor for the estates of Huntsman's third wife, Nancy Mosely Huntsman, Huntsman's son, George T. Huntsman, and acted as trustee for Huntsman's unmarried daughter America.

Chapter Ten

Stay at Home

1841–1849

*Old Adam Huntsman is one of those Democrats **who will do to take along**. When he says a thing will be so, it will be so! No man better knows the people—the great people—of Tennessee. The coons [Whigs] have tested his judgment, and when he tells them they are whipt, they at once **start down**.*
—Nashville Union, July 26, 1847

I have not applied either to the State or general government for any sort of appointment heretofore and confidently ask now for one at your hands (towit) That you will send me a commission under the great seal of the United States—to Stay at home and sleep with my wife ... and if you dont send it, I will sleep with her without it.
—Adam Huntsman, April 23, 1848

LIKE THE WHIGS after their defeat in the 1839 state elections, Democrats regrouped following their crushing loss in the 1840 presidential campaign and prepared for the upcoming gubernatorial contest in 1841. Polk realized his party's overconfidence had allowed their opponents to organize several months before the campaign began, enabling them to gain the upper hand and the victory. Attributing their losses to "the superior organization and industry of our opponents," he was determined not to make the same mistake again. In letters to Democratic leaders across the state, Polk tried to lift their spirits and encourage them to "take up

Tennessee state historical marker on Highway 70 near Jackson, Tennessee.

Photograph by the author

courage" and "lick the flint and try it again." He instructed them to organize five-man committees in each county that in turn would appoint committees for each congressional district. He hoped this grassroots effort would revive interest in the party's cause, ensuring that party newspapers and literature were well distributed and loyal Democrats made it to the polls in August.[1]

Huntsman went to work on the Democratic committee in Jackson and helped create a slate of candidates in the Western District. In the Gibson County state house race, he and fellow Democrats hoped to encourage "one strong Whig" to oppose the nomination of another for Congress. The two candidates would "lie upon each other to a sufficient extent to keep them from withdrawing" and enable a Democrat to enter the race and win. He told Polk he looked forward to antagonizing his opponents at the upcoming court day in Henderson County. "The prospect of engendering some mischief is quite flattering from all I learn," he wrote on March 9. "I find it affords me great amusement to play off a little Black dog philosophy amongst our Brother Whigs."[2]

On April 4, exactly one month into his administration, William Henry Harrison became the first president to die in office, and Vice President John Tyler assumed the presidency. Congressional Whigs expected him to adhere to the course already set out by the party, but Tyler—being a Jeffersonian and a former Democrat—twice vetoed legislation that would have created a new national bank, believing it to be unconstitutional. As a result, he was expelled from the Whig party and all but one member of his cabinet resigned.[3] Huntsman was delighted when a group of angry Whigs in Jackson were ready to burn the president in effigy. "I told them I would give as much to see that sight as I would to see a menagerie" and wanted nothing more than "to see one set of Whigs Singe another." But

---

1. Sellers, *Polk: Jacksonian*: 427-428
2. The Jackson Committee in 1843 included Huntsman, James A. Caruthers (president of the local branch of the Union Bank of the State of Tennessee), attorneys Archibald O.W. Totten and Thomas Ewell, and physician George Snider. Samuel H. Laughlin to JKP, December 25, 1843 CJKP 6: 394. The phrase "Black dog" seems to imply "depression of spirits" or ill humor.
3. Daniel Walker Howe, *What Hath God Wrought: The Transformation of America, 1815-1848* (New York: Oxford University Press, 2007): 589-592. Atkins, *Parties*: 118-119.

his teasing made them think better of their plan. He regretted that he had interrupted what would have been "glowing fun here."[4]

Polk was challenged in his bid for reelection by a novice politician and one-term legislator named James Chamberlain Jones, who had been a Whig presidential elector the previous year. The Whigs went back to what worked best for them, touting the simplicity and good humor of their candidate and nicknaming him "Lean Jimmy" for his rail-thin, six-foot frame. Huntsman predicted that Polk would "have a hard contest even if you succeed" in winning the election.[5] Polk discussed state and national issues while Jones entertained with his humor and satire. One disgusted West Tennessee Democrat, after attending a joint canvass between the two candidates, believed Polk "made an ass of himself, talking sense to a lot of d— fools." If he was Polk, he declared, he would not let Jones "make a laughingstock out of me" but would "get a stick and crack Jones' skull, and end this tomfoolery." Jones defeated Polk by more than 3,000 votes; it was the first loss of his eighteen-year political career.[6]

With a three-vote advantage in the state house of representatives and only two votes shy of a majority in the senate, Whigs looked forward to the rare opportunity to fill both of the state's two vacant U.S. Senate seats in the same session. (Felix Grundy had died a year earlier and his seat was filled temporarily by Alfred O.P. Nicholson, while Alexander Anderson had completed the last two years of Hugh Lawson White's term following his resignation in 1839.) Meanwhile, Democrats working behind the scenes hoped to persuade a few who were not "hearty Whigs" to vote for a Democrat instead. A month before the General Assembly convened, Huntsman reported to Polk that one newly elected Whig from a Democratic district had been pressured to do so, and he thought another reluctant Whig or two might do the same. There were plenty of national issues on which both Southern Democrats and Whigs could find common ground—opposition to a national bank and tariff among them—and he

---

4. AH to JKP, September 15, 1841. Williams, "Huntsman-Polk": 352-353. Also in CJKP 5: 757-758.
5. AH to JKP, March 9, 1841. Williams, ed. "Huntsman-Polk": 350-351.
6. Williams, *Beginnings of West Tennessee*: 278. Corlew, *Tennessee*: 261.

asked rhetorically if it would not be better for the state to have one senator from each party than none at all.[7]

When the session began, the Democratic majority—labeled by Whigs as "The Immortal Thirteen"—refused to convene a joint session with the house to elect the U.S. senators. It had been custom in previous elections for both houses to vote at the same time, but Democrats suddenly decided the procedure was unconstitutional and that each house should vote separately. Attempts to mediate a resolution between the two parties proved unsuccessful for the remainder of the session.[8]

Writing to Polk before the 1842 session, Huntsman thought it best that his fellow Democrats "bring on the election for senators by all means," though he still insisted that each party should have a senator. The matter should be resolved soon: "It would be much to our advantage to have that question disposed of before the next general election." In the Western District, he enjoyed minor success against the opposition. He attended a rally of about 600 Whig supporters in October at Jackson. The speakers generated very little enthusiasm for their cause, he believed, but his own prospects among the onlookers had been much more favorable. "I passed through the outskirts of the congregation, partook of their dinner and converted a few to democracy while the Whig speakers were defending the Bankrupt law."[9]

In Nashville, Democrats continued to block the elections as well as other Whig sponsored legislation. The impasse denied Tennessee representation in the United States Senate from 1841 to 1843. The state elections in 1843 proved that public opinion had sided against the Democrats. The actions of the "Immortal Thirteen" were considered obstructionist rather than principled tactics and resulted in the loss of their slim senate majority. Whigs also retained control of the house and reelected James C. Jones

---

7. AH to JKP, September 15, 1841. CJKP 5: 757-758. Also in Williams, ed. "Huntsman-Polk": 352-353.

8. Corlew, *Tennessee*: 261-262. Bergeron, *Antebellum Politics*: 69-70. The "Immortal Thirteen" controversy is discussed in more detail in Atkins, *Parties*: 120-123.

9. AH to JKP, September 27, 1842. Williams, ed. "Huntsman-Polk": 354-355. The "bankrupt law" refers to the Bankrupt Act of 1841, which the Whig majority in Congress passed during the special session in 1841.

to a second term as governor. It was Polk's second statewide defeat and called into question his future political prospects.[10]

In the winter of 1843, Huntsman lost his wife Elizabeth—to whom he had been married for close to fourteen years—on Saturday, January 7. She was buried at Salem Cemetery beside his first wife Sarah; both women had tragically died at the young age of thirty-three. He was left to care for their five children whose ages ranged from fourteen to two years old.[11]

IT SEEMED INEVITABLE that Martin Van Buren would be the Democratic nominee for president in 1844. The prospect of supporting his candidacy yet again was discouraging to most Tennessee Democrats. They had campaigned for him twice before in 1836 and 1840 and voters had rejected him each time. But Polk—knowing that a Southerner would be needed to balance the ticket—tied himself to the New Yorker's aspirations and hoped his reward would be the vice presidency. In March, Huntsman was concerned that Van Buren's former vice president Richard M. Johnson of Kentucky—who was now promoting himself as a presidential candidate—would instead seek to be his running mate again. If Johnson was successful, Huntsman advised Polk to be a state elector and campaign against his "Trusty Couzen John Bell" across the state. Such activism on Van Buren's behalf might be rewarded with a cabinet position or a U.S. Senate seat, "a kind of resting place untill better times."[12]

The nomination of Henry Clay for the Whigs seemed just as certain. While attending court at Huntingdon on February 8, 1844, Huntsman infiltrated a Whig convention that had nominated William T. Haskell—the son of his friend Judge Joshua Haskell—to be elector for the 12th Congressional District and George W. Gibbs as a delegate to the Whig national convention in Baltimore. Democrats had not yet chosen their electoral candidates for the upcoming election, and Huntsman boasted that he had "bluff[e]d them off" from starting their canvass without them. The excitement and competition of a political campaign always motivated

---

10. Bergeron, *Antebellum Politics*: 70. With control over the legislature following the 1843 elections, Whigs selected Ephraim H. Foster and Spencer Jarnigan to fill the vacant seats.
11. Elizabeth Huntsman tombstone, Old Salem Cemetery
12. AH to JKP, January 15, 1844. Williams, ed. "Huntsman-Polk": 357

Elizabeth (Todd) Huntsman tombstone, Old Salem Cemetery

Photograph by the author

him. He promised Polk he would "take an active interest in the Canvass next summer upon my own [ho]ok and for my own amusement" and "discharge a few speeches" in the Western District.[13]

Texas became an important issue in the campaign when the Tyler administration negotiated a treaty with the Republic of Texas for annexation and submitted it to the Senate for ratification in April. The probable candidates—Van Buren and Clay—both declared themselves against it, believing it would instigate war with Mexico. Notwithstanding his position, the Whigs nominated Clay unanimously; Democrats on the other hand felt Van Buren had made a fatal mistake and looked for other alternatives.

Andrew Jackson, still the patriarch of the party, regretted his friend's decision and bluntly told him "it was impossible to elect him."[14] The Old Hero set into motion a plan to save the election and make Polk the Democratic nominee. But Polk's Tennessee allies at the national convention in Baltimore also knew to keep his chances alive for the vice presidency should Van Buren secure the nomination. The Little Magician's inability to win a two-thirds majority at the convention enabled Polk's name to enter the contest and be nominated on the ninth ballot.[15]

Two weeks after his nomination, Huntsman congratulated him in his own humorous way: "I suppose miracles will not cease in the land. To have supposed it possible that such a Possum looking fellow as you were twenty five years ago would ever have been nominated for President of the United States would then have been deemed Quixotism. But so it is, and we must make the best we can out of you." He had been disheartened in the wake of Van Buren's announcement at the prospect of supporting an anti-annexation candidate. "I felt half killed myself," he admitted, and "considered we were beat." But the nomination of his friend Polk had brightened his outlook on the November election considerably. "I now think we can make a drawn Battle in the District," he enthusiastically wrote. "The Texas Question is a powerful lever in our hands and will give

---

13. AH to JKP, February 18, 1844. Williams, ed. "Huntsman-Polk": 357-358.

14. McCormac, *Polk*: 224-228. Remini, *Clay*: 638-644. David S. Heidler and Jeanne T. Heidler, *Henry Clay: The Essential American* (New York: Random House, 2010): 386-388.

15. Walter R. Borneman, *Polk: The Man Who Transformed the Presidency and America* (New York: Random House, 2008): 88-93, 97-106.

us many Whig votes and we have set every engine to work already to put our forces in motion."[16]

HUNTSMAN TOOK THE LEAD for Polk in the Western District, organizing party operatives and making speaking engagements. On July 6, he wrote Samuel H. Laughlin that Democrats there were "active, Confident and in fine spirits." He and William Fitzgerald had debated George W. Gibbs and Micajah Bullock in front of a large crowd at Trenton the first two days of July. Both Polk's candidacy and the Texas issue were on "the ascendancy" in the District and he felt confident that Democrats would "gain 12 or 1500 votes" in the region.[17]

Over the course of the campaign, Huntsman wrote to various Democratic leaders in New York, Pennsylvania, Maryland, Indiana, and Virginia to gather intelligence on Polk's chances there.[18] He made arrangements for state party leaders to canvass the District. In late September, he reported that Coe and Congressman Cave Johnson of Clarksville were "doing glorious work" but complained that he had heard nothing from elector-at-large Alfred O.P. Nicholson about following John Bell through the District in September. When Nicholson failed to appear, he enlisted Coe to follow Bell and recruited David Craighead, state senator from Davidson County, to take Coe's appointments. Craighead did "sterling business wherever we can get good meetings" despite the efforts of Whigs to "prevent any of their party from hearing him." Huntsman was also encouraged by Clay's recent efforts to back peddle on annexation to satisfy Southern Whigs. In doing so, he knew Clay would be "modifying himself out of many Northern votes."[19]

Huntsman was enthusiastic in the efforts to beat Clay, but he did not tolerate his fellow Democrats dredging up the twenty-year-old charge

16. AH to JKP, June 11, 1844. Williams, ed. "Huntsman-Polk": 360.
17. AH to Samuel H. Laughlin, July 6, 1844. Samuel H. Laughlin Papers TSLA.
18. AH to JKP, September 20, 1844. Williams, "Huntsman-Polk": 360-361. Huntsman wrote to many former colleagues in Congress during the 1844 campaign, including messmate Francis Thomas of Maryland; Ely Moore and Churchill C. Cambreleng, both of New York; and James Garland of Virginia. He also wrote to Senator James Buchanan of Pennsylvania, who would later become fifteenth President of the United States. Ibid.
19. Ibid

Adam Huntsman

Illustration by Wade Dillon

of a "corrupt bargain" between Clay and John Quincy Adams. When a party associate claimed it was true, Huntsman blasted him and called it "a base lie and slander...[H]e had pronounced it false in 1827, and so pronounced it again. He was for beating Clay *on his principles*, and not for LYING him to death!"[20]

Despite his best efforts, a month before the election, Huntsman conceded that a Whig victory was almost certain in the Western District by a majority of 950 votes. He felt Democrats would carry only nine of the eighteen counties, with Madison County likely going into the Whig column. In a letter on October 7, he predicted that Polk would carry Michigan, Maine, New Jersey, New York, Pennsylvania, Virginia, South Carolina, Alabama, Mississippi, Arkansas, Missouri, and Illinois. He believed Polk's "chances best" in Georgia, Tennessee, Ohio, Indiana, and Louisiana. "If the abolitionists in Ohio & Indiana vote a separate Ticket we have these [states]," Huntsman believed, otherwise "we are licked." If Georgia went for Clay, "she ought to be put in the mad house." Still, he was confident that Polk would win the election even if he lost his home state. "State pride makes it desirable to get Tennessee, but I do not consider it absolutely necessary."[21]

Huntsman's predictions were largely accurate: Polk carried every state but New Jersey and secured 170 electoral votes to Clay's 105 while falling short in the popular vote. The crucial state was New York, which he carried by 5,106 votes. James G. Birney, the anti-slavery Liberty party candidate, took 15,814 votes that likely would have gone to Clay.[22]

On the eve of Polk's victory, Huntsman made a mischievous observation about the example his friend would set as chief executive: "There is a pretty strong objection to you which is well founded, as Washington, Madison, and Jackson had no children. If you succeed, the world will believe that the qualifications of an American President lies *all* in his head, and *none* in his Breeches."[23]

20. *Jonesborough Whig*, December 6, 1843
21. AH to JKP, October 7, 1844. CJKP 8: 162-164. Also in Williams, ed. "Huntsman-Polk": 362-363.
22. Ibid
23. Ibid. Polk and his wife Sarah (Childress) Polk had no children.

A FEW WEEKS AFTER THE ELECTION Huntsman wrote the president-elect, emphasizing what he believed would be the primary issues of his administration: the tariff and Texas. "I am old *but chuck fu[ll] of fight upon these two subjects*," he wrote explicitly. The 1842 tariff—which he detested as a "Bill of abominations," much like the 1828 version—should be fought "on any & every occasion." If it came to taking action, he proposed doing "as our Fathers did in the Revolution, [and] refuse to use or wear their Northern Fabricks," but instead wear "nothing but our Western home made stuffs." Both issues would win Polk support in the South and West, Huntsman believed, and increase the Democratic party's chances in the Tennessee gubernatorial and legislative campaigns in 1845. He closed his letter with the salutation: "Please present me kindly to Mrs President and accept for yourself my hearty good wishes."24

It was custom for the president to choose someone from his home state to a cabinet position. Writing on December 20, Huntsman offered the names of Cave Johnson, Aaron V. Brown, Levin H. Coe, "or any good democrat." Fellow Democrats in the Western District believed Johnson to be the most deserving of a position and suggested that he become Secretary of the Treasury. Huntsman asked Polk to make his decision before the state Democratic convention in March 1845 to prevent someone being nomination to a state office that might be a prospective cabinet selection. Polk eventually chose his old congressional friend Cave Johnson for postmaster general.25

Victories in the 1845 legislative elections gave Democrats a four-seat majority in the General Assembly for the first time in six years. It also gave them the opportunity to install a Democrat to fill the expired U.S. Senate seat of failed Whig gubernatorial candidate Ephraim H. Foster. Prior to the election, Huntsman had been among nine potential candidates mentioned in Democratic circles for the office. President Polk tried to distance himself from the contest and avoid charges of executive influence on the decision. The candidates "had all been my personal and political

24. AH to JKP, November 17, 1844. CJKP 8: 327-328. Also in Williams, ed."Huntsman-Polk": 363-364.

25. AH to JKP, December 20, 1844. CJKP 8: 442. Also in Williams, ed. "Huntsman-Polk": 364-365.

friends, and…I could not with any propriety take any part between them," he wrote. But when nominations were made on October 21, Huntsman's name was not among them. Democratic legislators in both houses failed to unite behind one nominee and the election was deadlocked for two weeks between three candidates. One of them, Hopkins L. Turney, convinced the Whig minority that Alfred O.P. Nicholson was the preferred choice of the president. This knowledge was enough to give Turney all the Whig votes, which along with six Democrats won him the Senate seat.[26]

While Huntsman agreed that the preferred Democratic candidate should have been elected, he found Nicholson using his position as editor of the *Nashville Union* to publicly criticize Turney "in bad taste and selfish." Such tactics were used for Nicholson's personal benefit rather "than…to harmonize or strengthen the party" and hurt his standing within Democratic ranks in the Western District. Huntsman wanted Polk's name kept out of the intraparty squabble—writing to Turney himself to ensure that it be done—and advised the president to let the two men "scuffle this matter out" between themselves. "Such are the symptoms of divisions in our party about various little local matters [such as this] which are calculated to weaken us," he wrote, "that if another is added to them…(to wit the failure of the Tariff) I think there is great danger of loosing the State at the next election" in 1846.[27]

FOUR YEARS AFTER his wife Elizabeth's death, Huntsman married for a third time to Nancy Waller Mosely. The ceremony took place in Montgomery County, Tennessee on December 11, 1846. Nancy was fifty-seven years old and the widow of John S. Mosely of Montgomery County.[28] She owned 851 acres and thirty-eight slaves both in Montgomery

---

26. Milo Milton Quaife, ed. *The Diary of James K. Polk During His Presidency, 1845 to 1849* (Chicago: A.C. McClurg and Company, 1910) 1:112. Among the other potential candidates Polk mentions are Levin H. Coe, William C. Dunlap, and William Fitzgerald from the Western District, as well as William B. Turley, William T. Brown, and William Trousdale. Ibid. Atkins, *Parties*: 143. White, ed. *Messages* 4: 21-32.

27. AH to JKP, April 27, 1846. CJKP 11: 135-136. Also in Williams, ed. "Huntsman-Polk": 367-368.

28. Nancy Waller married John Mosely in Warren County, North Carolina on February 24, 1806. "North Carolina, Marriages, 1759-1979," index, FamilySearch <familysearch.org/pal:/MM9.1.1/F8BJ-KJP>

and Madison counties. Interestingly, the couple prepared a prenuptial agreement four days before their wedding that stated each would retain their own properties during the marriage.[29]

In his later years, Huntsman became something of a Democratic soothsayer for his prognostications on the outcome of state and national elections. Wrote one Democratic newspaper editor: "Old Adam Huntsman is one of those Democrats who *will do to take along*. When he says a thing will be so, it will be so! No man better knows the people—the great people—of Tennessee. The coons have tested his judgment, and when he tells them they are whipt, they at once *start down*."[30] His forecast of the 1844 presidential election had been generally accurate, but his predictions for two subsequent elections proved to be less reliable. In the 1847 gubernatorial election, Huntsman was confident that incumbent Democrat Aaron V. Brown would prevail over his Whig challenger, Neill S. Brown. "Not much money will be won or lost here," he told a Nashville editor. "The Whigs are not disposed to bet." It proved to be a close finish, but the governor lost by less than 1,500 votes.[31]

Still, when a Whig paper playfully bestowed upon him the title of prophet, Huntsman took advantage of the opportunity to send its editor his prophecies for the future of the Whig party. He expected that by the 1848 presidential election, "the whig party, by that name, is perfectly annihilated" and would have to change its moniker in order "to deceive the people before the next election." (Eight years later, the Whig party had indeed broken apart over the debate of slavery in the western territories; Northern members would join the Republican party.) Many of his predictions—that "Lean Jimmy" Jones would run for governor of Tennessee in 1847 and that many "honest, well meaning whigs" would "repent of their evil ways and join the Democrats" a year later—failed to come true. His most accurate prophecy was that once the 29th Congress

---

29. Nancy Huntsman tombstone, Old Salem Cemetery, Jackson TN. Madison County, TN Deed Book 11: 357-361.

30. *Nashville Union*, July 26, 1847. The raccoon (or coon) had become the accepted symbol of the Whig party.

31. AH to Editor of the *Nashville Union*, July 17, 1847, reprinted in *Boston Daily Atlas*, August 18, 1847.

convened in Washington, "the great whig mystery will be solved of 'who is James K. Polk.'"³²

Huntsman's letters to the president during the last two years of his term became less frequent out of sympathy for the increased responsibilities his old friend faced, "for I expect you are weighed down with correspondence without any addition from me." Because he handled even the menial tasks of government himself and was easily one of the hardest working occupants of the President's House, Polk must have appreciated his friend's consideration. When he did write, Huntsman touched upon national issues such as the tariff, Oregon, and a national bank. The bank was "the last remaining pillar that support[s] the tottering edifice" of the Whig party, he believed. With the prospect of war against Great Britain over the Oregon boundary dispute, Huntsman asserted that people in the Western District "do not believe in the Oregon War...nor do we care one copper if it comes. I discover there is no Whiggery or democracy about that, they are all Americans & ready for a frolic, and talk of it in that way rather than as a fight."³³

On April 23, 1848, he wrote what would be his last letter to Polk. It was the culmination of thirteen years of political advice, campaign strategy, and friendly banter with the man whom he first met in the Tennessee state senate in 1819. He shared his concern over party discord among the conservative and liberal Democratic factions in New York that threatened the party's chances in the upcoming presidential election. He was also concerned over the stand made by "hot-headed" Southern Democrats who had threatened to oppose any candidate that supported the controversial Wilmot Proviso.³⁴

Because Polk had pledged to serve only one term, there were many potential Democratic candidates seeking the nomination in 1848. Holding true to his independent nature, Huntsman for a time considered giving his support to General Zachary Taylor. A celebrated hero of the Mexican

---

32. *Nashville Union*, September 3, 1845. Huntsman's reputation as a "prophet" is alluded to in Moses G. Reeves to JKP, October 17, 1845. Reeves wrote: "I do not set up to be a Huntsman, Prophet or son of one..." (This phrase is taken from Amos 7:14 in the Old Testament.)

33. AH to JKP, January 15, 1846. CJKP 11: 25-26. Also in Williams, ed. "Huntsman-Polk": 366-367.

34. AH to JKP, April 23, 1848. Williams, ed. "Huntsman-Polk": 368-369.

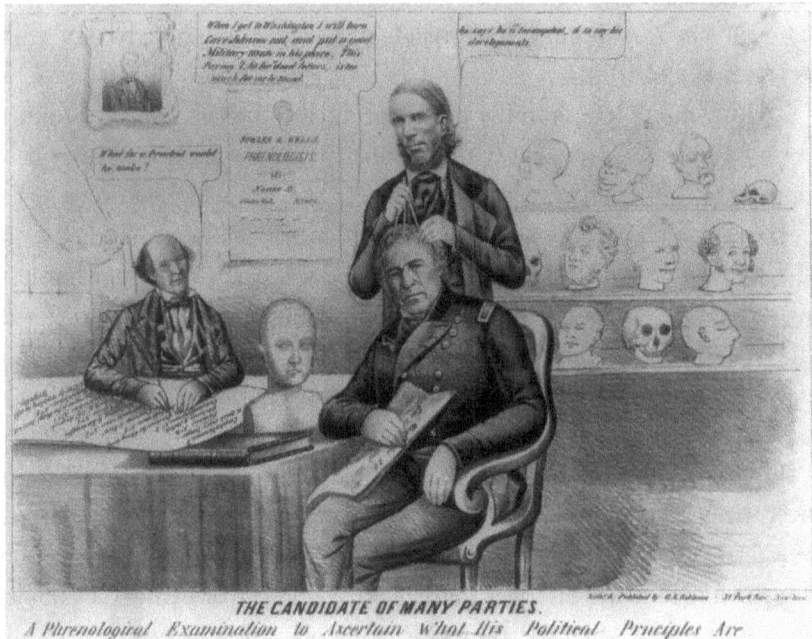

THE CANDIDATE OF MANY PARTIES.
A Phrenological Examination to Ascertain What His Political Principles Are

A hero of the Mexican War, General Zachary Taylor's candidacy was sought by both Democrats and Whigs for president in 1848. Initially, Huntsman favored the independent Taylor—until Taylor finally decided he was a Whig.

Courtesy of the Library of Congress

War, "Old Rough and Ready" seemed disinterested in politics and outwardly favored no party. Perhaps it was these independent traits that appealed to Huntsman. Taylor made it known that if he was nominated for the presidency, it would have to be a non-partisan selection. But pressure from Taylor's handlers who wanted him to secure the Whig nomination prompted him to be more specific. In a letter for publication in April 1848, he declared: "I am a Whig but not an ultra Whig."[35] This was all Huntsman needed to know to change his mind. "Now whether this means that he is a *soft whig*, or a *tender-footed* whig, I know—I care not," he wrote. "Of all the politicians which exist the soft or tender-footed are the most obnoxious to me. Instead of being a *no-party* man, as he at first declared, it turns out that he belongs to the *tender-footed whig* party, as

---

35. K. Jack Bauer, *Zachary Taylor: Soldier, Planter, Statesman of the Old Southwest* (Baton Rouge: Louisiana State University Press, 1985): 233

he himself shows." Based on what he had read about Taylor, he now concluded that the Hero of Buena Vista "has no qualifications to discharge the duties of chief magistrate. As Daniel Webster says, *he is a mere military man*."[36]

No longer enamored by Taylor's independent-turned-Whig candidacy—"I ought not, I cannot, and I will not vote [for] Taylor," he reiterated—Huntsman in mid April favored James Buchanan, Polk's secretary of state, for the Democratic nomination. He remained open minded to other possibilities such as Senator Lewis Cass of Michigan, Vice President George M. Dallas, U.S. Supreme Court Justice Levi Woodbury, or Senator John A. Dix of New York.[37] Huntsman eventually backed Cass, whom he believed to be "a man of first rate talents." In supporting his candidacy, he wrote, "I consider that I am carrying out those democratic doctrines, which I have been advocating for forty years, and expect to die in that faith." Cass lost the election to Taylor.[38]

With Polk's term nearing its end, Huntsman reassured him that as president he had "fought the good fight, and kept the faith amidst such storms and persecutions as I thought was wholly improbable would be heaped upon a man, who was not a candidate for reelection." The goals of Polk's administration—the reduction of the 1842 protective tariff, establishment of an independent treasury, settlement of the Oregon boundary, and the acquisition of California—had been accomplished and "placed you upon such ground as to be wholly [beyond] Whig defiance now and forever."[39]

IN THE SUMMER OF 1849, Adam Huntsman was sixty-three years old. He was less active than in years past and stayed close to his two-story brick home at Cotton Grove and his large family. His oldest daughter Ann and her husband Timothy P. Scurlock lived in Jackson with their five young children, two boys and three girls ranging in age from seven to

---

36. AH to Jackson (TN) Democratic Club, n.d. 1848, published in Columbus (OH) *Daily Ohio Statesman*, October 12, 1848.
37. AH to JKP, April 23, 1848. Williams, ed. "Huntsman-Polk": 368-369.
38. Ibid
39. Ibid

one. America, his oldest child by his second wife Elizabeth, was now a young woman about twenty years old; her brother George T. Huntsman was almost seventeen. His three youngest children—Paradise, Adam F., and Susan Jane—were about fourteen, eleven, and nine.

But politics was never far from Huntsman's active mind. He kept up with current affairs while leaving the campaign trail to younger, more energetic workers. No longer traveling the judicial circuit, he practiced law in Madison County with his son-in-law and legal partner. For his labors on behalf of his party and his state, all Huntsman asked from his friend Polk was "a commisson under the great seal of the United States—to Stay at home and sleep with my wife…and if you dont send it, I will sleep with her without it."[40] Many of his past friends, rivals, and associates in law and politics such as John Williams, Hugh Lawson White, Andrew Jackson, Felix Grundy, William Carroll, and David Crockett were now gone. Even James K. Polk—nine years younger than he—died on June 15, 1849, three months after leaving office and retiring to Nashville.

Huntsman's own health took a turn for the worst that summer. He developed what nineteenth-century physicians called dropsy, or swelling caused by fluid retention in the body tissues or cavities, likely the result of congestive heart failure. A neighbor, John E. Stewart, was his physician at the time.[41] Huntsman died at home on the evening of Thursday, August 23, 1849. His body was taken by a horse-drawn hearse a mile southwest to Salem Cemetery and laid to rest—likely with Masonic honors—beside his first wife Sarah.[42]

As a former congressman, epitaphs announcing his death appeared in newspapers close to home and across the nation. "Mr. Huntsman has borne a conspicuous part in the politics of the State," wrote the *West Tennessee Whig*, "and occupied a high stand at the Bar of which he was long a member." The *Weekly Memphis Eagle* noted: "He had filled many public stations, and filled them well, and enjoyed a high measure of the

---

40. Ibid. Huntsman and Scurlock were listed as legal partners in a lawsuit settled after Huntsman's death. Madison County, Tennessee Circuit Court Minutes, 1848-1850: 177.

41. Stewart owned land to the west of Huntsman's property in the Cotton Grove community.

42. Adam Huntsman tombstone, Old Salem Cemetery, Jackson TN. The *Weekly Memphis Eagle*, August 30, 1849, specified that Huntsman died "on the evening of the 23rd instant, of dropsy," while the notation at the top of AH to Samuel H. Laughlin, July 6, 1844, states he died "of fever."

Adam Huntsman tombstone, Old Salem Cemetery

Photograph by the author

respect and esteem of his fellow citizens." A Mississippi paper made the coarse remark that he had been "the primary cause of the death of David Crockett."[43] The most respectful tribute came from those who knew him best—his colleagues in the Jackson bar, of which he had been a member for twenty-six years. They met at the law offices of Milton Brown and Hervey Brown in Jackson to express their regret at the passing "of one of its most aged and esteemed members."

> For more than thirty years Mr. Huntsman has been an active, efficient and distinguished member of the [legal] profession, receiving a full share of its confidence and respect, its honors and its profits. He was a favorite of the Bar, especially of its junior members, towards whom his learning was ever kind, respectful, and obliging.
>
> Often a member of the State Senate, whilst he resided in the Middle Division of the State and after his removal to the Western Division, a prominent and leading member of the State Convention of 1834, which framed our present Constitution. Mr. Huntsman has greatly influenced the Legislative policy of the State, and indelibly impressed his name upon its history.Finally, he was transferred to a larger *arena*—the Congress of the Union, where in that numerous body, he approved himself an able, efficient and independent representative.
>
> Often before the people, he was ever a popular favorite, and was never defeated in a popular election. He never held office from any other source of power. In both professional and personal life, therefore, he has had a long

---

43. *Weekly Memphis Eagle*, August 30, 1849. Jackson *West Tennessee Whig*, August 30, 1849. *American* (MS) *Sovereign*, reprinted in Greenville (SC) *Mountaineer*, September 21, 1849. Huntsman's death was also mentioned in the *Knoxville Register*, September 8, 1849; *Boston Daily Atlas*, September 14, 1849; Charleston (SC) *Mercury*, reprinted in *Greenville Mountaineer*, September 14, 1849; Raleigh (NC) *Register*, September 15, 1849; and *Milwaukee* (WI) *Sentinel and Gazette*, October 6, 1849. The *Boston Daily Atlas* erroneously reported that Huntsman was "one of the oldest men who ever served in the House."

and distinguished career, but few comparatively, have attained to so great success.

But Mr. H. was no ordinary person—he possessed a powerful and discriminating mind, much energy and steadiness of purpose, was disinterested, sincere and active in his friendship, frank, affable in intercourse.

In this brief retrospect of the life and character of Mr. Huntsman, we may see how great has been our loss and that of his numerous friends and family.[44]

After his death, Huntsman's children were split up. While America stayed with her stepmother at Cotton Grove, Paradise and Adam went to Shelby County, Tennessee and lived with their aunt Sarah Todd McNeill and her husband Philip McNeill. His oldest son George T. Huntsman and George's sister Susan Jane likely moved to Shelby County as well, but stayed with other relatives.[45]

It was determined three months later that Huntsman had died insolvent and without a will. From the time he settled in Madison County in 1823, indebtedness had burdened him and brought him to court as often as defending his clients. It was especially true in his later years. On November 29, 1848, he borrowed $2,000 from the Jackson branch of the Union Bank of Tennessee and gave as collateral his 457 acre farm. A loan for an additional $3,258 was taken five months later on the same property with fellow attorney Micajah Bullock acting as trustee for the bank. When Huntsman died, the loans remained unpaid. Bullock was forced to sell the house and farm to the highest bidder on February 11, 1850, what would have been Huntsman's sixty-fourth birthday.[46]

---

44. *West Tennessee Whig*, August 31, 1849. Madison County, Tennessee Circuit Court Minute Book, 1848-1850: 170-171.

45. 1850 U.S. Census for Shelby County, Tennessee: 196 A (11th Civil District). Transcribed by Kathy Balestrini, April 2004 <files.usgenarchives.org/tn/shelby/census/1850/1850-dist11.txt> The whereabouts of George T. and Susan Jane Huntsman at the time of the census is uncertain. Both children eventually made it to Shelby County, where George married Anna M. Henry in 1857 and Susan married Samuel Ragland in 1860. 1850 U.S. Census for Madison County, Tennessee.

46. Madison County, TN Deed Book 12: 191, 422. Jackson *West Tennessee Whig*, January 18, 1850. Madison County, Tennessee Deed Book 14: 200, 532. Madison County, Tennessee Chancery

The property was bought on Nancy's behalf by Joseph Fogg, however, and she continued to live there with her stepdaughter America until her death on December 4, 1858. Meanwhile, two court-appointed administrators tried for over five years to satisfy Huntsman's heirs and numerous creditors to whom he owed money. Not even his funeral expenses could be paid. In her will, Nancy specified that what remained of her estate after debts had been paid should be used "in fixing up my grave and that of my husband, the late Adam Huntsman, with proper enclosures [and] tombstones."[47]

A CENTURY LATER, historian Chase Curran Mooney visited Old Salem Cemetery three and a half miles northeast of Jackson, Tennessee. There he found the graves of Adam Huntsman and his three wives. Nancy Huntsman's last wishes had been fulfilled as the graves were enclosed by a wrought iron fence and both she and her husband had tombstones of similar shape and design. But like Huntsman himself, the cemetery had been forgotten over time and their neglected graves were "heavily overgrown" with vines and vegetation.[48]

Twenty years later, the Altrusa Club of Jackson found the historic cemetery to be "a mass of tangled vines, thickets, fallen trees, and broken tombstones." Through their efforts, it was cleared and tombstones were repaired, including those of Huntsman and his three wives. The cemetery was designated as a historic landmark in 1975. Over the years, various local groups held additional cleanups to keep it in good repair.[49]

Because of its secluded location, the cemetery often fell victim to vandalism as people damaged tombstones and littered the area with discarded trash. Finally in 1994, the Sons of Confederate Veterans John Ingram Camp 219 took the initiative to protect it and at the same time commemorate the Civil War skirmish that was fought there on December

---

Court Minutes Vol. 1: 136, 147, 191, 197, 199, 206, 233, 263, 305-306, 340, 354. Nancy Huntsman's will may be found in Madison County, Tennessee Will Book 7: 32-34.

47. Ibid
48. Mooney, "Huntsman": 125fn
49. "Bicentennial Project: Restoration of Old Salem Campground Cemetery." *West Tennessee Historical Society Papers* 30: 141-142.

The graves of Elizabeth, Sarah, Adam, and Nancy Huntsman.

Photograph by the author

19, 1862. Today, Old Salem Cemetery is well maintained with a covered pavilion and monuments that interpret the battle. It has become a point of interest on the Tennessee Civil War Trails with the addition of an interpretive marker there in 2010.[50]

AS A STATE SENATOR, constitutional convention delegate, and congressman, Adam Huntsman left his mark on the times in which he lived. He worked to improve the efficiency of the state judicial system, promote infrastructure improvements for his district, and fund public education for children across the state. He played a conspicuous role in the creation of the amended 1835 state constitution that governed the Volunteer State for thirty-five years until the end of Reconstruction. But in that capacity, he also deprived free black men the right to vote that had been granted them in the original constitution and ensured that slaves could not be emancipated by the state legislature. Although he proposed no enduring legislation in his brief time in Congress, he witnessed the beginning

---

50. "Vandals Mar Historic Cemetery." *Jackson Sun*, June 11, 1994. "Civil War Site to Be Marked." Ibid: December 12, 1994. "Battle Scars." Ibid: December 18, 1994. Salem Cemetery and Battleground website <www.salemcemeterybattlefield.com/index.html>

of the tumultuous slavery debate in its halls that twenty-five years later would lead to disunion and civil war.

Huntsman thoroughly enjoyed politics—the nuisances of strategy, stump speaking, and campaign rallies. He had no qualms about attending a Whig rally and using his powers of persuasion to win over a few undecided voters in the crowd. He was a leader of the Democratic party in West Tennessee and responsible for party organization in the region. In later years he labored on the campaign trail not for the rewards of higher office or political appointment, but for the sheer fun of it. He helped arrange and publicize speaking engagements for prominent Democratic leaders and grassroots lieutenants in various local and statewide campaigns to spread the Jacksonian gospel to the electorate. "If I [lose], I will have fun sufficient to pay me for the defeat," he wrote. Whether in person or letters, he mingled with important state and national political figures of his lifetime such as John Williams, Hugh Lawson White, John Quincy Adams, John C. Calhoun, James K. Polk, and Andrew Jackson. Indeed, his letters to Polk reveal a man who truly considered the game of politics "glorious fun."

The question could be asked: what if Huntsman had *not* beaten David Crockett in 1835? In the predawn hours of March 6, 1836, Crockett likely would have been asleep at a boardinghouse or hotel in Washington. He would not have been among a group of volunteers defending a makeshift garrison in Texas against an army that outnumbered them. He would not have died a heroic death at the Alamo or become the cultural icon of the American frontier that he is today. The Davy Crockett craze that swept American households in 1954 and 1955 would never have occurred. The song that became a cultural classic would never have been written. Children would never have learned that Davy Crockett was born on a mountaintop and killed him a b'ar when he was only three (neither of which is true).

Consequently, the childhood memories of millions of Americans—as well as the companies that profited from the craze with vinyl records, toys, lunch boxes, and coonskin caps—perhaps owe a debt of gratitude to an obscure frontier lawyer and politician from Tennessee named Adam Huntsman.

Appendix A

Huntsman Genealogy

Descendants of (Unknown) Huntsman

First Generation

1. UNKNOWN[1] HUNTSMAN died in 1764 during an Indian attack on his homestead. He married Barbara ? date and place unknown.

The author believes he may have been Lawrence Huntsman, who died in Augusta County, Virginia in 1764. Lawrence's daughter, Elizabeth Huntsman, later married Joseph Ward June 5, 1775, in Charlotte County, Virginia. Adam[2] Huntsman was listed as surety for the marriage bond.

Children of Unknown and Barbara (____) Huntsman

2 i. Adam Huntsman

ii. Jacob Huntsman, born circa 1745; died April 18, 1825, at his home near Monroe, Overton County, Tennessee. He married (1) Mary Devine, December 29, 1782, in Charlotte County, Virginia; (2) Elizabeth Hunt, June 25, 1787, in Charlotte County.[1]

---

1. Jacob Huntsman's obituary published in *Sparta* (TN) *Review*, May 4, 1825. It noted: "During the whole course of his life, he has distinguished himself as an undeviating patriot and soldier, firmly devoted to the cause of freedom." His obituary mentioned him being survived by a widow and two daughters. Though an old man, he outfitted his 15-year-old son "at his own expense" to serve in the War of 1812.

iii. John Huntsman, died 1807 in Knox County, Tennessee². He married Elizabeth "Betsy" Kenner on May 3, 1796, in Hawkins County, Tennessee.³

iv. Unknown son, killed as an infant in 1764

Second Generation

2. ADAM² HUNTSMAN (Unknown¹) was born circa 1750, place unknown; died circa 1803, Charlotte County, Virginia. He married (1) Jeane Francis, date and place unknown. Jeane was a daughter of James and Obedience (Carrington) Francis. She died before 1793 in Charlotte County, Virginia. (2) Nancy Tiller Pugh, December 29, 1796, in Charlotte County.⁴

There is no definitive evidence that Adam Huntsman (the subject of this book) is the son of the elder Adam Huntsman, though circumstantial ties do make it a reasonable conclusion. At the time of the younger Adam's birth in 1786, there were three male members of the Huntsman family in Charlotte County: Adam, Jacob, and John. Their relationship as brothers is established in affidavits in two lawsuits (both Jacob Huntsman v. Adam Huntsman) filed in Charlotte County Chancery Court in 1784 and 1787, which also identifies their mother as Barbara Huntsman. (Their unnamed father "being then dead" as early as 1774.) Both Jacob and John settled in Knox County, Tennessee as early as 1799—where the younger Adam eventually located, but not until about eight or ten years later. Jacob's obituary in the *Sparta* (TN) *Gazette*, May 4, 1825, stated that he died near Monroe in Overton County on 18 April 1825 (where the younger Adam lived a few years earlier). As prominent a public figure as Adam was in Monroe, the obituary mentions no kinship between them, much less that he was Adam's father. John Huntsman's widow, Elizabeth Kenner Huntsman, applied for a pension based on his service in the Revolutionary War. She too indicated no paternal relationship with Adam; she did mention that her late husband was " a near relative to the Hon. Adam

---

2. John Huntsman's wife Elizabeth (Kenner) Huntsman claimed in her Revolutionary War Pension application that he died in October 1809. However, his estate sale after his death took place about October 1807.

3. Elizabeth Huntsman Revolutionary War Widow's Pension application. Her application was denied, as she could not prove to the satisfaction of the congressional Committee on Revolutionary Pensions her marriage to John Huntsman prior to 1800 or his military service in the war. Serial Set Vol. No. 584, Session Vol. No. 2. 31st Congress, 1st Session. House Report 361. newsbank.com website.

4. Nancy Tiller Pugh's maiden name found on Descendants of William Tiller of Old Rappahannock County, Virginia website at tiltill.tripod.com/WilliamTillerPage.htm.

Huntsman Decd late a member in Congress from Tennessee..." Having eliminated Jacob and John as potential fathers, it seems most likely that Adam Huntsman—his namesake who remained in Charlotte County until his death about 1803—was Adam's father. It is certain that Jeane (Francis) Huntsman was Adam's mother; this is proven in an affidavit he wrote on behalf of Lucy Cook Williamson, whom he had known as a child in Charlotte County, which is contained in Rains Cook Revolutionary War Pension <www.footnote.com> Adam wrote: "James Reese, Married my aunt." Reese married Anne (Frances) Ward, the widow of William Ward, in Charlotte County on May 19, 1800. Anne Frances was a sister of Jeane Francis Huntsman, whose children were listed as Adam, Ann, John, and James Huntsman, according to her mother Obedience Carrington Francis's will in Charlotte County, VA Will Book 2: 40, dated October 1, 1793.

Children of Adam and Jeane (Francis) Huntsman

3 i. Adam Huntsman

ii. Ann Huntsman[5] married _____ Street

iii. John Huntsman

iv. James Huntsman died about 1825 in Overton County, Tennessee. He married Mary Farmer, June 20, 1805, in Charlotte County, Virginia.

Notes for JAMES HUNTSMAN

James made his older brother Adam administrator of his estate.[6]

Child of James and Mary (Farmer) Huntsman

i. Stephen Huntsman

Notes for STEPHEN HUNTSMAN

Stephen resided in Madison County, Tennessee as early as March 23, 1829, when he appointed his friend Garten Petty of Pittsylvania County, Virginia "to sell my land in Charlotte County, Virginia, which came to me from the estate of my grandfather Stephen Farmer." A year later, he was listed in the 1830 census for Madison County as between 20-30 years old. He was in Madison County as late as November 1834.[7]

---

5. Adam and Jeane (Francis) Huntsman may have been another daughter. Catherine Huntsman married Christley Deniard in Charlotte County on December 8, 1783. Her father, Adam Huntsman, was surety for the marriage bond. Catherine Lindsay Knorr, ed., *Marriage Bonds and Ministers' Returns of Charlotte County, Virginia, 1764-1815*: 22.

6. As administrator of James Huntsman's estate, Adam Huntsman sold to Valentine Matlock a slave named Melinda for $350 on January 23, 1826. Overton County, Tennessee Deed Book F: 261.

7. Charlotte County, Virginia Deed Book 19: 114. Madison County, Tennessee Wills and Inventories, Vol. 1 (1822-1835): 511. Stephen's name appeared on a list of accounts to the estate of the late Robert Dickson.

Third Generation

3. ADAM³ HUNTSMAN (Adam², Unknown¹) was born February 11, 1786, Charlotte County, Virginia; died August 23, 1849, at Cotton Grove, Madison County, Tennessee. He had an unwed relationship with Elizabeth Witt, date and place of birth unknown; died December 1811 or January 1812 in Knox County, Tennessee. Elizabeth was the daughter of George and _____ Witt. Adam married (1) Sarah Wesley Quarles, circa 1820-22 in Overton, Jackson, or White County, Tennessee. She was born about 1792 in Albermarle or Bedford County, Virginia; died October 1825 in Madison County, Tennessee. (2) Elizabeth Todd, on June 14, 1829, in Madison County, Tennessee. She was born about 1810 in North Carolina; died January 7, 1843 in Madison County, Tennessee. (3) Nancy (Waller) Mosely, on December 11, 1846, in Montgomery County, Tennessee. She was born in 1789 in North Carolina; died December 4, 1858 in Madison County, Tennessee.

Child of Adam Huntsman and Elizabeth Witt

4 i. MELINDA JANE HUNTSMAN

Child of Adam and Sarah (Quarles) Huntsman

5 i. ANN HUNTSMAN

Children of Adam and Elizabeth (Todd) Huntsman

6 i. AMERICA HUNTSMAN
7 ii. GEORGE T. HUNTSMAN
8 iii. PARADISE HUNTSMAN
9 iv. ADAM FRANKLIN HUNTSMAN
10 v. SUSAN JANE HUNTSMAN

Fourth Generation

4. MELINDA JANE HUNTSMAN (Adam³, Adam², Unknown¹) was born August 25, 1811, in Knox County, Tennessee; died August 3, 1826, in Lincoln County, Tennessee. She was born Rutilia Witt, but her name was changed when her father legally adopted her on October 9, 1812. She may have been living in the home of her maternal uncle, Thomas Witt, in Lincoln County at the time of her death.

5. ANN⁴ HUNTSMAN (Adam³, Adam², Unknown¹) was born October 25, 1823, in Madison County, Tennessee; died May 12, 1882, at her home in Jackson, Madison

County, Tennessee. She is buried at Riverside Cemetery in Jackson, Tennessee. She married Timothy P. Scurlock in Madison County on December 22, 1840.[8]

Children of Ann[4] and Timothy P. Scurlock

i. Catherine L. (Kate) Scurlock, born in 1842 in Madison County, Tennessee. She married William D. Clark in Madison County on May 24, 1869.

ii. Joseph M. Scurlock, born in 1843 in Madison County, Tennessee.

iii. Fanny B. Scurlock, born January 1845 in Madison County, Tennessee; died between 1900-1910 in Mount Pleasant, Maury County, Tennessee. She married Dr. Henry Long on September 9, 1872, in Madison County, Tennessee. Long was born on September 28, 1835, and died on June 2, 1919. He was surgeon for the Ninth Tennessee Cavalry C.S.A. during the Civil War. He is buried at Lawrence Cemetery in Mount Pleasant, Tennessee.

iv. Clarence H. Scurlock, born January 1847 in Madison County, Tennessee.

v. Martha E.A. Scurlock, born in 1848 in Madison County, Tennessee.

vi. Ann Scurlock, born in 1849 in Madison County, Tennessee. She married A.L. Milner on December 2, 1885, in Madison County.

Notes for ANN HUNTSMAN

Upon her mother's death when she was about two years old, Ann was sent by her father to White Plains, where she was raised by her maternal grandmother and namesake, Ann (Hawes) Quarles. She may not have returned to Madison County until she was sixteen, despite the fact that her father had remarried in 1829. On October 28, 1836, her grandmother gave her two slaves as a gift, a five-year-old girl named Ella and a boy named Bob. (The deed was not registered in Madison County until January 21, 1840, after she returned to the county.)[9]

Ann's father was reportedly upset with Gov. James K. Polk over her husband Timothy Scurlock not being appointed attorney general for the 10th Judicial District of Tennessee.[10] A year later, Huntsman asked Polk not to "interfere" in a contest between Scurlock and two other candidates for solicitor in the Western District. "I do not expect you to aid Scurlock after giving the pro tem to [Joseph H.] Talbot," he wrote. "[A]ll we expect

---

8. Ann Scurlock obituary in the Memphis *Weekly Appeal*, May 24, 1882. Copy given to the author by Charlene McClain.

9. Jonathan K.T. Smith, *Genealogical Gleanings from the Deed Books 1-9, 1822-1845, Madison County, Tennessee*: 36

10. West H. Humphreys to JKP, May 23, 1840 CJKP 5: 459-460

is that you will not interfere between him and Scurlock as they are both democrats and your friends." Scurlock eventually became attorney general, serving from 1846 to 1850.[11]

During the Civil War, a Federal officer stationed in Jackson described Ann Scurlock as "a rebel, though a most excellent & kind hearted woman…" as she sought the release of her half brother Adam F. Huntsman, who was a Confederate prisoner of war.[12] Upon her death, her obituary noted: "She had been a citizen of Jackson over fifty years. She was a member of the Episcopal Church, and was loved and respected by all who knew her."[13]

6. AMERICA HUNTSMAN (Adam[3], Adam[2], Unknown[1]) was born circa 1829 in Madison County, Tennessee; died May 30, 1859, in Marshall County, Mississippi. She is buried at Riverside Cemetery in Jackson, Tennessee. She never married or had children.

Notes for AMERICA HUNTSMAN

The 1850 U.S. Census for Madison County listed her as residing with her stepmother, Nancy Waller Moseby Huntsman. In her will, Nancy left America a slave named Charlotte and her four children as well as "a choice of my beds, bed-stead and suitable quantity of bed clothing" and "the carpet and window curtains now in use in my parlor." She also left her $400 to be used to settle America's "present indebtedness," to be held by trustee Timothy P. Scurlock.[14] She was baptized at St. Luke's Episcopal Church in Jackson on May 20, 1857.[15] After Nancy's death a year later, America may have lived with her sister Paradise and her husband Nathaniel W. Williams in Marshall County, Mississippi, where she died of pneumonia on May 30, 1859. She was returned to Jackson, Tennessee and buried in an unmarked grave in the Scurlock

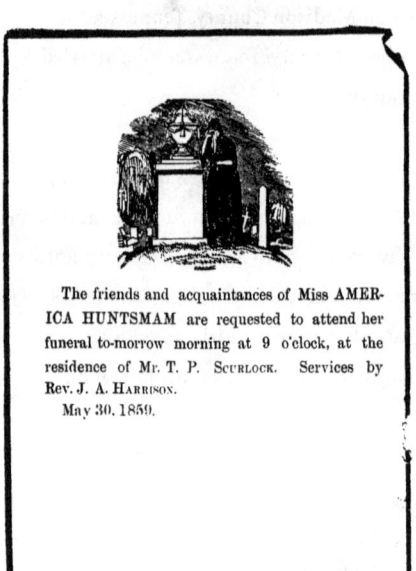

The friends and acquaintances of Miss AMERICA HUNTSMAM are requested to attend her funeral to-morrow morning at 9 o'clock, at the residence of Mr. T. P. SCURLOCK. Services by Rev. J. A. HARRISON.
May 30, 1859.

11. AH to JKP, September 30, 1841 AH Papers TSLA. CJKP 5: 460fn
12. A.F. Huntsman Confederate Civil War Service Records. fold3.com
13. Ann Scurlock obituary, *Memphis Weekly Appeal*, May 24, 1882.
14. Madison County, Tennessee Will Book 7: 32
15. Jonathan K.T. Smith, *A Genealogical Miscellaney, Madison County, Tennessee.* Vol. 4: 80

family lot at Riverside Cemetery. On September 6, 1859, the Madison County Court reported that America's will had been proven and she had slaves remaining in Madison County worth about $7,000.[16]

7. GEORGE T. HUNTSMAN was born September 16, 1832, in Madison County, Tennessee; died April 1, 1859, in Memphis, Shelby County, Tennessee. He is buried at Elmwood Cemetery in Memphis. He married Anna M. Henry in Shelby County on December 17, 1857. George and Anna had no children.[17]

Tombstone of George T. Huntsman
Elmwood Cemetery, Memphis Tennessee
Courtesy of Dale Schaefer

Notes for GEORGE T. HUNTSMAN

The author believes George likely was named for his maternal grandfather, George Todd. After his father's death in 1849, the sixteen-year-old probably lived with one of his mother's married sisters in Shelby County, Tennessee. Three months after his marriage to Anna Henry, she died from "inflammation of [the] stomach and bowels" in Memphis at the age of 22.[18]

A year later, in 1859, George was a salesman for Candee, Mix & Company, a dry goods business in Memphis, and he resided on Madison Street at the corner of Front Row.[19]

In March 1859, George became ill with congestive fever and drafted his last will and testament on March 31, but appeared to be too feeble to sign it. He made his brother-in-

---

16. Jackson, Tennessee City Council Minute Book A (April 15, 1858-January 12, 1869): 82. Transcribed in Jonathan K.T. Smith, *My Riverside Cemetery Tombstone Inscription Scrapbook*. Vol. 4. (Jackson, TN: Self-published, 1993).

17. Edythe Rucker Whitley, ed., *Marriages of Shelby County, Tennessee, 1820-1858* (Baltimore, MD: Genealogical Publishing Company Inc., 1982): 94.

18. Mrs. John Trotwood Moore, ed. *List of Deaths in the City of Memphis, May 1848-December 1859*: 201

19. Edythe Rucker Whitley, ed. *Marriages of Shelby County, Tennessee, 1820-1858*. Baltimore, MD: Genealogical Publishing Company, Inc., 1982: 94. 1859 Memphis City Directory: 101. Mrs. John Trotwood Moore, ed., *List of Deaths in the City of Memphis, May 1848-December 1859*: 201. In *List of Deaths*, George T. Huntsman's date of death is given as March 30, 1859, which conflicts with the inscription on his tombstone, which is April 1. Ibid: 228.

law, Timothy P. Scurlock, executor of his estate. He specified that two slaves, Mary and Nancy, be sold and $1,000 applied to the settlement of his late wife's funeral expenses and "suitable monuments & cemetery lot if necessary." He left a slave named Robert to his sister Susan and $250 to his brother Adam which had been left to him by his stepmother. The remainder of his estate was to be divided into one-fourth portions to his siblings and his wife's brother and sister, George J. Henry and Jane F. Henry. George died the next day and was buried beside his wife Anna at Elmwood Cemetery in Memphis.[20] His obituary was published in the *Memphis Daily Appeal* on April 2, 1859:

> The friends and acquaintances of the late George T. Huntsman are respectfully invited to attend his funeral this day, Saturday, April 2, at 2 ½ o'clock p.m. from the First Baptist Church, corner of Adams and Second streets. Services by Elder T.J. Drane. Hacks will be attendance at the church.[21]

8. PARADISE[4] HUNTSMAN (Adam[3], Adam[2], Unknown[1]) was born about 1834 in Madison County, Tennessee; died September 10, 1883, in Little Rock, Pulaski County, Arkansas. She is buried at Mount Holly Cemetery in Little Rock. She married Nathaniel Washington Williams in Madison County on May 30, 1855. He was born in North Carolina circa 1826; died October 9, 1894, in Wellington, Collingswood County, Texas.

Notes for PARADISE HUNTSMAN

After her father's death in 1849, Paradise and her younger brother Adam lived with their aunt Sarah (Todd) McNeill and her husband Phillip McNeill in Shelby County, Tennessee. There she was baptized and became a member of Salem Presbyterian Church (later Collierville Presbyterian Church) in southeast Shelby County on October 13, 1850. Her aunts Sarah McNeill and Susan (Todd) McIver and their husbands Phillip McNeill and Roderick McIver were also members.

The day before her wedding on May 29, 1855, Paradise's older brother George became trustee for sixteen slaves she and her siblings had inherited, to be kept for her personal benefit.[22] By 1856, Paradise and Nathaniel lived in Marshall County, Mississippi, where she joined the Holly Springs Church on March 19. (Nathaniel had joined on November

---

20. Shelby County, Tennessee Probate File 1944, MSCL. George T. Huntsman and Anna Huntsman tombstones, Elmwood Cemetery, Memphis, Tennessee, provided by Jonathan K.T. Smith.
21. Memphis *Daily Appeal*, April 2, 1859.
22. Madison County, Tennessee Deed Book 18: 177-178.

23, 1850.) The couple may have lived for a short time in Tippah County, Mississippi, as she had attended the Presbyterian church at Salem prior to joining Holly Springs Church.[23]

Upon the death of her stepmother in 1858, Paradise and her younger sister Susan received the balance of her estate (after allotments to their other siblings), with her portion entrusted to executor Timothy P. Scurlock "in paying for or in part payment of a home for her."[24]

On November 3, 1867, Paradise joined Wattensas Prebyterian Church in Prairie County, Arkansas. A year later, she and her family moved to neighboring Lonoke County, then back to Prairie County again. Her husband Nathaniel "received the ordinance of baptism" at the same church on May 16, 1869. The 1880 census shows Paradise and Nathaniel living in Caroline, Lonoke County, Arkansas.

Children of Paradise[4] and Nathaniel Washington Williams

i. Fannie Erwin Williams, born 1855 in Madison County, Tennessee

ii. Bettie Williams, born 1857 in Holly Springs, Marshall County, Mississippi; died before 1860.

iii. William Williams, born in 1860 in Holly Springs, Marshall County, Mississippi.

iv. Sallie Williams, born March 24, 1862, in Holly Springs, Marshall County, Mississippi; died December 8, 1936, in Brownwood, Brown County, Texas. Buried in Brownwood, Texas.

v. Joseph Lanier Williams, born August 25, 1865, in Holly Springs, Marshall County, Mississippi; died November 3, 1947, in Brownwood, Brown County, Texas. Buried at Greenleaf Cemetery in Brownwood, Texas.

vi. Robert L. Williams, born 1868 in Austin, Arkansas; died November 24, 1946, in Brownwood, Brown County, Texas. Buried at Greenleaf Cemetery, Brownwood, Texas.

vii. Timothy Hart Williams, born February 6, 1869, in Des Arc, Prairie County, Arkansas; died March 20, 1954, in Austin, Travis County, Texas. Buried at Austin Memorial Park, Austin, Texas.

9. ADAM FRANKLIN[4] HUNTSMAN (Adam[3], Adam[2], Unknown[1]) was born January 1838 in Madison County, Tennessee; died August 26, 1918, in Little Rock, Pulaski County, Arkansas. He married (1) Kate Beatty on December 10, 1865, in Prairie County, Arkansas. They had no children. (2) Mary Katherine Fletcher on June 1, 1873,

---

23. Members of the Holly Springs Church page on the Marshall County, Mississippi MSGenWeb Project website at marshallcountyms.org/church/hsmemn.php. Accessed July 17, 2012. The church record showed her first name as "Paralee," but indicated that she was Mrs. N.W. Williams.

24. Madison County, Tennessee Will Book 7: 33.

Tombstone of Adam Franklin Huntsman
Lonoke Cemetery, Lonoke, Arkansas
Courtesy of Harmony and Heritage

in Lonoke County, Arkansas. They had four children.

Notes for ADAM FRANKLIN HUNTSMAN

Adam F. was one of two of Adam Huntsman's children listed in Dictrict 14 of the Madison County School Census/Scholastic Population in 1838. Following his father's death in 1849, Adam lived with his aunt Sarah (Todd) McNeill and her husband Phillip in Shelby County, Tennessee. He returned to Madison County as early as July 29, 1855, when he was baptized at St. Luke's Episcopal Church in Jackson. He was also a witness to the marriage of James N. Acres and Mary Melley in that county on June 6, 1857. Three years later, he had moved to White River in Prairie County, Arkansas and was living with his aunt Susan (Todd) McIver and her husband Roderick McIver, employed as a laborer on his farm.[25]

Adam received $250 in the will of his stepmother, Nancy Waller Mosely Huntsman, who died in 1859. It was held in trust by executor Timothy P. Scurlock, husband of his half sister ANN (HUNTSMAN) SCURLOCK. He later received his older brother George's $250 share "to be held or invested in Land for his benefit" upon George's death in 1859.

Adam enlisted in Company L of the Sixth Tennessee Cavalry C.S.A. at Jackson, Tennessee, on March 10, 1862, and served under the command of Col. W.H. Stephens. Capt. M.D. Meriwether thought Adam was "a gallant Soldier and a true Veteran though...but a boy in years." He was wounded at the Battle of Perryville in Kentucky on October 8, 1862, suffering "a Compound Fracture wound in the right leg 6 inches below the knee." He almost endured his father's misfortune as surgeons "were anxious to amputate" the limb, but decided otherwise. A physican in 1901 described the wound as being a "Fracture of the upper 1/3 of [the] tibia and fibula" from a "Minie ball, resulting in extensive necrosis of [the] leg (tibia)." (Necrosis is the death of living cells or tissues resulting from a lack of blood flow.) It left a "Depressed scar 10 in[ches] long, 3/4 in[ch] wide...to show [the] removal of bone."[26]

25. Smith, *A Genealogical Miscellaney, Madison County, Tennessee.* Vol. 4: 79. 1860 U.S. Census for Prairie County, Arkansas for "R. McKeever," page 121.
26. Adam F. Huntsman Arkansas Confederate Pension Record. Arkansas History Commission,

Adam was taken prisoner at Perryville the day after the battle and his comrades thought he had been killed. He was sent to City Point, Virginia, but was apparently paroled at Harrodsburg, Kentucky by Provost Marshal Capt. Joseph P. Black and sent instead to Jeffersonville, Indiana. For some reason, his name also appeared as a prisoner at Fort McHenry in Maryland on January 9, 1863, though this appears to be a mistake.

His half sister ANN (HUNTSMAN) SCURLOCK sought his release and asked a Federal officer named E. Durham, who was stationed at Jackson, Tennessee, for assistance. He wrote the following letter to his superior:

> HdQrs 2nd Brigade
> Jackson Tenn
>
> General
>
> There is boarding at _____ Reads Jeffersonville Ind a young Confederate prisoner badly wounded His name is *AF Huntsman* private in the 6th Tenn Regiment He has a sister living She is very anxious for him to come she is a Rebel but a most excellent & kind hearted woman and I do not think _____ anything by these little animosities even in War He is now upon his parol[e] reporting to Genl Boyle Cant you get Genl Boyle to permit him to come here Others have been permitted to do so I should take it as a favor if you will get this accomplished as soon as possible though I will [admit] the woman is neither young nor handsome but the mother of a "*large and respectable*" family
>
> Yours truly,
> E Durham

His half sister's concern for him led to Adam's release, and he returned to Jackson in late February 1863. Jackson resident and diarist Robert H. Cartmell noted on February 25: "I saw Adam Huntsman yesterday. [H]e was wounded at Perryville [in] october, a ball passing through one leg below the knee and lodged in the other leg."[27] He continued having difficulty with the injury and underwent an operation that year in Little Rock.

27. Robert H. Cartmell Papers 1849-1915, on microfilm at TSLA. Upon his release, Huntsman was ordered to report to the commander of Federal occupation forces at Jackson on or about February 14, 1863. Huntsman Military Record.

Jackson to remove "a portion of the bone" from the leg. It would affect him the rest of his life. Adam applied for a Confederate disability pension from the state of Arkansas on August 4, 1893, stating that the leg injury coupled with a double hernia prevented him from performing manual labor. He was granted a pension and in 1909, he sought a pay increase owing to his age (71 years old) and being "still in indigent circumstances."[28]

Before the war ended, Adam returned to Arkansas and married Kate Beatty, who was born in 1842 in Tennessee; died circa 1873 in Arkansas. After Kate's death, he married Mary Katherine Fletcher, who was born in June 1853 in Mississippi; died in 1912 in Arkansas. On May 12, 1872, he made a confession of faith at Wattensas Presbyterian Church in Prairie County, Arkansas. During his residence in the state, he served as deputy sheriff for Lonoke County and was mayor and postmaster for the county seat at Lonoke. In 1900, he moved back to Shelby County, Tennessee, but ten years later he returned to Arkansas and lived with his widowed son-in-law Sam D. Morgan in Little Rock and was a member of First Baptist Church.[29]

Children of Adam Franklin[4] and Mary Katherine (Fletcher) Huntsman

i. Susan Jane Huntsman, born in April 1874 in Arkansas; died between 1900-1910 in Arkansas. She married Samuel D. Morgan on July 24, 1892, in Lonoke County, Arkansas.[30] He was born in February 1894 in Little Rock, Pulaski County, Arkansas; died November 1, 1915, in Little Rock, Pukaski County, Arkansas.[31] They had two children.

ii. Mary Ella Huntsman, born in April 1876 in Arkansas. She married Charles L. Morgan and had three children.

iii. Adam Hugh Huntsman, born June 1, 1878, in Lonoke, Pulaski County, Arkansas; died December 17, 1953, in Fayette County, Kentucky. He married his cousin Gertrude Huntsman on November 18, 1912.

Notes for ADAM HUGH HUNTSMAN

"Hubie" enlisted on April 25, 1898, as a private in Company E, Second Regiment of the Arkansas Infantry during the Spanish-American War. He was discharged on February 15, 1899.

iv. Edith Huntsman, born in July 1885 in Arkansas.

28. Huntsman Arkansas Confederate Pension Record.
29. Margaret White genealogical record supplied by Patricia Grames Pollock.
30. Lonoke County, Arkansas Marriage Record Book G, page 258. Familysearch.org. Accessed August 6, 2012. Adam F. Huntsman served as surety for the marriage bond.
31. Arkansas Death Index, 1914-1950. Familysearch.org. Accessed August 6, 2012.

10. SUSAN JANE[4] HUNTSMAN (Adam[3], Adam[2], Unknown[1]) was born October 30, 1840, in Madison County, Tennessee; died February 14, 1924, in Austin, Travis County, Texas. She is buried at Oakwood Cemetery Annex in Austin. She married (1) Samuel William Ragland on July 25, 1860, in Prairie County, Arkansas;[32] (2) Dr. Powell Erwin Hogue on April 27, 1880, in Lonoke County, Arkansas.[33]

The son of prominent Memphis physician Nathaniel Ragland and his wife Elizabeth, Samuel William Ragland died on January 7, 1861, in Prairie County, Arkansas.

Dr. Powell Erwin Hogue was born in 1829 in South Carolina; died November 22, 1882, in Pulaski County, Arkansas. He is buried in an unmarked grave, presumably in the Hogue family lot, at Oakland Cemetery in Little Rock. Susan was his second wife; his first was Nancy Margaret Wall, with whom he had at least five children: John Brown Hogue, James A. Hogue, Louie George Hogue, Charlie Watson Hogue, and Nellie Hogue.[34]

The 1850 Census showed Hogue living in Tippah County, Mississippi and owning several slaves. In 1874, he filed a claim with the Southern Claims Commission (which was denied), indicating that he had been loyal to the Union during the Civil War. The 1880 U.S. Census listed his residence as being in Little Rock, Pulaski County, Arkansas, and his occupation as doctor.

Tombstone of Susan Jane (Huntsman) Ragland Hogue
Oakwood Cemetery Annex, Austin Texas
Courtesy of Robert Sage

---

32. Bernice Taylor Cargill and Brenda Brenda Bethea Connelly, eds. *Settlers of Shelby County, Tennessee and Adjoining Counties* (Memphis, TN: The Descendants of Early Settlers of Shelby County, 1989): 139. Prairie County, Arkansas Marriage Record, Vol. C: 260. familysearch.org

33. Lonoke County, Arkansas Marriage Record, Vol. C: 322. Susan's brother Adam F. Huntsman was security for the marriage bond.

34. Dr. P.E. "Powell Erwin" Hogue page. http://findagrave.com website. Accessed July 17, 2012.

Notes for SUSAN JANE HUNTSMAN

Susan, with her older brother Adam F., attended school in District 14 according to the 1838 Madison County School Census/Scholastic Population. On October 1, 1853, on the same day her aunt Susan (Todd) McIver joined Wattensas Presbyterian Church in Prairie County, Arkansas, Susan made a "profession of faith in Christ" and was baptized there. The 1860 census for Prairie County, Arkansas listed her with her husband Samuel Ragland, living next to her maternal aunt Susan McIver and her family, whose household included her brother Adam.[35]

In 1910, Susan lived in the town of Newport in Jackson County, Arkansas, with her daughter Samuella (listed as "Samantha N.," also a widow), age 49, and granddaughter Pattie Ann Ragland, age 8. The epitaph on Susan's tombstone reads: "The best and sweetest Mother and Grandmother that ever lived."

Child of Susan Jane[4] (Huntsman) and Samuel Ragland

    i. Samuella Elizabeth Ragland, born April 15, 1861, in Arkansas; died June 4, 1939, in Austin, Travis County, Texas. She married James Hart Davis, who was born October 7, 1861, and died November 29, 1901. Samuella was Davis's second wife. They had one child, Patricia Sue Davis, born May 26, 1901, in Texas; died May 7, 1942 in Corpus Christi, Nueces County, Texas. Patricia is buried at Oakwood Cemetery Annex in Austin, Travis County, Texas. She married George Clyde Hengy Sr.

Samuella was baptized on May 18, 1862, at Wattensas Presbyterian Church in Prairie County, Arkansas. She is buried at Oakwood Cemetery Annex in Austin, Travis County, Texas.[36]

---

    35. Smith, *A Genealogical Miscellaney, Madison County, Tennessee.* Vol. 4: 23. Sessional Records of the Wattensas Presbyterian Church, Prairie County, Arkansas, October 1, 1853 to September 12, 1886. argenweb.net/prairie/Church/Wattensas/WattMin.htm. 1860 Census for Prairie County, Arkansas, page 121.

    36. Sessional Records of the Wattensas Presbyterian Church, Prairie County, Arkansas, October 1, 1853 to September 12, 1886. argenweb.net/prairie/Church/Wattensas/WattMin.htm. Samuella (Ragland) Davis Death Certificate. Susan J, Huntsman tombstone page on findagrave.com, accessed August 5, 2012.

Appendix B

The Huntsman Farm

After settling in Madison County, Tennessee by the fall of 1823, Adam Huntsman made his home in the Cotton Grove community four miles east of the county seat at Jackson. The property that became Huntsman's farm was originally part of the unclaimed Revolutionary War warrants owned by the University of North Carolina. At some point, George Hicks (1796-1878) purchased it from the university and sold twenty-five acres to Huntsman in an unrecorded transaction. The earliest recorded deed involving Huntsman in Madison County was his purchase of 698 acres on July 20, 1825, from his future father-in-law George Todd. This tract was located "on the head waters of Butlers Creek...lying betweene [sic] said Huntsman and Todds [sic] dwelling houses." These initial land purchases are believed to be his home and farm on which he lived and worked over his twenty-six year residence in Madison County.[1]

---

1. Madison County, Tennessee Deed Book 1: 581-582. The initial 25-acre land purchase between Huntsman and Hicks is mentioned in Ibid 14: 3 and Madison County, Tennessee Court Minute Book 8: 169-170. The author is greatly indebted to Jonathan K.T. Smith, from whose research much of the details of the Huntsman property transactions contained in this section were obtained. Smith, "Ownership Sketch of the Adam Huntsman Place Near Jackson, Tennessee." June 1998.

In the late 1830s, perhaps after his return from Congress, Huntsman may have enlarged his existing home or built a completely new one.[2] Brothers John R. Norvell and Thomas G. Norvell, builders of the Madison County Courthouse and later St. Luke's Episcopal Church, were employed to lay brick at the exterior walls. On April 20, 1840, Huntsman jointly sold them fifty acres, perhaps as partial compensation for their work.[3]

Indebtedness forced Huntsman to sign a deed of trust with his home and property held as collateral for a $2,000 loan acquired from the local branch of the Union Bank of Tennessee. On November 29, 1848, he authorized fellow attorney Micajah Bullock as trustee for 457 acres. Another deed was executed five months later for about 455 acres "on which I now reside," his debt having increased to $3,258 by April 12, 1849.[4]

After Huntsman's death on August 23, 1849, Bullock was forced to auction the home and surrounding property to satisfy the unpaid debts. He placed an advertisement for the auction in the *West Tennessee Whig* on January 18, 1850:

Sale of Valuable Land

BY virtue of two Deeds of Trust, executed to me by the late Hon. Adam Huntsman, and duly recorded in the Register's office of Madison county, I will expose to public sale to the Highest bidder, for cash, at the court house door in the town of Jackson, on the 11th day of February, next, the valuable tract of Land on which Mr. Huntsman resided, containing 457 acres, more or less.

This land lies about four miles East of Jackson on the road to Lexington, adjoining the land of Judge [Milton] Brown, Alex[ander] Greer and others. It is known to be a excellent farm: has several never failing springs of water,

---

2. According to Joseph Fogg, George Hicks believed Huntsman may have "made over his property to keep from paying his debts." Perhaps this implies the building of a new home on the site. Joseph Fogg document, October 9, 1850, in the author's collection.

3. Madison County, Tennessee Deed Book 7: 66-67. Jonathan K.T. Smith to the author, September 26, 1995. Huntsman sold the property to the Norvells for $1,100.

4. Madison County, Tennessee Deed Book 12: 191, 422.

& large and thrifty Apple and Peach orchards. The dwelling house is of brick and is large and commodious, and it has all the necessary out houses.

About 250 or 300 acres are cleared and under good fence, and the whole place is in excellent order, and is one of the best farms in West Tennessee.[5]

Joseph Fogg purchased the home and property,[6] but he allowed Huntsman's widow and family to continue living there until her death on December 4, 1858. Fogg died that same year and left it to his children, one of whom sold his interest to John Irvin and Samuel Lucky on January 19, 1860. The remaining Fogg heirs sold the home and property on December 15, 1860, to Madison County sheriff John J. Brooks, who subsequently sold the 457 acres "known as the Huntsman place" to James R. Malone for $6,000 on January 18, 1866. Ten months later, indebted to Birdsal & Brother of Cincinnati, Ohio and Caroline W. Malone assuming that debt, Malone sold the property to her for $5,904.90 on November 16.[7]

Although it had various owners, "the Huntsman place" remained in the Malone family for the next fifty years.[8] On March 14, 1916, the brothers and sister of W.G. Malone sold the home and 290 ¾ acres to Robert Lee Hill of Clarksburg, Tennessee, for $8,000. Hill's granddaughter, Ruthie Pritchard Henderson, remembered the property boundaries at this time being Cotton Grove Road to the north, Leiper Lane to the east, the present-day Fraternal Order of Police Lodge property to the west, and "halfway down Leiper Lane" to the south.[9]

---

5. *West Tennessee Whig*, January 18, 1850

6. The 457-acre tract was described in 1850 as being located on the Lexington-Cotton Grove Road. It was bounded to the north by the property of Milton Brown and Alexander Greer; to the west by John E. Stewart (physician for the Huntsman family), to the south by Robert Hurt; and to the east by the White family. Madison County, Tennessee Deed Book 14: 200-201. Smith, "Ownership Sketch": 1.

7. Madison County, Tennessee Deed Book 14: 3. Ibid 21: 630-631. Ibid 23: 552. Ibid 24: 412. Madison County, Tennessee Court Minute Book 8: 169-170. Madison County, Tennessee Deed Book 23: 456.

8. Ibid 41: 113. Ibid 50: 384. Ibid 58: 607. Ibid 87: 403.

9. Ibid 87: 403. Interview with Ruthie Pritchard Henderson by Jonathan K.T. Smith, June 15, 1998. Notes courtesy of Jonthan K.T. Smith.

Hill and his wife Fannie sold it (less some 190 acres) to William Henry Collier for $12,048 on August 27, 1923. Collier was vice president of the Southern Engine and Boiler Works located at 342 North Royal Street in Jackson. As a mechanical engineer seventeen years earlier, he had created the Southerner automobile (later renamed the Marathon), which became the first automobile manufactured in the South. From 1906 to 1909, about three hundred were produced in Jackson before the Marathon division was purchased by Nashville investors and relocated there in 1910. But financial mismanagement eventually led to the automobile's demise in 1914.[10]

Collier became indebted for $4,785.50 and placed the house and 100 acres under three successive trustees between 1932 and 1942. On November 17, 1942, they were foreclosed to the First National Bank for $12,500. The bank rented the home and property over the next three years before selling them to Robert A. Caldwell on September 12, 1945. Caldwell and his wife Angelyn sold the home to Ray Monger and his wife Lavenia on October 29, 1947, but reduced the surrounding land to ten acres. This would remain the property configuration for all subsequent purchases of the former Huntsman farm.[11]

Less than a year later, the house was foreclosed once again and sold to Abner Utley Taylor Jr. of City Lumber Company, to whom the Mongers owed a portion of the mortgage. Taylor lived there until City Lumber sold to home and property to Robert E. and Martha M. Branham for $30,000 on June 24, 1954. The Branhams sold them back to City Lumber two years later. City Lumber held onto the home and property for over fifteen years before selling them to James and Jean L. Thompson on May 22, 1970.[12]

Local attorney John Van Den Bosch Jr. purchased them from the Thompsons on September 29, 1972, and acquired Elizabeth Van Den

---

10. Ibid 103: 294. Philip Thomason, "Southern Engine and Boiler Works." The Tennessee Encyclopedia of History and Culture Version 2.0. <www.tennesseeencyclopedia.net/entry.php?rec=1234> Margaret D. Binnicker, "Marathon Motor Works." Ibid. <www.tennesseeencyclopedia.net/entry.php?rec=832>

11. Collier's trustees are recorded in Madison County, Tennessee Trust Deed Book 162: 245.; Ibid 318-199; and Madison County Deed Book 134: 615-616. The foreclosure is recorded in Madison County Deed Book 134: 615-616. The Caldwll purchase is recorded in Ibid 143: 395. The Monger purchase is recorded in Ibid 150: 83.

12. Madison County, Tennessee Deed Book 154: 71. Ibid 169: 326. Ibid 256: 634-636.

Bosch's interest in the property almost three years later. Van Den Bosch lived there for close to twenty years before selling to the current owners, Roy Houston Callahan and his wife Peggy Jane Callahan, on January 16, 1992.[13]

The Huntsman Home

The two-story home built by Adam Huntsman in the mid to late 1830s was described as "a substantial brick residence" located "on a knoll on the right side of the [Lexington-Cotton Grove] road going east."[14] Unfortunately, no photographs are known to exist. However, Ruthie Pritchard Henderson (1915-2003), whose grandfather Robert Lee Hill owned it from 1916 to 1923, remembered its floor plan and features.

Turning off the Lexington road (present-day 260 Cotton Grove Road), visitors traveled a cedar tree lined drive toward the house, which had a two-story, full-length porch supported by large posts at each end and posts beside the steps. Chimneys were embedded into the side (east and west) walls. There was a large front door bordered with narrow sidelights and a rectangular transom above it. Two windows were on each side of the door. Inside was an entry hall with a large staircase on the right side, its newels and balusters a dark mahogany color. Through a door to the left was a large room with a plain fireplace mantel on the east wall that could have been the dining room during Huntsman's residence. To the right of the entry hall was a parlor with another plain mantel on the west wall. There were two rooms on the second floor of equal dimensions to the ones downstairs. A "secret door" built into the west wall allowed access to a small stairway leading to the house-length attic. Another small stairway downstairs in the kitchen—a post-Huntsman addition to the rear of the existing structure—led to the cellar, which was used primarily for food storage. The house had a back porch and a covered walkway leading to a

---

13. Madison County, Tennessee Deed Book 278: 285-286. Ibid 318: 280-282. Ibid 515: 62-63. The Callahans were the owners as of 2012.

14. Jay Guy Cisco, "Adam Huntsman." Public Men of Tennessee collection, Manuscript Division, TSLA. "Historical Happenings in Jackson." *The Jackson Sun*, n.d. T.M. Gates Scrapbook , 1912: 48. The Tennessee Room, JMCL.

separate, two-story brick building that could have been Huntsman's law office. There were a few buildings behind the house, which were reached by field roads.[15]

Madison County historian Emma Inman Williams claimed the cedar trees leading to the house were planted by Huntsman as payment for a bet between he and David Crockett. She gave no source for the story, however, and it seems unlikely it would be true.[16]

During William Collier's residence, the home burned on or about Christmas Day 1929. One local resident recalled his uncle having stoked the fires in the fireplaces on the morning of the blaze.[17] A new structure was built on top of the existing foundations, meaning the present-day house is likely the identical length and width of the original. The cause of the fire is uncertain.

Slavery on the Huntsman Farm

Adam Huntsman owned slaves as early as 1807 or 1809, when he first settled in Knoxville, Tennessee. As he prospered in his legal practice in the Mountain District and the Western District, he acquired and sold more until his death in 1849.

Huntsman's overseers between 1829 and 1836 were William Smith, John E. Irvin, and Gibson Whittington. Smith was employed in the late 1820s and though he had been replaced by Irwin in December 1830, he continued to stay on the farm in some capacity for at least two more years. Irvin was born in Wilkes County, Georgia on November 3, 1802, and died in Madison County on January 15, 1889. He married Elizabeth H. McFadden in Williamson County, Tennessee, on November 8, 1832. Irvin acted as Huntsman's overseer from Christmas week of 1830 until December 1832. According to Irvin his wife was Huntsman's second

---

15. Interview with Ruthie Pritchard Henderson by Jonathan K.T. Smith, June 15, 1998. Notes courtesy of Jonthan K.T. Smith.

16. Emma Inman Williams, Marion B. Smothers, Mitch Carter. *Jackson & Madison County: A Pictorial History* (Norfolk, VA: The Donning Company, 1988): 26

17. Interview with J.B. Hurt by Jonathan K.T. Smith, June 15, 1998. Notes courtesy of Jonathan K.T. Smith.

cousin, though their relationship has not been verified. Whitington was overseer from August 1833 until about 1836.[18]

The Madison County tax list for 1830 shows Huntsman with 17 "black polls," which includes slaves between the ages of 12 and 50.[19] Between 1829 and 1832, he incurred many personal debts as well as business debts resulting from the failure of a mercantile business in which he was a partner with John K. Chester. The predicament left him "much embarassed [sic]" according to one neighbor. "I had heard Mr Huntsman say some time in 1833 that he had thought that he was broke," recalled Whittington in July 1851, "but that he then saw his way through..." One way he raised money was to sell many of his slaves. Irvin said several had been sold in the fall and winter of 1829-1830, and more were sold during his time as Huntsman's overseer. He believed Huntsman sold some for less than he should have received.[20]

Based on the recollections of Irvin and Whittington as well as a few neighbors, it is possible to know the identities of some of Huntsman's slaves during the 1829-1836 period.[21]

Chloe	Child of Hall and Fanny
Cynthia (or Cindy)	Child of Hannah. 15 years old in 1831. Worked outdoors. She and her children were sold to James L. Lyon between 1831-32.
Dick 1	Husband of Rose. Described as an "old man." Sold after Huntsman's death by his estate's administrator Burwell Butler, who described him as "very old and infirm."
Dick 2	Child of Hannah. 14 years old in 1831. Sold to David Wallick between 1831-32.

---

18. Information for this section of Appendix B was obtained from documents in the author's collection. John Irvin document dated July 9, 1851. Irvin genealogical data found at <wc.rootsweb.ancestry.com/cgi-bin/igm.cgi?op=GET&db=stevensp&id=I12684> Gibson Whittington document dated July 9, 1851. Gibson Whittington is shown in the 1850 census as a 43-year-old farmer, born in North Carolina and living in District 17 of Madison County. He married Elizabeth Williams in Madison County on August 20, 1840.

19. Jonathan K.T. Smith, *Antebellum Militia, Justices, and Some Early Taxpayers, Madison County, Tennessee* (Jackson, TN: Self-published, 1998): 249. Fogg document.

20. Whittington document. Irvin document.

21. Information based on mutiple (and often conflicting) recollections.

Eliza	Child of Hannah. About 6 years old in 1831.
Fanny	Wife of Hall. Child of Hannah. House servant. Died before 1851.
Hall (or Hal)	Husband of Fanny. Belonged to "Mr. Brown" but lived on the Huntsman farm because his wife was one of Huntsman's slaves. Told Huntsman "he was dissatisfied living in town [Jackson]" and allowed to stay a short time. Later sold to Dr. William A. Murchison and taken away by him.
Hannah	Child of Dick and Rose. Older sister of Mary 2. Family cook and house servant. About 15 to 18 years old in 1831. Sold with two of her children to Gabriel Anderson between Janaury and spring 1831.
Henry	Adult originally owned by Huntsman and sold to George Todd in 1831. Bequeathed by him to Elizabeth Huntsman and her children. Sold by Huntsman to George Hicks in 1840. Described at the time as having "good general health" and being "a boy of good habits."
Jesse 1	Child of Hannah. Field hand. Sold to Milton Brown between Janaury and spring 1831.
Jesse 2?	Sold to J__ P. Horton between Janaury and spring 1831.
Julia	Child of Mary 1
Laura	Child of Hannah. About 9 years old in 1831.
Lewis	Given to Huntsman's wife Elizabeth by her father, George Todd. Later sold or exchanged with John Copender for Hannah's husband.
Lindy?	Field hand?
Lotty?	Female slave remaining after Huntsman sold many of his slaves between 1831-32. She had children.
Male child of Hannah	Sold by Huntsman between Janaury and spring 1831.
Male child of Nancy	Sold with his mother to Joseph Johnson between January and spring 1831.
Mariah 1 (or Maria)	Daughter of Hall and Fanny. Described by Whittington as an adult and "a tolerable bright Mulatto." Stayed with Ann Huntsman at her maternal grandmother's home at White Plains until about 1840. May have had a child by 1840.
Mariah 2	About 5 years old in 1834. Sold to Roderick McIver for $150 as trustee for George Todd's estate, 1834,

Mary 1	House servant. Described by Whittington as "old Mary" and had about five or six children.
Mary 2	Child of Dick and Rose. Younger sister of Hannah by 18 months to two years. House servant. Her husband may have been Coter, who was owned by Joseph Fogg. She was later sold to Fogg. She had one child eight or nine months old when she was sold to him.
Miley (or Milley)	Child of Hannah. House servant. Sold to J__ P. Horton between Janaury and spring 1831.
Moses	Field hand. Sold to James Vaulx and McIver(?) between Janaury and spring 1831.
Nancy	House servant. Described as an older woman. Sold to Joseph Johnson between Janaury and spring 1831.
Patsy	House servant. About 13 years old in 1834. Later sold to Milton Brown.
Phoebe	Child of Hall and Fanny. House servant. Had at least two children (names not known). Later she and her children were sold to Stephen Huntsman, nephew of Adam. However, she still lived on the Huntsman farm as late as 1850, when Huntsman's administrator, Burwell Butler described her as "very old and infirm."
Robert	Child of Hannah. About 7 years old in 1831.
Rose 1	Wife of Dick. House servant. Sold to "Anderson & Fusel"? Died before 1851.
Rose 2	Eight or nine years old in 1834. Sold to Roderick McIver for $300 as trustee for George Todd's estate, 1834,
Saley (Sally?)	Slave belonging to Huntsman's nephew Stephen Huntsman
Sam	Field hand. Sold to Joseph Johnson between Janaury and spring 1831.
Silas	Child of Mary 1
Solomon	Field hand. Sold for $525 to William Armour between Janaury and spring 1831.
Tom	Field hand. Sold for $525 to William Armour between Janaury and spring 1831.

Hannah and Mary were described by Irvin as "favorite family Negroes," as "were all of the family of Rose and Dick..." He recalled that some of the women who normally stayed in the house would work in the fields during "Crop time."[22]

After Huntsman paid most of his debts, Irvin named the following slaves that remained on the farm: Dick and his wife Rose; Hall and his wife Fanny; Jesse, Patsy, Rose (young girl) and Lottey and her children. (Phoebe, Chloe, and Saley[?] belonged to Huntsman's nephew Stephen Huntsman.) The 1840 census reveals that Huntsman acquired more slaves after his debts were paid. He is shown with 40 slaves: seven males under 10 years old; two males 10-24; three males 24-36; one male 55-100; six females under 10; six females 10-24; two females 24-36; one female 36-55; and two females 55-100.[23]

In 1997, historian Jonathan K.T. Smith identified the slave cemetery on the former Huntsman farm as possibly being "located on the east side of Jones Creek," about 0.1 mile southwest of the home, "on a rise of ground among [old] cedars." Two residents who lived in the Cotton Grove area for many years related to him that older generations mentioned there being a slave cemetery on the property, although no surviving markers identify it as such.[24]

Legal Battles over Huntsman's Slaves

On March 10, 1831, Huntsman's father-in-law George Todd executed a deed of trust with son-in-law Roderick McIver as trustee for three slaves—a man named Henry and two girls Hannah and Mary—he had purchased from Huntsman to help with payment of his debts. (Henry was sold for an unspecified price, Hannah for $250, and Mary for $200.) Todd intended for the three slaves and their future children to be used for the benefit of Huntsman's wife Elizabeth and her children.[25] In his last will and testa-

---

22. Irvin document
23. Irvin document. 1840 Madison County, Tennessee Census
24. Johnathan K.T. Smith, *Tombstone Inscriptions from Black Cemeteries in Madison County, Tennessee*. Vol. 2., 2000, p. 21; Jonathan K.T. Smith to the author, February 1, 1997, January 26, 2008. Interview with Andrew Longstreet by Jonathan K.T. Smith, June 15, 1998. Notes courtesy of Mr. Smith.
25. Madison County, Tennessee Deed Book 2: 635-636

ment dated October 26, 1833, Todd left Elizabeth these slaves in trust as well as one named Lucy "and their increase."[26]

On November 1, 1834, McIver purchased three additional slaves on behalf of Todd's estate to help Huntsman raise money for his debts: Patsy (about 13 years old) for $300, Rose (eight or nine) for $200, and Mariah (about five) for $150.[27] Huntsman's relationship with McIver was described by Irvin as "friendly as such as fair [far] as I no [sic] and [they] visited Each other as Relatives wo[u]ld..." The brothers-in-law "lived som[e] three miles apart."[28]

Although these slaves legally belonged to Todd's estate and were intended for Elizabeth and her children, they continued to live and work on Huntsman's farm and he agreed to clothe them and pay taxes for them. Yet Huntsman subsequently sold the three slaves and/or their increase. Henry was sold to George Hicks for $600 on March 8, 1840. Mary (27 years old) and her two daughters Sucky[29] (about 11) and Nancy (age not specified) were sold to Joseph Fogg in 1848 as partial compensation for money loaned to Huntsman almost 20 years earlier and a contracting arrangement he had made with Huntsman for use of the slaves.[30] Four months before Huntsman's death, Micajah Bullock sold two of Hannah's daughters, Cynthia (about 14 years old) and Fanny, to satisfy a deed of trust initiated by Huntsman and held by Bullock. Both girls were sold to George Hicks. At some point, he also acquired Hannah's son Dick.[31]

When Huntsman died on August 23, 1849, he left no last will and testament. In fact, upon examination by Burwell Butler (appointed by the Madison County Court as administrator of his estate), he determined in December 1849 that Huntsman had died insolvent. Butler was required to publish such notice for three consecutive weeks in the *West Tennessee Whig* as well as post it on the door of the Madison County Courthouse

26. Madison County, Tennessee Will Book 1: 444-446
27. Madison County, Tennessee Deed Book 4: 22-23
28. Irvin document
29. Perhaps Sucky's name was pronounced "Sooky."
30. Madison County, Tennessee Court Minute Book 8: 287. Fogg document.
31. Madison County, Tennessee Chancery Court Minute Book 1: 286. Hicks purchased Cynthia for $450, but the price for Fanny is not known.

in Jackson to allow Huntsman's creditors sufficient time to make claims against his estate.[32]

Before his appointment, however, Butler had purchased two of Hannah's children, Robert (about seven years old) for $200 and Laura (about nine) for $300 on November 5, 1849, from James D. McClellan at a public sale in Jackson to satisfy a deed of trust made by Huntsman to McClellan dated April 10. On the same day, William Croom acquired Eliza (about six years old), another daughter of Hannah.[33]

On January 15, 1851, Roderick McIver, as trustee for the slaves Henry, Hannah, and Mary and their offspring and representing the interests of Adam Huntsman's children, filed three separate lawsuits in Madison County Chancery Court against George Hicks and son Benjamin Hicks; Joseph Fogg; and Burwell Butler, James D. McClellan, and William Croom. McIver, now a resident of Shelby County, Tennessee, stated that the Huntsman children "are orphans and destitute and their only hope of support is derived from the provision made by their grandfather [George Todd] in the aforesaid Trust..."[34]

McIver eventually won all three suits. Attempts by the defendants to appeal the verdicts to the state supreme court proved unsuccessful. In March 1853, the slaves were recovered and the defendants were ordered by the court to reimburse the plantiffs for the services given by the slaves while in their possession.[35]

On December 3, 1855, Huntsman's children asked the Madison County Court to divide their inheritance among them, which now numbered sixteen slaves. A month later, five court-appointed commissioners allocated the following: America Huntsman received Cynthia, Mary, and Susan valued at $1,850; George T. Huntsman was given Mary, Nancy, and Robert valued at $2,050; Paradise Huntsman Williams received Fanny, Eliza, and Patsy valued at $1,900; and Adam F. and Susan Jane Huntsman jointly

---

32. Madison County, Tennessee Court Minute Book 6: 89
33. Bill of complaint, Roderick McIver, trustee v. James D. McClellan, Burwell Butler, and William Croom.
34. Ibid. Madison County, Tennessee Chancery Court Minute Book 1: 286-289. Madison County Court Minute Book 8: 287-289. Refer to page 209 of this book for details on the Huntsman children's circumstances following their father's death.
35. Madison County, Tennessee Chancery Court Minute Book 1: 330-331

received Hannah, Chloe, Dick, Laura, William, Susan, and Margaret valued at $3,790. Paradise's slaves were held in trust by her brother George for her own benefit separate from her husband Nathaniel W. Wiliams.[36] Once they reached maturity, the two youngest children, Adam and Susan, petitioned the court to have their joint allotment divided as well. On November 2, 1857, commissioners gave Adam title to the slaves Dick, Chloe, and Margaret valued at $2,650 total and Susan received Laura and her son Will, Hannah and her daughter Rose, Will, and Susan valued at $2,650 total.[37]

---

36. Madison County, Tennessee Court Minute Book 7: 464-465; 480
37. Madison County, Tennessee Court Minute Book 8: 81, 91-92. Initially, Adam and Susan petitioned the court for division of the slaves on January 6, 1857, then asked that their petition be dismissed shortly thereafter for reasons unknown. The judge did require them to pay court fees. Ibid 7: 713, 761.

Appendix C

Selected Letters

To "Fellow Citizens" of Overton County, Tennessee, November 27, 1819[1]

Murfreesborough, *November 27, 1819.*
FELLOW CITIZENS,

The important session of 1819 is now drawing to a close, and we think it the duty of the representatives of the people to afford all the means of information in their power to their constituents, at this earliest practicable moment after measures are adopted, which is to have a general operation on society.

In performance of this duty, we take great pleasure in stating to you, that by the liberal policy adopted by the general government towards this state, in granting us the liberty of satisfying land claims South and West of the congressional reservation line, this state has had it in her power to bring all the lands lately ceded by the Cherokee Indians within the chartered limits of this state, South of the Tennessee river into market for the benefit of Tennessee.

The terms on which these lands are to be sold will be found substantially as follows—One fourth of the purchase money payable in good circulating bank notes, is required to be paid down, the balance to be paid by the end of ten years, with interest to be paid thereon, in three install-

---

1. Early American Imprints (2nd Series). Shaw-Shoemaker Bibliography, 1801-1819. Jean and Alexander Heard Library, Vanderbilt University, Nashville TN.

ments. It is believed by these persons who are best acquainted with this desirable country, that the sale thereof will produce to the stat two millions of dollars; this sum will enable Tennessee to take a respectable stand amongst the sister states of the Union, in promoting internal improvement, navigation, build a penitentiary, (if it should be the opinion of the people of this state that such an establishment should go into operation) and likewise to give proper encouragement to seminaries of learning. And at the same time it affords an opportunity to the poor men to purchase a situation for themselves; as no one man is permitted to purchase more than six hundred and forty acres for himself, and three hundred and twenty acres for each of his children. These sales are to take place on the first Monday in November next, at the town of Knoxville.

Provisions have been made for the satisfaction of land claims in the congressional reservation, and each occupant in possession on the first of September, is entitled (provided he has a warrant when the office opens) to enter one hundred and sixty acres, including his own improvement, and if he has no warrant he is entitled to receive pay for the value of his improvement. This law is not altogether satisfactory in all its features to your representation, but owing to the great diversity of opinion which existed upon that subject, it is the best that could be procured. The Cherokee lands North of the Tenn. River, are subject to the same regulations, as those in the congressional reservation. A statute of limitation has passed, which in its influence, it is hoped, will greatly benefit the honest, industrious & uninformed man, by giving him an indefensible right to his land, if he has lived upon it seven years, under any title that he believed was a good one, at the time he purchased it.

A law has passed requiring all creditors who have heretofore or may hereafter obtain judgments to endorse on the back of the execution that he will take bank notes, on the state bank & her branches, & other bank notes at par with them, or he is prevented from the collection of said judgment for two years; this measure was deemed indispensable to the country, as an exaction of specie, at this time, would be a total sacrifice of property without either paying the debt, or leaving the defendant the means of ever paying it. There has been at this session, six additional counties laid off, three in East and three in West Ten. in consequence of which it became necessary to divide our silicitorial [sic] district, which now consists of the counties of White, Warren, Overton and Jackson, and for which James Rogers, esq. was elected Solicitor, and the honorable Nathaniel Williams was elected Judge for the third circuit.

An act has passed revising the militia laws of this state—this law repeals all former laws on that subject, each field and staff officer, and the captains of the several companies are to be furnished with one copy thereof, there are to be four company musters in each year, one on the Saturday preceding the regimental and battalion masters; two others at such times as the commanding officers may direct. The first battalion is to hold their muster on the first Friday in April, and the second, on the second Friday in the same month. There are to be regimental battalion, and company court martials. The regimental court martials are to be held on the fourth Thursday in November every year; the battalion courtmartial, are to be held in the month of June, annually.

It appears that the treasury of this state, is in a more flourishing condition than every known; after paying all demands of government their [sic] will be a balance remaining of about fifty thousand dollars, which may be applied together with other sums (if the people so will it) to the improvement of the navigation of one rivers, to building a Penitentiary and supporting seminaries of learning, and it gives us much pleasure to state that while our prospects seems to brighten in this respect there is an ample sufficiency of land in the Congressional reservation to satisfy the Warrant holder for his claim.

The dispute between this State and Kentucky in regard to the boundary line is assuming a serious aspect. [W]e have appointed two commissioners to go to Kentucky to endeavour to settle the same and if they cannot settle the differences amicably, said commissioners are to agree upon some tribunal by which said dispute may be determined, and the Governor is authorized in case an amicable adjustment cannot be made by the commissioners, to employ a mathamitition [sic] to extend Walkers line from Tennessee to the Mississippi River.

It was with great difficulty the line between the counties of Morgan and Overton could be settled, about one half of Morgan county petitioned to have the territory west to McClellands line and some other citizens of Morgan wished it to come up further than the Turnpike at length the representation from that county, agreed to give up all claims to territory west of a line from Johnsons stand to where French now lives, thence to the dividing ridge between Wolf and White-oak, thence due north to the state line; this is all we could get, consequently it was impossible to strike off a new county as contemplated by some petitioners, as Morgan would give up no more and Overton according to their lines has not quite one third more than her constitutional limits, and if we shall loose [sic] territory by the approaching dispute with Kentucky, Overton will be reduced below her constitutional limits.

We have on all occasions acted as we thought best calculated to promote the public interest; but if we have acted otherwise, we hope you will attribute it to the falibility [sic] of mankind, please make the contents of this letter known to your neighbours [sic].

Respectfully your Fellow-Citizens,
ADAM HUNTSMAN
JOHN B. CROSS[2]

To James Chisum (circular), July 4, 1823[3]

4th July 1823.

TO JAMES CHISUM, ESQ.[4]

Sir,

A circular of yours dated the 30th of May, addressed to the Voters of White, Overton and Jackson, was this day handed to me, wherein you call upon the voters of this district to enquire who wrote the presentment of the Grand Jury of Overton against your legislative conduct. I presume you have been informed that I drew it up for and at the request of the Grand Jury, or some of them, and as you respect the people to enquire into *that matter*, with a view to point them to me I suppose, I

---

2. John Bolling Cross (1775/77-1852) represented Overton County in the Tennessee house of representatives during the 10th and 13th General Assemblies 1813-15 and 1819-21.

3. Chisum and Robinson Small Collection, Box 1, Folder 4. Manuscript Division, Tennessee State Library and Archives, Nashville TN.

4. James Chisum (1774-1834) was a trustee of Fiske Academy in Overton County, Tennessee, one of the first female academies in the South. Chisum succeeded Huntsman as senator for Overton, White, and Jackson counties in the 14th and 15th General Assemblies (1821-25).

will proceed to satisfy both you and them as well as the facts therewith connected will enable me. When you was a candidate for the Senate in 1821, a considerable number of the north, north west and centre parts of Overton county voted for you, because you was their county man, and because they believed it impossible for you to vote for the seat of justice in Overton county to be removed, or for any bill which would have that effect, they had two good reasons for believing so, 1st they knew the seat of justice was placed as near the centre of the county as an eligible situation with water could be had, and which is in less than three poles of the centre. And 2ndly, they knew that you were one of the commissioners who originally placed it where it stands now at Monroe, upon oath. Therefore, the idea never struck their minds, that it was possible *you* would set it down where it now stands on oath as a commissioner, and remove it away on oath as a Senator. This you positively did do as commissioner, and the bill you tryed to get passed as a Senator, would as certainly have had the effect to have removed it away from where you placed it. Therefore, when the Grand Jury understood that the bill you introduced in the Legislature had a dark and covered design in it, that instead of reducing Overton county to her constitutional limits as its caption pretended, by a strange and unheard of mathematical process, you tried to reduce Overton county to her limits by taking off a considerable piece from the south west end of Morgan that was mountain, and had not ten inhabitants in it, and adding it in your bill to a part of Overton, in order to make said reduced county as long and as narrow as possible, which if passed into a law, would directly have had the effect to make the seat of justice down in a direction towards your own neighborhood. They begin to think it was time to inquire into your legislative conduct. To reduce one county to her limits by adding a part of another to it, was a species of mathematicks they did not understand, and by that kind of wily contrivance, cutting it down on one side, adding from Morgan on another, you could at last get the seat of justice out of the centre, and get the centre towards your own neighborhood; and this you did against the wish of a large majority of Overton county, and when these facts came to the knowledge of an honest Grand Jury of your county, they on their oath presented your legislative conduct as being destructive of their best interests. What excuse you have for these things I know not. I have in two or three instances in the legislature voted to give the people the right to move their seats of justice, when either by design or mistaken views they had been placed much out of the centre in the first instance, this I did in relation to Jackson, Campbell, and Bledsoe counties[,] and I would forever do it under similar hardships. But the idea never once struck my mind, that it was possible any man could think it right, when the seat of justice was placed in the centre in the first instance, to vote to cut it down and add to it in such a way as to throw it out of the centre, for the purpose of moving it afterwards; this you attempted to do absolutely, without allowing the people the right of voting for or against the measure, as was done in Campbell and Jackson counties, and which should be done in all cases. The above facts I know to be indisputably true, for the bill you introduced for that purpose I have seen, and it is now on the files in the Secretary's office, and can be seen by any person, and I have now the map you drew in conformity therewith; in doing this you deceived a majority of Overton county, and the Grand Jury was the proper organ through whom they expressed their disapprobation of your conduct. The reason why it lay from last September until its publication, was in consequence of your moving a part of your property to the Forked Deer country, and telling publickly every where your intention of moving there with the balance this fall, they thought it probable your would not again interfere with the concerns of the county, and therefore it would be unnecessary to publish it. But when they found that notwithstanding you had moved a considerable part of your property to the lower country, and made public declarations of your going with the balance this fall. You all at once to serve your friends, came out as a candidate for the Senate, altho' not ten days before you came out, you told some of your acquaintances you would move this fall; they believed you did this for the purpose of moving the seat of justice from the centre where it now stands down amongst your friends before you moved away, and therefore they thought it necessary to publish the presentments, as I suppose, for I was not in the country when it was published. Thus Sir, I have answered the inquiry in your circular as far as my knowledge or information extends, and so far as it relates to me. This I have done Sir, without malice or ill will, nor would I have answered it but that I believed that the inquiry directed at me, and I felt justified in vindication of my own conduct to answer it. As to your private conduct, character and talents, as a man and a neighbor, I have seen much to approve. But as to your public or political opinions, I have always believed them to be dangerous to the local concerns of the district. Because, I have heretofore thought, and yet believe, that Sampson Williams (a name I mention without either praise or censure,) was connected in opinion and movements with you, to cut up the counties of White, Overton and Jackson so as to answer your own purposes at the expence of the Courthouses, and counties therein concerned, and as I have always acted independently on all subjects, I shall give some of the reasons why I entertain that opinion.

1st. In the year 1811, you used vast exertions in support of a petition while Sampson Williams[5] was in the Senate, giving aid to lay off a new county, composed of part of the counties of White, Overton, and Jackson, leaving the centre of said county near your own plantation or Williams' Quarter in Overton county; and this attempt was partially renewed by you both in 1812, and this if I am correctly informed, was after you, yourself, had aided to reduce Jackson county to her limits, and she had none legally to spare. The limits of the new county were to run within less than ten (perhaps eight) miles of Sparta. This county, which you in the country and Williams in the Legislature, supported with all your means (had it not been prevented by the vigilance and activity of Gen. Bird Smith[6], who then represented White,) would have been established. What would have been the consequence? It would certainly have moved Sparta and Monroe. It would have established Williamsburg, and the new Court-house near Williams' Quarter: for both Monroe and Sparta would

---

5. Sampson Williams (1762-1841) was a justice of the peace and sheriff of Davidson County, Tennessee in the 1790s. He later served in the Tennessee state senate for three terms (1799-1801, 1805-1807, 1811-1813) representing Sumner, Jackson, Smith, Wilson, Overton, Franklin, Warren, and White counties. The county seat of Jackson County from 1806 to 1817—Williamsburg—was named for him. McBride and Robison, *Biographical Directory* 1: 797.

6. Bird Smith (1761-1815) represented Overton, White, Jackson, Franklin, and Warren counties for two terms in the state house of representatives (1809-1813). He served as a brigadier general in the Tennessee militia under Maj. Gen. William Carroll and fought at the Battle of New Orleans. He died at New Orleans over a month later. Ibid: 679.

have been thrown considerably out of the centre of White and Overton. Then sir, you would, in conjunction with Williams, have destroyed two Court houses for the purpose of establishing one in your own neighborhood. These facts appear from the petition you took so active a part in, and from the Bill that Williams introduced in the Legislature, which is likewise in the Secretary's Office amongst the rejected bills, and may be inspected by any person.

2ndly. In the year 1817, when I had published my sentiments to the people of Jackson county that I would pass a law, if elected, authorising them to vote for moving their seat of Justice, inasmuch as it had been placed far from the centre in the first instance, in order to prevent the people of that county from redressing their grievances about their Seat of Justice, Sampson Williams came out against me himself, and to support your old friend and confederate Williams, you wrote several publications against me, and put no names to them, and so vehement was you in trying to elect Williams, (by which the people in Jackson would have been deprived of their rights) that on the morning of the election, you and Williams at Sparta, opened a new set of publications that had never before seen the light, and you and him got up in a piazza in Sparta, called the congregation, and read the publications you had written, you made a speech for Williams, altho' I never heard one sentence of opposition from either of you until I declared my sentiments in favor of allowing the people to move their Seat of Justice in Jackson to the centre, as it was a great distance from it. These are the circumstances which induced me to believe there was a clear understanding and confederacy between you and him on the subject of these Court-houses as the policy you then both adopted, and which you singly have since pursued, precisely corresponds with that idea.

Then, as an additional reason why I think your politicks are dangerous, although I do not know that you have a direct connection with the plan, but it so exactly accords with the policy adopted for many years by you and Williams, that I will mention it in order that the people of Overton and Jackson, may be prepared to meet any attempt that may be made to their prejudice. The people in some parts of Smith county are getting... restless about their Seat of Justice and dividing their county. I believe there is a plan formed by some designing persons, to throw a part of the east boundary of Jackson to Overton, and a part of the eastern boundary of Smith to Jackson, by that means the Seat of Justice of Overton could be moved lower down, that in Jackson back to Williamsburg, and the disorganizers in Smith, effect something in view. The reason why I believe it is, that one of your near neighbors and warmest supporters, told me positively, it was the plan. Another told Col. Matlock[7] of Overton, in substance the same thing. I know not that you have given encouragement to this contrivance, but it is in the same train of policy, which I think is injurious to the people, but of that, they are to be the best judges, they will act on it cooly and impartially, and do you justice I have no doubt. As I am not your personal enemy, I will act more generously with you than you did with me in 1817, for I will put my name to this, in order that I may be responsible for any thing set forth herein as of my knowledge, and also give it in time sufficient to allow you to make any explanations in your power, whereas in 1817, you brought out a parcel of Circulars against me on the morning of the election. Now, if it is the wish of the people after understanding the subject fairly that you should be their Senator, and that they can run the risque, I am content it should be so; I believe you possess talents, but that your political tenets are erroneous, but if so, the people are to be effected by them, consequently they are the judges.

Adam Huntsman.

To the Editor of the *Jackson Gazette*, June 27, 1828[8]

SIR:—From the number of applications which have been made to me, by citizens of the Western District, added to the one in your last paper, requesting that I will offer for Congress, at the next election, I deem it my duty to state publicly and candidly, the reasons why I must decline a compliance with the wishes of my friends in this instance.

First: Since I have been of age to act for myself, nearly one half of that time has been devoted to the service of the people in a public capacity.

---

7. Valentine Matlock, sheriff of Overton County and nephew of John Sevier, Tennessee's first governor.

8. Published in the *Jackson* (TN) *Gazette*, July 2, 1828.

This has been extremely detrimental to my private concerns, which at this time needs my undivided attention for sometime to come; otherwise they will suffer; and if a man is incapable of taking care of his own affairs, or neglects them, he cannot be qualified to take care of all the interests of a community, nor is he the man who should be trusted with them.

Secondly: The practice of *electioneering* has become so extremely disgraceful on the part of some candidates, that I cannot condescend to the little arts and contemptible contrivances which are frequently adopted on such occasions. To go up creeks, down valleys, over hills, and into dales for the purpose of collecting votes, as a tax gatherer would his tax, or a cow driver to buy cattle; and in doing this, frequently propagates or gives currency to lies, slanders and detractions against other candidates, is so far descending beneath the dignity of man, or the independence of a correct politician, that I would not condescend to such an act of degradation to be President of the United States. Add to this the pitiful practice of endeavoring to buy up freemen's votes with a half pint of *white-face* CORN WHISKEY; all of which, sooner or later, meets with the merited condemnation of an enlightened public.

When I see a candidate adopt such degrading and contemptible means, he is the last man on earth I will vote for—the last man I will trust—such great anxiety is suspicious. Does he not want to serve himself at the expense of the public?—I have no doubt if sufficient temptations were thrown in his way, he would sacrifice the interest of his constituents to his own advantage; for it is impossible that he can have either dignity of mind or independence of character, which would form safeguards or protections to our rights and liberties.

The most ignorant man in society should know, that those vile arts are attempts to cheat him out of his birthright; his badge of freedom. I mean his right of suffrage, & that sometimes by a half pint of *still burnt whiskey*. It is an indignity offered to his independence, an insult to the freeborn sons of America.

I am not opposed in principle to a candidate on public occassions mixing with the people, so far as to enable him to ascertain their wants and wishes and affording them an opportunity of becoming acquainted with him, his talents and qualifications for their service. This may be advantageous to both—but further than this is reprehensible.

Lastly: If I were a member of Congress, it would be my pride and pleasure to be placed at least in such a scale of respectability in that body as to do some honor to my constituents. At present, in my own opinion, I do not possess the high qualifications, requisite for that station amongst the members, with the early disadvantage of a limited education, added to poverty & indigence at my outset in life, and dependent entirely upon my profession for a support, I have not had the opportunity of making the science of government and politics in all its aspects and bearings a subject of study or contemplation, to such an extent as to satisfy even myself on that point; though I may have better opportunities hereafter probably; therefore I cannot request the suffrages of the people.

To be elected to Congress for the name without the qualifications of a member is an imposition I will not put upon the people. I owe these explanations to the public. I am under great obligations to the people of Tennessee, for their kindness to me; I came to this state poor and pennyless: I have been fed and cloathed here; what property I have has been accumulated amongst them, every appointment I ever asked for, they have given me; and in declining to come forward as a candidate for Congress I conceive I am acting honestly towards both them and myself.

A. HUNTSMAN.
Madison county, June 27, 1828.

To the editor of the *United States Telegraph*, April 4, 1836[9]

DEAR SIR—My attention has been called to an article in the Telegraph, of the 2d instant, in the following words:

"We ask the reader to bear in mind the fact, that Messrs. J.Q. Adams, Bouldin, Conner, Harregan, Samuel S. Harrison, *Huntsman*, Jarvis, Loyell, Lucas, Manning, McKay, Schenck, and Webster,[10] all known to be the

---

9. Reprinted in the *Randolph* (TN) *Recorder*, May 6, 1836.
10. Congressmen John Quincy Adams of Massachusetts, James W. Bouldin of Virginia, Henry W. Conner of North Carolina, Edward A. Hannegan of Indiana (Huntsman's messmate at Dowson's No. 1 boardinghouse in Washington D.C.), Samuel S. Harrison of Pennsylvania, Leonard

admitted partizans of Mr. Van Buren, refused to perjure themselves by voting that Mr. Newload[11] was entitled to the seat when they did not believe he had been elected."

I do not choose (as far as I am concerned) that false impressions shall go abroad in relation either to my political preferences, which are erroneous, and which the above article is calculated to give currency to.

You have either been misinformed or you are in error, in relation to my sentiments. I have no motive for concealment, and supposing that you have been unintentionally misled in regard to this subject, I will, for that reason and others which are satisfactory to myself, state that you are mistaken in supposing that I am the partizan of Mr. Van Buren. I am the partizan of no man. I never intended to be so. I have turned the leaves of my Dutch dictionary,[12] to ascertain what is the precise definition of the word *partizan*. It is rendered thus: "a thorough going partizan is a man who is always ready to tell lies for his party, and swear to them if it becomes necessary." I beg to be excused from this service, if you please. Every vote which I have given, or shall give, as a member of Congress, was and shall be given, upon the same principles, exactly, as if there was no President to be elected for fifty years to come. The people whom I have the honor to represent, sent me here to attend to other business; and especially reserved the right to make a President themselves. Individually, I shall vote for Judge White, if he gets no other upon earth. I shall afford him all honorable support in my power. This must consist in urging his fitness, qualifications, and honesty, instead of twisting up my votes to that point upon measures which have no relation to it, and which Congress should not be influenced by. I am now, and have always been a supporter of the main principles of this Administration. I expect to continue so—my constituents expect it of me. I have not joined in a *crusade* against Mr. Van Buren for two reasons.

Jarvis of Maine, George Loyell of Virginia, Edward Lucas of Virginia, Richard I. Manning of South Carolina, James I. McKay of North Carolina (another messmate), Ferdinand S. Schenck of Maine, and Taylor Webster of Ohio.

    11. The identity of Mr. Newload is uncertain.
    12. Reference to Huntsman's Dutch ancestry.

1st. When Mr. Van Buren was thrown out of the contest of the Vice Presidency (he being my choice) I began to cast about for some other choice. An overwhelming majority of the people of Tennessee began to cry like a whip poorwill in the evening, *Van Buren, Van Buren, Van Buren, Van Buren.* I did not know very much about it, and upon examination, I cried out *Van Buren* some too. Now, sir, if there was any statute of limitations by which these recollections could be cut off from memory entirely, it would then be in my power, without a charge of *inconsistency,* if I chose to cry out, Crucify him! Crucify him! But there is no such statute in Tennessee (whatever there may be in Congress.) To praise him then and abuse him now, wants explanation.—The second reason is, that I have always deprecated the principle of *supporting one man by the abuse of another.* I have total[l]y abstained from it in practice. My preference for Judge White is as well known to Mr. Van Buren, and the administration, as it is known to my constituents. This was communicated to *him* at his own table, in company with many of his friends. If by a set of political contingencies, the election of President shall be thrown into the House of Representatives, and by possible events, I shall be compelled to make a second choice, the path for me to travel, is a plain and smooth one. I consider the vote unquestionably belongs to that man who will be the most acceptable to a majority of my District, and that I am the organ only through which that vote is to be conveyed. These great and fundamental principles were inculcated upon my mind when I went to school in the old fi[e]lds of Virginia in my boyhood; in the forests of the far west they have grown to maturity, I am pertinaciously in favor of the holy and sanctified right of institution. *No twistification, no dodging*—and I shall obey the wish of a majority of my constituents in this instance, *or resign.* I consider it not only the corner stone, but the pillar also, of our political edifice. The essence and quintessence of our republican institutions, require the representative to speak freely, and truly, the voice of his constituents. Whenever he fails to do that, he is a misrepresentative. He is a man whom republicans despise, and fools laugh at as an aristocrat in republican clothing.

Yours respectfully,
A. HUNTSMAN.

John Read[13] and others to Adam Huntsman, September 20, 1836[14]

Jackson, Ten, Sept. 20th, 1836.

Hon. A. Huntsman,
Dear Sir:

The Hon. Hugh L. White having accepted the invitation of the citizens of Madison county, to partake of a free barbecue, to be given in honor of himself, near Jackson, on Thursday the 29th inst., we the committee in behalf of the citizens of Madison county and for ourselves, do hereby invite and solicit your presence on that occasion.

Amongst the faithful representatives of Tennessee who have yielded their support to the Hon. Hugh L. White, the peoples candidate for the Presidency the people of Madison county are proud to number you.

The slanders which were repudiated by those unfriendly to Judge White, in placing you in the ranks of the opposition, made no impression on your constituents.—knew you—knew your unwavering attachment to Judge White and his cause—they set the charge sown as false; and they are happy to find they were right when they done so.

With sentiments of high regard,
    we remain,
        Your's &c.

John Read,	W.B. Miller,
Samuel Lancaster,	John Greens,
P. M. Miller,	Samuel Givens,
H.W. M'Corry	& others,

Committee.

To John Read and others, September 24, 1836[15]

Jackson, Sept. 24th, 1836.

---

13. John Read was a Jackson attorney and judge.
14. Published in the *Knoxville Register*, October 19, 1836.
15. Published in the *Knoxville Register*, October 19, 1836.

Gentlemen:

I have had the honor of receiving your letter of the 20th instant, in which you inform me that the Hon. Hugh L. White, has accepted the invitation given him by the citizens of Madison county, to partake of a public dinner with them on the 29th; and also the invitation on part of those citizens conveyed through you, requesting my attendance at, and participation in said dinner.—accept the invitation with the deepest sensibility; coming as it does, from that portion of my fellow citizens who are my county men, with whom I have been associated in the professional, political and social relations of life, who were the earliest settlers of the country with me, and who have known me long and known me intimately, would have been a subject of gratitude at any time. But it possesses a double value at this moment, because it affords me an opportunity of joining my fellow-citizens in paying that tribute of respect to Hugh L. White, which his pre-eminent talents and sterling integrity, so richly merit from the wise, the good and the great; such a man the citizens of Madison county will always delight to honor, merit shall receive its just reward, and incorruptible integrity, its proper estimate.

Having been acquainted with him for 30 years; having voted for him 29 years ago as a Senator for Knox county, (the first vote I ever gave) having served with him in the Senate of this State 10 years ago, having voted for him as Senator in Congress nine years ago, having as Lawyer practised before him, while he presided in the Supreme Court of this state; and having lived in the same town with him some years, I think I have had a thorough opportunity of forming an accurate opinion of his talents, integrity and business habits. The result of all is, that I consider him pre-eminently qualified to fill the Presidential chair with honor to himself and usefulness to his country.

As soon as his friends obtained his consent for his name to be used as a candidate for the chief magistracy, I formed the determination (which is unchanged and unchangeable) to give him all fair and honorable support in my power, and I have done so. This determination was made known to the people of this District in all the public addresses which I had the honor to make during the late Congressional canvass. I then urged his superior talents, unquestioned integrity, and business habits as an inducement to others to support him, without following the beaten track of abusing others who were likely to come in competition with him for that high appointment.

I have considered and yet consider that those high qualifications ought to insure his success, and the most powerful lever to be used in the attainment of that object is at public dinners, or in the primary assemblies of the people; where his merits may be discussed and properly understood. I know that Judge White has been an inflexible supporter of the main principles which brought the present Chief Magistrate into power, and that his support has been unwavering in those principles from that time to this. He may have differed with the administration in the selection of some of the men who was to act as agents to carry out those principles, or he may have differed in some principles of recent adoption.

Yet, in the great and fundamental principles of this Government, which has separated the Federal from the Republican party, since the days of ninety-eight, and which defined the boundaries between those two doctrines, Judge White has given Gen. Jackson's administration an unshaken [support?] therefore the __?__ attempted to be put __?__ that Judge White abandoned Gen. Jackson's administration are totally unfounded As Tennessee was conspicuous in bringing forward the present Chief Magistrate in order to carry out these principles, we have the most gratifying evidences, that in the coming election she will ably and firmly stand by the Hon. HUGH L. WHITE with the same degree of and energy that she stood by Gen. Jackson in 1828.

In the next place I will speak something in respect to the reports alluded to in your esteemed letter, which have been put [in] circulation, alledging that I had abandoned the support of Judge White for the purpose of espousing the Van Buren cause. That some of the propagators of this deep and malignant falsehood in this district acted willfully, [insidiously],[6] and knowingly, I have but little doubt. My reasons for thinking so are the following—

1st. I had proclaimed my preference for Judge White not only in public speeches throughout the District, but also in private conversation, here and at Washington City, and particularly to Gen. Jackson and Mr. Van Buren both.

2nd[l]y. An incident occurred at Washington, which gave me an opportunity of declaring my sentiments publicly, and which was published in the principal newspapers of this city, in the newspapers of this district, and in many [other?] [...][16] the active propagators of this report could have been ignorant that they were circulating falsehoods with the view of deceiving many well meaning men who were friendly to me.

These few w[...][17] [workers?] will confer a singular favor upon me *by voting against me at the next election.*

After such open and repeated declarations in favor of Judge White, or these men to say I was in favor of Mr. Van Buren, Harrison, Webster, or any other, is neither more nor less than giving me the lie directly, and I shall (if I have energy sufficient) hold them responsible if repeated, to the same extent precisely that I [would?] do if a man was to give me the lie to my face.

I have not changed my political preferences or political opinions within the last 20 years, and it cannot be expected at my time of life, that I should now fluctuate between the Federal and Republican opinions, to which I class all the subordinate doctrines under new and assumed names and slight variations.

I tender you my best wishes, Gentlemen, both for yourselves and the good cause you are engaged in.

ADAM HUNTSMAN.

To the Jackson (TN) *District Telegraph*, April 1837[18]

The beginning of the original letter, according to the Nashville Republican, *May 2, 1837, gave "an account of his stewartship" as a member of Congress.*

As I have declined being a candidate for Congress at the ensuing election, I consider the proceeding explanation necessary in addition to what the Journals will show, upon which I am willing to stand or fall.

---

16. The original newspaper appear to be crimped when it was microfilmed, making this portion of the letter impossible to decipher.
17. See footnote 12
18. Reprinted in the *Nashville Republican*, May 2, 1837.

I have many reasons for the step I have taken. Since I arrived at the age of twenty-one years more than one half of my time has been spent in public life. The sympathies excited for the melancholy fate of the late Col. Crockett, is such, that many wish to pay a tribute of respect to him, by electing his son; I will not stand in the way of this generous sympathy; besides, in the last two years, I was only four and one-half months at home; my own affairs need my attention much. Furthermore, I find young Crockett possesses (in the main) sound republican principles. He is opposed to a protective Tariff—for reducing it to the wants of the Government administered with economy.—He is against the power claimed by the General Government to make Internal Improvements, but is for leaving that to the States.—He is against the re-charter of the U. States Bank—for a strict construction of the constitution of the United States.—He is against Federalism, Abolition, and has always been against the doctrines of Nullification, most especially—and I shall most unquestionably support him against any man possessing *contrary doctrines in these particulars.*

It may be said by some, that I declined because I supposed he (Crockett) might have beat me; to these, I answer—if so, I have only followed the example set by some very great men: Judge M'Lean[19] declined when he was a candidate for the Presidency. P.M. Miller[20] declined when a candidate in this District, against Col. David Crockett. Now, if such great men as these declined from an apprehension of being beat, I may be pardoned for following their example, even if that is the true grounds upon which I act. Be my motives what they may I have formed my determination and intend to act upon it with vigor. I have to thank the people of the Western District most sincerely for the many manifestations of their favour upon me. Their kindness will always occupy a place near my heart, and I fervently pray that in their next Representative; they may find a man able, capable and honest, one who will do credit to himself and honor to his constituents.

With respect, &c.
A. HUNTSMAN.

19. John McLean, U.S. Supreme Court justice appointed by President Andrew Jackson in 1829.
20. Pleasant M. Miller

To Dr. Felix Robertson and others, October 30, 1838[21]

Jackson, Ten., 30th October, 1838.

Gentlemen—I have received the invitation the Republican party of Davidson county has so kindly sent me, to participate in a Barbacue to be given to the Hon. James K. Polk, near the City of Nashville, on the 6th of November. I regret that professional business which cannot be dispensed with, requires my attendance at our Courts in the District on that day, otherwise I should be proud to be with you. Of the Virginia doctrines of '98[22] I have been a uniform supporter. Mr. Randolph's[23] proverb was: "If a man changed his politics after he was thirty years of age, he suspected some dishonest motive." In nine cases out of ten he was right. That an attempt would be made to transfer the State of Tennessee to Mr. Clay, Webster, or Harrison, has been strongly suspected by me ever since the winter of 1835. So strongly was that object pressed upon me indirectly by a p[erson] whom I suspected to be a leader in this pr[...] (not Judge White) that I felt myself constra[ined] to draw up in writing my objections somewh[ere?] the form of my political creed, and give it t[o the] gentleman. As a supporter of Judge Whi[te, I] felt perfectly justifiable in this course I [had] known him for nearly thirty years to be the [un]compromising opponent of the U.S. Bank, [the] Tariff, Internal Improvement by the General [Gov]ernment, and a strict construer of the Federal [Con]stitution. I knew that Webster, Clay, and H[arri]son, entertained the reverse of all those princi[ples] which separated the Federal from the Republ[ican] party in '98. In that contest the Republicans [pre]vailed; I consider that under various names [and] disguises, the Federal party are now rallying o[nce a]gain the power they have lost.

---

21. Published in the *Nashville Union*, November 12, 1838.
22. The Virginia doctrines of '98 refer to the Virginia and Kentucky Resolutions written by James Madison and Thomas Jefferson respectively. In declaring the Alien and Sedition Acts passed by Congress to be unconstitutional, the resolutions argued that individual states could nullify any federal law they deemed unconstitutional.
23. John Randolph of Roanoke, longtime congressman and U.S. senator from Huntsman's native Virginia.

What has Tennessee to gain by this? She [has] stood at the Republican post with unflinching f[irm]ness, battling Federalism in every form in w[hich] it has been presented. Shall she desert this p[...] and go over horse, foot and dragoons, to the [Fed]eral ranks? I believe no one contends, that [...] Clay has changed his political principles in the [last] 20 years. He is the same ardent supporter of [the] Bank, Tariff, Internal Improvement, or what [he] calls his American System, as he was then. H[ow] does this accord with our politics? Tennessee [...][24] her elections and the various resolutions w[ill] stand unrescinded upon her Legislative records. [They] not only denounced these doctrines, but their gi[ven] author by name. Is Tennessee to change her [po]litics in toto, and say that these various resoluti[ons] upon her journals are legislative falsehoods, [and] then go over to the support of Mr. Clay and [his] principles, as he will not come to us or ours? Th[ose] who are prepared for this sacrifice may throw [a] somerset; for myself, I am still a democrat of [...]. But this leap requires some caution[.] I remem[ber] right well, that in the fall of 1827, when som[e of] the most conspicuous of the new converts to C[lay?]ism, who now sit in high places, but, were [...] attendant upon, or members of the Tennessee [le]gislature, at that time concerted in the form [of a] Preamble to a Resolution, nominating Gen. Jack[son] for the Presidency; the most rare and exqui[site] dose of vituperative abuse (and perhaps a li[ttle] slander) upon Mr. Clay and Adams, that can [be] found in any production of the same length. [It] charged Mr. Clay and Mr. Adams with every th[ing] except being honest and clever men. This was t[hen] taken upon oath, and spread upon the journ[al.] It passed accordingly, by almost a unanim[ous] vote. I could not swallow the dose, because [I did] not believe the half of it, although I was a Jack[son] man. My advice to the new converts is to get [the] Preamble expunged from our journals before [it] progresses one atom further; for I, a Jackson m[an,] had to enter upon the journals my solemn pro[test] against this preamble, but there was but tw[o or] three voted with me. If Mr. Clay's friends [will] not (as I strongly suspect) consent to the pro[spect?] of expunging, then it must remain upon the

---

24. Portions of the text were cut off the newspaper page.

[jour]nals forever. Let those who voted for it look [...].[25] It is said by some of Mr. Clay's friends in [this] quarter, that if elected, he is willing to drop [the] principles which heretofore have been so ob[nox]ious to Tennessee. I can best answer this by [a] reference to one of Aesop's Fables. It runs thu[s:] Wolves soon found out a pretence to break th[e] league, and devour all the sheep in the absenc[e] of the dogs. So with the Government; give it int[o] the hands of the Federalists, American Syste[m] men, &c. let them promise what they will, the[y] will soon find a pretence to eat up our substane[nce] and reinstate the whole mass of Federal principl[es] upon us forthwith. In conclusion, I will send yo[u] a toast.

As the salutation to the Kings of Babylon wa[s]—"O King, live forever"— So let the salutation [of] every true Republican be—O Democracy, live fo[r]ever

ADAM HUNTSMAN

Dr. Felix Robertson and others,
Committee.

To Aaron Vanderpoel, August 26, 1839[26]

Jackson Ten, Augt 26th 1839

D sr

You will have learned before this reaches you the glorious result of our last elections We fought a hard battle to make the people understand the nature of the contest In many places in the State the Whig Electors hoisted the Clay Flag most incautiously—the moment that was done our success became certain Vanburen can beat Clay tomorrow ten thousand votes in Tennessee and the longer the worse for Clay

What can you do in the empire State, what can you do this fall I shall be glad to hear from you I was truly Glad to hear of your election to congress where I think you can do [so much?] good

---

25. See footnote 20

26. Courtesy of the New York State Library, Manuscripts and Special Collections. Vanderpoel Family Papers, 1815-1839. SC 14626, Box 1, Folder 1. Aaron Vanderpoel (1799-1870), a native of President Martin Van Buren's hometown of Kinderhook, NY, he served with Huntsman in the 24th Congress.

Accept my best wishes &c
ADAM HUNTSMAN

To the Editors of the *Nashville Republican*, August 1845[27]

Dear Sirs—As some of the Whig Editors have consecrated me a *Prophet* because I thought proper to send some calculations upon the late election to a Democratic friend, I will, for the satisfaction of the whigs, accept of their appointment and utter a few prophecies for their benefit.

Item 1st. I predict that the whig party, by that name, is perfectly annihilated and that they will never engage in another Presidential canvass under the cognomen, but that they will change their name to that of *Native American*, or some other, to deceive the people before the next election.

Item 2d. I prognosticate that the whigs will try to claim the Annexation of Texas as a whig measure, unless there is a likelihood that it will produce war, and then they will swear it is a Democratic movement.

Item 3d. I prophesy that in less than two years they will proclaim to the world that they never were for any other than a revenue tariff, especially after it shall be reduced to that point by Congress by equitable principles.

Item 4th. I prophesy that the whigs, Northern abolitionists, and federalists, are to join heart and hand in the acquisition of the Oregon Territory, notwithstanding their opposition to Texas on the ground of making our territory too large.

Item 5th. I prophesy, predict, and foretell, that at the next Presidential election the whig party is to make a powerful effort to coalesce with the abolitionists to defeat the Democratic party, it being their forlorn hope.

Item 6th. I prophesy that the whig party has changed their priorities so often the abolitionists will not trust them.

Item 7th. I prophesy that the whigs in this State will endeavor to bring out James C. Jones as their candidate for Governor at the next election.[28]

---

27. Published in the *Nashville Republican*, September 3, 1845.
28. While James C. "Lean Jimmy" Jones was not the Whig candidate for governor in 1847, the party's nominee—Neill S. Brown—did beat incumbent Democrat Aaron V. Brown.

Item 8th. I prophesy and predict that in the event that he offers for Governor aforesaid, that Aaron jr. with the aid of the Brownlow funds, will make a larger Bull Calf of him than Aaron of old did out of the gold rings, bracelets and jewelry of the Children of Israel on Mount Sinai.[29]

Item 9th. I prophesy and predict that about the first Tuesday in December next, the great whig mystery will be solved of "who is James K. Polk."

Item 10th. I prophesy that before and at the next Presidential election, a large number of honest, well-meaning whigs will repent of their evil ways and join the Democrats, as they hate minorities any way.

Item 11th. I prophesy and predict that my old friend, W.W. Gates,[30] Editor of the West Tennessee Whig, will not stop at his contemplated settlement on Salt River,[31] but will move to Oregon, turn Democrat, and Edit the first State paper printed for the new *State of Oregon*, when it shall be established.

Item 12th. I prophesy that W.W. Gates will not charge me any thing for taking his paper from last fall up to the late election.

Now, Messrs. Editors, if it shall so turn up that the whigs shall need another chapter of prophecies, as they conferred the title upon me, I feel bound to give it to them.

ADAM HUNTSMAN.

To John C. Calhoun, April 10, 1846[32]

Jackson Ten, April the 10th, 1846

DEAR SIR I received your speech which you was so kind as [to] send me upon the Oregon controversy. It is a masterly exposition of the question, one that I heartily approve of, and I have the satisfaction to inform you

---

29. Aaron Jr. could refer to Democratic Gov. Aaron V. Brown. William G. Brownlow was the editor of the *Tennessee Whig* newspaper based in Jonesborough.

30. William Ward Gates established the *West Tennessee Whig* newspaper in 1842, which was published in Jackson until federal occupation of the town in June 1862 during the Civil War. The paper was revived after the war and eventually was incorporated into another publication in 1877. Williams, *Historic Madison*: 265-267.

31. The phrase "Salt River" implies political defeat.

32. Published in U.S. Congress, Annual Report of the American Historical Association for the Year 1929. In One Volume and a Supplemental Volume. House Serial Set Vol. No. 9314, Session Vol. No. 91, Seventy-first Congress, 2nd Session. House Doc. 447, Vol. 1.

that nine tenths of the people of Tennessee are heartily with you. There are a few Hotspurs here as well as elsewhere, who desire to settle that controversy (as well as others) by fighting first, and explaining the question afterwards. But the great body of our people are for an honorable compromise, and will be perfectly satisfied with the 49th. You know the people of Tennessee too well to suppose they fear war. If they find that one is inevitable they will go to it like they would to a frolick.

ADAM HUNTSMAN

To the *Nashville Union*, July 17, 1847[33]

Jackson, July 17, 1847

Dear Sir:—Candidates for Governor will finish the canvass in this district today. I think we will gain 500 votes in this district. If your section of the State and East Tennessee shall do equally well, we must elect Aaron V. by double the majority he beat Foster.[34] We shall gain one or two members in the Legislature in the West, and Gardiner[35] is making admirable speeches in the canvass for Congress. Not much money will be won or lost here. The Whigs are not disposed to bet.

Respectfully yours, &c.
ADAM HUNTSMAN

Excerpt of letter to Jackson Democratic Club, 1848[36]

I spoke of Gen. Taylor[37] favorably until he came out in a letter that he was not an *ultra whig*. Now whether this means that he is a *soft whig*, or a *tender-footed whig*, I know—I care not. Of all the politicians which exist the soft and tender-footed are the most obnoxious to me. Instead of

---

33. Reprinted in the *Boston* (MA) *Daily Atlas*, August 18, 1847.
34. Aaron V. Brown and Ephraim H. Foster.
35. John A. Gardner (1809-1892) was an unsuccessful Democratic candidate for Congress in the 1847 election. McBride and Robison, eds. *Biographical Directory* 1: 276-277.
36. Reprinted in the Columbus *Daily Ohio Statesman*, October 12, 1848.
37. Gen. Zachary Taylor, Whig nominee for president in the 1848 election.

being a *no-party* man, as he at first declared, it turns out that he belongs to the *tender-footed whig* party, as he himself shows.

I never did, nor never will vote for a political officer, who will not come out frankly with his opinions upon all subjects connected with that office. If he has got no opinions, then I consider him a fool upon those subjects; if he has any, as our government is peculiarly founded upon the opinions of the people, we have a right to his, if he wants to conduct that government as its chief. I never wish to see a man exalt himself to such a high and mighty position, in his own estimation as to refuse to give his opinion to his countrymen, when he is asking them to confer office upon him. This is precisely or worse than the practice of Kings, and should be scouted by every man in a free government. We should never vote for a man, who would not condescend to inform his countrymen of his opinions.

Since I have seen Gen. Taylor's letters and correspondence, they have convinced me that he has no qualifications to discharge the duties of chief magistrate. As Daniel Webster says, *he is a mere military man.* In that capacity he will always do honor to himself and country.

I am personally acquainted with Gen. Cass[38]—was much in his company when he was Secretary of War. His conduct and services, since as Minister of France and as Senator in Congress, has satisfied all the world that he is a man of first rate talents, and qualifications for any civil appointment. For the foregoing reasons, I ought not, I cannot, and I will not vote Taylor and M. Fillmore[39] but if spared I shall vote for Cass and Butler.[40] In doing so, I consider that I am carrying out those democratic doctrines, which I have been advocating for forty years and expect to die in that faith.

ADAM HUNTSMAN

---

38. Lewis Cass, Democratic presidential nominee in 1848.
39. Millard Fillmore, Whig vice-presidential nominee in 1848 and, upon the death of Zachary Taylor two years later, the 13th President of the United States.
40. William O. Butler, Democratic vice-presidential nominee in 1848.

Appendix C

The Book of Chronicles

The initial chapter of Adam Huntsman's political satire "The Book of Chronicles, West of the Tennessee and East of the Mississippi rivers" was first published in the Jackson (Tennessee) *Southern Statesman* on June 25, 1831. It was followed by a second chapter on July 16, 1831. Written in Biblical prose, both stories describe the rise and fall of "David" (David Crockett) as a member of the great "Sandedrim" (Congress). Huntsman wrote other Books of Chronicles on Andrew Jackson and Martin Van Buren that were published in the same paper on September 15 and 22, 1832.

CHAPTER 1

1. And it came to pass in those days when Andrew was chief ruler over the children of Columbia,[1] that there arose a mighty man in the river country, whose name was David;[2] he belonging to the tribe of Tennessee, which lay upon the border of the Mississippi and over against Kentucky.

1. President Andrew Jackson
2. David Crockett

2. Now David was chief of the hosts of Forked Deer, and Obion, and around about the Hatchie, and the Mississippi rivers, and behold his fame had spread throughout all the land of Columbia, insomuch, that there was none to be found like unto him, for wisdom and valour; no, not one in all the land.
3. David was a man wise in council, smooth in speech, valiant in war, and of fair countenance and goodly stature, such was the terror of his exploits, that thousands of wild cats and panthers did quake and tremble at his name.
4. And it came to pass that David was chosen by the people in the river country, to go with the wise men of the tribe of Tennessee to the grand Sanhedrim[3] held yearly in the twelfth month, and on the first Monday in the month, at the city of Washington, where the wise men from the east, from the west, from the north and from the south gathered themselves together to consult on the welfare of Columbia and her twenty four tribes.
5. In those days there were many occupants spread abroad throughout the river country; these men loved David exceedingly, because he promised to give them lands flowing with milk and honey.
6. And it came to pass in the 54th year after the children of Columbia had escaped from British bondage, and on the first month, when Andrew and the wise men and rulers of the people were assembled in the great Sanhedrim, that David arose in the midst of them saying, *Men and brethren, wot ye not that there are many Occupants in the river country on the west border of the tribe of Tennessee, who are settled down upon lands belonging to Columbia; now I beseech you give unto these men each a portion for his inheritance, so that his soul may be glad and he will bless thee and thy posterity.*
7. But the wise men from the south, the south east, the west, and the middle country, arose with one accord and said *Lo, brethren, this cannot be done. The thing which our brother David asketh is unjust, the like hath never been done in the land of Columbia. If we give the*

---

3. The U.S. Congress. Huntsman consistently misspells the Great Sandedrin, the supreme religious body of the Jewish religion during the time of Jesus.

lands away, it must be to the tribe of Tennessee, so that they may deal with the occupants as it may seem good in their right. This has been the practice in old times and with our fathers, and we will not depart therefrom. Furthermore, we cannot give this land away, until the warrants are satisfied.

8. Behold, when David heard these sayings, he was exceeding[ly] wroth against the wise men and the rulers of the congregation, and against Andrew, and made a vow unto the lord that he would be avenged of them. Then John, one of the wise men of the tribe of Tennessee who lived at the rocky dity,[4] arose in the midst and said, *If we give this land, unto the occupants instead of the tribe, all the occupants in the land of Columbia will beseech us for lands, and there will be none left to pay the debt which redeemed us from bondage; no not one acre, and this saying pleased the wise men and the rulers and they did accordingly.*

9. Now there were in these days wicked men sons of Beleal,[5] to wit: the Claytonites, the Holmesites, the Burghesites, the Everettites, the Chiltonites, and the Bar[t]onites, who were of the tribes of Maine, Massachusetts, Rhode Island, Kentucky and Missouri,[6] and who hated Andrew and his friends of old times, because the children of Columbia had chosen him to rule over them instead of Henry whose surname was Clay, who they desired for their chief ruler.

10. And lo, when those men saw that David was sorely troubled in spirit, they communed one with another, and said, *Is this not David from the river country in the west, who of old times was very valiant for Andrew to be ruler, and who perplexed our ranks in the Sanhedrim, and who was foremost in battle against our great chiefs Henry & John Q.[7] when they were defeated by Andrew?* Now Tristam, whose surname was Burgess, answered and said, Men and brethren, *as the Lord liveth it is he.*

---

4. John Blair of Jonesborough, representative of the 1st Congressional District in the House of Representatives.

5. In Hebrew, Belial is a name for Satan; it also implies wickedness.

6. Congressmen John M. Clayton of Delaware, John Holmes of Maine, Tristam Burges of Rhode Island, Edward Everett of Massachusetts, Thomas Chilton of Kentucky, and David Barton of Missouri each opposed President Jackson.

7. Henry Clay and John Quincy Adams

11. Then Daniel, whose surname was Webster, and who was a prophet of the order of Balaam,[8] said, Let us comfort David in his afflictions, his wrath is kindled against Andrew and his friends, and against the wise men of Tennessee; peradventure he will come over to us at the next election, to fight for Henry against Andrew; and Thomas whose surname was Chilton, said, Thou speaketh wisely, let what thou sayest be done according to thy words.

12. Then Daniel drew nigh unto David and said unto him, *Wherefore O, my brother, doth thou seem sad & sorrowful? Why is thy soul bowed down with affliction? Hath famine and pestilence destroyed thy land and all thy beloved occupants? [O]r has the wise men and rulers been unkind to thee?* I pray thee tell me and I will comfort thee.

13. And David lifted up his eyes and wept, and said O, Daniel! live forever. If the wise men and rulers had given my occupants the lands according to the manner I beseeched them I could have been wise man and chief ruler in the river country for life. But if I join the wise men and give it to the State of Tennessee then they will share the honor with me, and the council of the state of Tennessee will give it to the occupants at twelve and one half cents per acre, and they will receive the honor instead of me; then the people of the river country will not have me for their wise man and chief ruler forever, and it grieveth me sore.

14. And Daniel answered, and said unto David, swear unto me [allegiance] and all thy people in the river country will come over unto me, and fight with me at the next election against Andrew and his people, in favour of Henry for chief ruler of Columbia; then I will help thee to get the lands for thine occupants, and David swore accordingly, and there is a league existing between them, even unto this day.

15. Now there was a man in the river country, about the centre thereof, whose name was William.[9] He loved David as he loved his own soul; his soul and David's were knet as tho' they were but one; he was David's chief counsellor. When David wept he wept, when David

---

8. Balaam was considered a "wicked man" in the Old Testament.
9. William Fitzgerald, Crockett's opponent in the 1831 congressional election.

rejoiced he rejoiced, if David bid him go he went, if David bid him come, he come.

16. So it came to pass when David returned from the Great Sanhedrim, that William ran and fell upon his neck, and wept for joy. Then David said unto him, I have been discomfitted in all my plans, I could not get my beloved occupants their lands without dividing the honor with the wise men of my state, and giving it to the whole tribe of Tennessee; I wot not but the council would give it to them as cheap as I, but it would rob me of the honor and then I cannot be the wise man and chief ruler for life. I have therefore engaged to forsake Andrew and join the ranks of Henry for the chief ruler over the children of Columbia, for the wise men of my tribe and the friends of Andrew hath forsaken me. Wilt thou, in whom my soul delighteth, go with me in these things?

17. And William answered, and said, Where thou goest I will go; where thou stayest I will stay; what thou doest, I will do; and will have none other God but thee—when I forsake thee, let the Lord forsake me, do as thou wilt.

18. And David said unto William, draw near unto me, I will counsel thee, for thou art my beloved disciple, in whom I am well pleased; Go thou through all the river country, and every neighborhood thereof, tell the people I will be elected by five thousand votes, as though art a baptist, they will put trust in thee.

19. If thou dost come to a people who knoweth thee not, if they are for me, say unto them be strong and valiant on the day of the election; if they are against me, say unto them thou art against me also, but thou hast been all through the river country and I will be elected by a mighty host, this will terrify them and they will join me; if thou shalt come to an ignorant people, say unto them my adversary is guilty of corruption; if a Jackson man approach thee say unto him, I have always been for Jackson.

20. If a Clay man encounter thee then mayesy thou tell him of the bargain with Daniel; If a baptist greet thee, say unto him, I am religiously disposed and think highly of the baptists; If a methodist shall enquire of thee, say until him I always attend their camp-meetings;

If cumberland Presbyterian shall call upon thee say unto him I have joined his society.

21. But be thou circumspect in all things, and do not say unto the people that I have franked sack bags full of books into the river country against Andrew at their expense. Thou shall not say unto the people that I have franked Humes' history of England or a sack of feathers; be careful to inform Roland, the High Priest, of all these things, so that he may direct his congregation accordingly.[10]
22. Remember now, my beloved disciple, that I am thy light and thy life; I have sent thee big coats, bibles, hymn books, and many articles of the great Sanhedrim, for thyself and family; I will send thee many other things if thou art faithful unto the end; go forth, and the lord prosper thee.
23. And William went unto all the river country, and did according to all that David commanded him; but the people were a stiff necked generation, and would not agree that David should bring in Henry to be chief ruler over the children of Columbia, instead of Andrew; but with one accord said unto William, David hath beguiled us, we will desert him, and stick to Andrew, who hath brought us out of British bondage and we will vote for William, whose surname is Fitzgerald—and the people all said AMEN!

Chapter 2

1. And it came to pass when William returned with these sorrowful tidings, he said, O, David! mayest thou rule and reign as our wise man forever. I have been throughout all the hill country, and [*page torn*] vallies; I have been to the great river [Missi]ssippi, and the Indian border; I [ha]ve been over against Kentucky, in the north, and on [the] Tennessee river in the east, and the people by mighty hosts, sayest

---

10. "Roland the High Priest" refers to Rev. Roland Cook (1771-1843) of Henderson County, who founded the first Baptist Church in West Tennessee near present-day Wildersville about 1822. "Reverend Roland Cook, Founder of the First Baptist Church in West Tennessee." *Memphis Commercial-Appeal*, 20 May 1905. <homepages.rootsweb.ancestry.com/~reburke/lines/data/cook/roland_cook_article.html>

thou shall not bring Henry of Kentucky[11] to reign and rule over them, instead of Andrew, whose surname is Jackson. They furthermore say, that thou hast dealt deceitfully with them in this thing, and that thou didst promise them hereto fore, when they chose thee for their wise man, that thou wast the friend of Andrew, who led us in battle and kept us out of British bondage.

2. But thou hast betrayed them and gone over to the sons of Belial,[12] and joined them, to fight for Henry, whose surname is Clay, against our beloved Andrew. And this stiff necked and ungovernable generation, doth moreover say, that thou hast voted away all our money to make roads and canals in Yankee land, and the middle regions of Columbia, and hast not *asked of the great Sanhedrim one dollar for thine own country; no, not even one cent, but hath wholly neglected them.* And lo, they swore with a mighty oath, that as the Lord liveth, they will no more follow thee, or go out after thee, for their wise man; but they will choose William, whose surname is Fitzgerald, to rule over them in time to come, in thy stead.

3. Now when David heard these things, he rent his garments and put on sack cloth and ashes, and wept until eventide, and about the ninth hour of the next day, David lifted up his eyes and said unto William: my deciple whom my soul loveth, let us send for Roland the High Priest,[13] to commence with us in our afflictions; peradventure he can council us what *I must do to be saved in this election*; and peradvanture, also, the Lord will permit him to curse William, whose surname is Fitzgerald and all his followers on my account.

4. And it came to pass when Roland was come and heard all these things, that William said unto David, he was gently troubled in spirit, in so much that he walked to and fro, through the Creek nation, and unto the borders of Spring Creek, and Independence, he could find no rest.[14] Roland got the Bible, the Testament, and occupant law, and enquired

---

11. Henry Clay, U.S. Senator from Kentucky
12. In the Hebrew Bible, the Sons of Belial refer to worthless, lawless people.
13. Rev. Roland Cook was a personal friend of David Crockett.
14. Spring Creek, likely in Madison County, and Independence in Hardeman County.

of the Lord concerning this matter; but the Lord had departed from David, and he could get no answer.

5. Behold, when David heard these things, he said unto them, is there a Witch in all the river country, that we may inquire of her? And they answered and said unto him; no not one; for since Thomas, whose surname is Smith, and Samuel, whose surname is Hodge,[15] has been preaching in the river country, all wizzards, witches, demons and familiar spirits, hath departed; yea, even into the land of Arkansas, and not one remaineth.

6. Then Roland spake and said unto them, let not their heart die within us, but let us take courage and acquit ourselves like men, for I will put off my Priestly garments, and girt the armour of election about my loins. I will get me into all the Synagogues and neighborhoods thereof, and I will assemble the *true believers in David* in congregations throughout all the river country, and I will scoff at Andrew, and all the acts of his Administration; I will impeach him and the wise men of the great Sanhedrim, of sin, and of wickedness; I will say that David is the only righteous man left amongst them to come and tell us the tale.

7. Behold, I will further say unto the multitudes, that the Legislature of the Tribe of Tennessee are wicked and corrupt, that they have not the fear of God before their eyes, but are bribed against the occupants. I will speak strongly against common schools and education, *for brethren we all know if the people get learning and information, they will quickly discover that David is unqualified to be our wise man, and they will choose another; therefore our policy is to keep them as ignorant as possible.* I will try and confirm the trust that the occupants putteth in David. I will bestir me from this until the election; *go thou, and do likewise.*

8. And David said, well done thou good and faithful servant; enter thou seven times into the joy of thy lord; what thou sayest pleaseth me exceedingly. I will arouse myself also; I will charge William, whose

---

15. Thomas Smith was a Methodist preacher in Madison County in the late 1820s. Samuel Hodge was undoubtedly a preacher as well, though of which denomination is uncertain. Williams, *Historic Madison*: 294.

surname is Fitzgerald, with sin, with iniquity, with bribery, with lying, and all other crimes; peradventure, I can make the weak and ignorant men in the river country, believe me.

9. I will get records against them; if it does not show enough I will add to, I myself. If the whole record would make against me, I will only take so much as in my favor. I will get such Jurors to [c]ertify for me as I can deceive by reading the certificate contrary to the way it is written.

10. I will deny voting one hundred and fifty thousand dollars to the Washington Turnpike Road[16], to please the Kentuckians, and I will deny there ever was such a Bill before the Sanhedrim. Peradventure no body in the river country has got a copy of the Journals, and they cannot detect me before the election. I have never sent them any of the Journals for fear they would see how I voted away their money. If I can be elected only this once, I care no more for them and I will provide for myself and thee.

11. I will also write a book against William, whose surname is Fitzgerald. I will abuse him very much; I will put any thing in it by which I can get votes; this election is approaching; yea, even so nigh, that the people will not discover it in time to contradict me.

12. Now when David had made an end of speaking, William arose and said, *my soul is revived within me.* What David and the High Priest saith, let it be done accordingly. I will take unto me my two sons, and we will carry these sayings of David and Roland, also David's circulars, through every neighborhood, and border of the river country, and unto the people in every direction; and we will try and deceive the people in every direction, and we will try and deceive the very elect if they are against David. So they all arose with one accord, and went their respective ways to act accordingly, and I saw them no more.

13. Now when these things come to be known in the river country, the love of many waxed cold for David, and many, yea, very many, deserted from him and went over to William, whose surname is Fitzgerald,

---

16. The Washington Turnpike bill passed by Congress in 1830 was vetoed by Congress in 1830. He believed federally funded internal improvements were unconstitutional.

and they said unto him, lo! we have come from following David, to join thy standard, and we will cleave unto thee so long as thou shalt walk in the laws and ordinances prescribed for the children of Columbia, and so long as thou shalt not go lusting after other chief rulers than Andrew.

14. If thou shalt prove faithful to the end in all things, we entrust unto thee, then we will never forsake thee. If after we elect thee our wise man, thou shalt go like unto David over unto the uncircumsized Yankees and the Clayites, the Websterites and the Chiltonites, then we will curse thee and thy posterity forever, and we will burn both thee and thy house with fire.

15. For behold, we have been the supporters of David, and he hath departed from the law of our political forefathers, and hath not kept our ordinances and our constitutions, but hath sin[n]ed exceedingly in the sight of the Lord, in somuch so that great and mighty plagues hath come upon us, and upon our land. Behold! we have been sorely afflicted with Buffaloe [g]nats, which hath destroyed much cattle, and all the river country hath been grievously afflicted with cut worms, which hath destroyed our crops; whereas east of the river Tennessee, in the hill country, where Cave[17] is the wise man and chief ruler, there is no Buffalo [g]nats or cut worms; no not so much as one. The reason whereof was this: Cave done that which was wise, righteous in the sight of the Lord and had walked in the statutes and ordinances prescribed for the children of Columbia, and had obeyed the voice of his constituents and did not lust after Henry as chief ruler, and his district was not afflicted with plagues, which destroyed the cattle and crops, like unto the manner in David's districr.

16. And it came to pass that on the day appointed to select a wise man in the river country, the people assembled in might congregations, and elected William by a mighty host. Now all the rest of the acts of David, and what he did are they not written in the Chronicles of Adam the scribe, and Roland the highest, and he was gathered to his fathers in the Priestly land of wild cats and Panthers.

---

17. Cave Johnson, Democratic representative for the 11th Congressional District

DAVID CROCKETT'S RESPONSE TO THE CHRONICLES[18]
David from the River country to Adam the Chronicle writer.

Adam, David feareth that thou hast wilfully misrepresented David without having the fear of God before thine eyes. Wilt thou recollect that thou hast been a distinguished Senator from Tennessee, and also that thou hast received a letter franked by Andrew the Chief ruler over the tribe of Columbia, enclosing a prospectus of the Globe a Van Buren type, for the purpose of procuring subscribers, in order to mislead the people of the District which David has had the honor to represent for the last four years.[19]

Know then Adam, David calleth on thee to explain how this league has been entered into between thyself and Andrew the Chief ruler, and also what is to be thy reward for thy services, and if thou art to be Foreign Minister, and where to—for thy witty Chronicles which thou hast been pleased to furnish to the people of this river country. How is this come to pass, when thee thyself told David of the river country, that at the close of the legislative council in 1819, when thee was filling the station of distinguished Senator in Tennessee, and after Andrew our Chief ruler, had come before the Legislature and made a speech before them against the People's Bank, which was established at that Session, and that it had kindled thy wrath against Andrew so that thee and thy friend from East Tennessee[20] went down to the Rocky city to fight against Andrew, and avenge thyself for the insult cast upon the body to which thou was a distinguished Senator? Now how has this all happened that the lion is to lie down with the lamb?[21] David is exceedingly anxious to know how this has come to pass? Will thee be so good as to tell David what is to be thy reward for this strange somerset of this distinguished Senator, who was carrying on a correspondence with Andrew the Chief ruler, during the last Congress, and at the same time was writing deceitful letters to

---

18. Published in the Jackson *Southern Statesman*, July 30, 1831
19. For an explanation of Huntsman being a "distinguished Senator," see pages 75-77.
20. David Wallace of Smith County
21. Crockett refers to the battle over the loan office bill in the 1820 special session of the Tennessee General Assembly. Andrew Jackson personally berated senators—including Huntsman—who supported it. See pages 35-38 for a detailed explanation.

David and exhibiting David's letters and Andrew's publicly, and saying that David or the President had one or the other lied. This shows what little reliance can be placed in this distinguished Senator. David charges Andrew with dealing deceitfully with him, and he will not neglect Adam: no not even when Adam shall make the attempt to go to the great Sanhedrim. David will pay the utmost farthing.

David calls on Adam to retract his statement concerning David's franking books to his friend in Trenton. Here David charges Adam of a wilful mis[s]tatement, to deceive the people.—Adam states that David franked one hundred and fifty dollars worth of postage on books. David is sorry to say that a distinguished Senator should write down a wilful fals[e]hood to injure David in his election. David never did at any time frank any books to Trenton to his friend, over the two ounce weight, which is given to all members of Congress. The books perhaps, that Adam has allusion to, were the American Biography. These books were franked by the Clerk of the House of Representatives,[22] and directed to John W. Crockett, at Trenton.[23] David told the Clerk that if he would frank them, he would bring his Journals of Congress and Diplomatic correspondence, and other books, which he had a right to frank, to the amount of four or five times the weight of what the Clerk did frank. David's name was never on a book sent to Trenton, not any where else over lawful franking privilege; therefore he does pronounce Adam's late address to William, particularly what relates to the franking books a barefaced falsehood.

David did have a better opinion of Adam than to believe he would have joined the little yelpers, which have been after his heals to bear the slang and pole-cat abuse of every little parasite of a partizan, that could lift a pen, and they have hurt him just as much as the moscheto[24] can hurt the ox, when he lights on his horn to suck his blood. Here David disposes of Adam, by laying him away with the unfinished business for the remainder of his days.

DAVID, from the river country.

---

22. Matthew St. Clair Clark was the House clerk and a friend to Crockett during his congressional terms.

23. John Wesley Crockett was the oldest son of David, who would later run for his father's congressional seat. At this time, he was a practicing attorney in Trenton.

24. Mosquito

Bibliography

Books

Abernathy, Thomas Perkins. *From Frontier to Plantation in Tennessee: A Study in Frontier Democracy.* Chapel Hill: University of North Carolina Press, 1932.

Adams, Charles Francis, ed. *Memoirs of John Quincy Adams, Comprising Portions of His Diary from 1795 to 1848.* Philadelphia: J.B. Lippincott and Company, 1876.

Ailsworth, Timothy S., Ann P. Keller, Lura B. Nichols, Barbara R. Walker. *Charlotte County: Rich Indeed.* Charlotte Court House, VA: Charlotte County Board of Supervisors, 1979.

American Colonization Society. *The African Repository, and Colonial Journal.* Washington D.C.: James C. Dunn, 1831.

Atkins, Jonathan M. *Parties, Politics, and the Sectional Conflict in Tennessee 1832-1861.* Knoxville: University of Tennessee Press, 1997.

Bauer, K. Jack. *Zachary Taylor: Soldier, Planter, Statesman of the Old Southwest.* Baton Rouge: Louisiana State University Press, 1985.

Bergeron, Paul H. *Antebellum Politics in Tennessee.* Lexington: University of Kentucky Press, 1982.

Bergeron, Paul H. *Paths of the Past: Tennessee, 1770-1970.* Knoxville: University of Tennessee Press, 1979.

Bigelow, Melville, ed. *Reports of Cases Argued and Adjudged in the Supreme Court Errors and Appeals of Tennessee.* New York: Hurd and Houghton, 1870.

Booraem, Hendrik. *Young Hickory: The Making of Andrew Jackson.* Dallas, TX: Taylor Trade Publishing, 2001.

Borneman, Walter R. *Polk: The Man Who Transformed the Presidency and America.* New York: Random House, 2008.

Bowden, Catherine Drinker. *Miracle at Philadelphia: The Story of the Constitutional Convention, May to September 1787.* Boston: Little, Brown and Company, 1966.

Boylston, James R. and Allen J. Wiener. *David Crockett in Congress: The Rise and Fall of the Poor Man's Friend.* Houston, TX: Bright Sky Press, 2009.

Brownlow, William G. *A Political Register, Setting Forth the Principles of the Whig and Locofoco Parties in the United States, with the Life and Public Services of Henry Clay.* Spartanburg, SC: The Reprint Company, 1974.

Burnett, Peter H. *Recollections of an Old Pioneer.* New York: D. Appleton & Company, 1880.

Caldwell, Joshua W. *Studies in the Constitutional History of Tennessee.* Cincinnati, OH: The Robert Clarke Company, 1907.

Cole, Donald B. and John J. McDonough, eds. *Witness to the Young Republic: A Yankee's Journal, 1828-1870.* Hanover, NH: University Press of New England, 1989.

Congressional Quarterly's Guide to U.S. Elections. Washington D.C.: Congressional Quarterly, 1985.

Cobia, Manley F. Jr. *Journey into the Land of Trials: The Story of Davy Crockett's Expedition to the Alamo.* Franklin, TN: Hillsboro Press, 2003.

Corlew, Robert E. *Tennessee: A Short History.* Knoxville: University of Tennessee Press, 1981.

Crockett, David. *A Narrative of the Life of David Crockett of the State of Tennessee.* James A. Shackford and Stanley J. Folmsbee, eds. Knoxville: University of Tennessee Press, 1973.

Culp, Frederick and Mrs. Robert E. Ross. *Gibson County, Past and Present.* Jackson, TN: McCowat-Mercer Press, 1961.

Cutler, Wayne, Earl J. Smith and Carese M. Parker, eds. *Correspondence of James K. Polk.* Vol. 5. Nashville: Vanderbilt University Press, 1979.

Cutler, Wayne and Carese M. Parker, eds. *Correspondence of James K. Polk.* Vol. 6. Nashville: Vanderbilt University Press, 1983.

Cutler, Wayne and James P. Cooper Jr., eds. *Correspondence of James K. Polk.* Vol. 7. Nashville: Vanderbilt University Press, 1989.

Cutler, Wayne, Robert G. Hall and Jayne C. Defiore, eds. *Correspondence of James K. Polk.* Vol. 8. Knoxville: University of Tennessee Press, 1993.

Cutler, Wayne and Robert G. Hall, eds. *Correspondence of James K. Polk.* Vol. 9. Knoxville: University of Tennessee Press, 1996.

Cutler, Wayne and James L. Rogers II, eds. *Correspondence of James K. Polk.* Vol. 10. Knoxville: University of Tennessee Press, 2004.

Cutler, Wayne, James L. Rogers II and Benjamin H. Severance, eds. *Correspondence of James K. Polk.* Vol. 11. Knoxville: University of Tennessee Press, 2009.

Davis, William C. *Three Roads to the Alamo: The Lives and Fortunes of David Crockett, James Bowie, and William Barret Travis.* New York: HarperCollins, 1998.

Derr, Mark. *The Frontiersman: The Real Life and Many Legends of Davy Crockett.* New York: William Morrow and Company, 1993.

Dickens, Charles. *American Notes for General Circulation.* Vol. 1. London, England: Chapman and Hall, 1842.

Durham, Walter T. *Balie Peyton of Tennessee.* Franklin, TN: Hillsboro Press, 2004.

Eddlemann, Sherida K., ed. *Genealogical Abstracts from Tennessee Newspapers, 1821-1828.* Bowie, MD: Self-published, 1991.

Elliot, Jonathan. *Historical Sketches of the Ten Miles Square Formed the District of Columbia; Etc.* Washington D.C.: J. Elliot Jr., 1830.

Elting, John R. *Amateurs to Arms! A Military History of the War of 1812.* Chapel Hill, NC: Algonquin Books of Chapel Hill, 1991.

Everett, Dick. *The Dixie Frontier: A Social History of the Southern Frontier from the First Transmontane Beginnings to the Civil War.* Norman: University of Oklahoma Press, 1993.

Ford, Lacy K. *Deliver Us from Evil: The Slavery Question in the Old South.* New York: Oxford University Press, 2009.

French, James Strange. *Sketches and Eccentricities of Colonel David Crockett, of West Tennessee.* New York: J & J Harper, 1833.

Friedman, Lawrence M. *A History of American Law*. New York: Simon & Schuster, 2007.

Force, Peter. *The National Calendar for MDCCCXXXI* [1831]. Washington D.C.: Peter Force, 1831.

Goldman, Perry M. and James S. Young, eds. *The United States Congressional Directories 1789-1840*. New York: Columbia University Press, 1973.

Goodpasture, A.V. and W.H. *Life of Jefferson Dillard Goodpasture*. Nashville, TN: Cumberland Presbyterian Publishing House, 1897.

Guild, John C. *Old Times in Tennessee, with Historical, Personal, and Political Scraps and Sketches*. Nashville, TN: Tavel, Eastman & Howell, 1878.

Gunderson, Robert Gray. *The Log-Cabin Campaign*. Lexington: University of Kentucky Press, 1957.

Hargreaves, Mary W.M. and James F. Hopkins, ed. *The Papers of Henry Clay, Volume 6, Secretary of State 1827*. Lexington: University of Kentucky Press, 1981.

Haywood, John, and Robert L. Cobbs. *The Statute Laws of the State of Tennessee, of a Public and General Nature*. Knoxville, TN: F.S. Heiskell, 1831.

Heidler, David S. and Jeanne T. Heidler. *Henry Clay: The Essential American*. New York: Random House, 2010.

Holt, Michael F. *The Rise and Fall of the American Whig Party: Jacksonian Politics and the Onset of the Civil War*. New York: Oxford University Press, 1999.

Howe, Daniel Walker. *What Hath God Wrought: The Transformation of America, 1815-1848*. New York: Oxford University Press, 2007.

James, Marquis. *The Life of Andrew Jackson in One Volume*. Indianapolis, IN: The Bobbs-Merrill Company, 1937.

Keating, J.M. *History of the City of Memphis and Shelby County, Tennessee*. Syracuse, NY: D. Mason & Company, 1888.

Livingston, John. *Portraits of Eminent Americans Now Living: Including President Pierce and His Cabinet; with Biographical and Historical Memoirs of their Lives and Actions*. New York: R. Craighead, 1854.

Lofaro, Michael A., ed. *Davy Crockett: The Man, the Legend, the Legacy 1786-1986*. Knoxville: University of Tennessee Press, 1985.

Mahon, John K. *The War of 1812*. Gainesville: University of Florida Press, 1972.
Masterson, William H. *William Blount*. New York: Greenwood Press, 1969.
May, Robert E. *Manifest Destiny's Underworld: Filibustering in Antebellum America*. Chapel Hill: University of North Carolina Press, 2002.
McBride, Robert M. and Owen Meredith, eds. *Eastin Morris's Tennessee Gazetter 1834 and Matthew Rhea's Map of the State of Tennessee 1832*. Nashville, TN: The Gazette Press, 1971.
McBride, Robert M. and Dan M. Robison, eds. *Biographical Directory of the Tennessee General Assembly*. Vol. 1. Nashville: Tennessee State Library and Archives and Tennessee Historical Commission, 1975.
McCormac, Eugene Irving. *James K. Polk: A Political Biography*. New York: Russell and Russell, 1965.
Meacham, Jon. *American Lion: Andrew Jackson in the White House*. New York: Random House, 2008.
Meine, Franklin J. *The Crockett Almanacks: Nashville Series, 1835-1838*. Chicago: The Claxton Club, 1955.
Miller, Charles A. *The Official and Political Manual of the State of Tennessee*. Nashville, TN: Marshall & Bruce, 1890.
Miller, William Lee. *Arguing About Slavery: The Great Battle in the United States Congress*. New York: Alfred A. Knopf, 1997.
Mitchell, John L., ed. *John L. Mitchell's Tennessee Gazetteer, and Business Directory, for 1860-61*. Nashville: J.L. Mitchell, 1860.
Moore, John Trotwood and Austin Powers Foster. *Tennessee, the Volunteer State*. Chicago: S.J. Clarke Publishing Company, 1923.
Morrell, Z.N. *Flowers and Fruits in the Wilderness: Forty-Six Years in Texas and Two Winters in Honduras*. St. Louis: Commercial Printing Company, 1882.
Moser, Harold D., David R. Hoth, George H. Hoemann, eds. *The Papers of Andrew Jackson*. Vol. 4. Knoxville: University of Tennessee Press, 1994.
Overton County History Book Committee. *History of Overton County, Tennessee*. Dallas, TX: Unknown publisher, 1992.

Parks, Joseph H. *Felix Grundy: Champion of Democracy.* Baton Rogue: Louisiana State University Press, 1940.

Penick, James Lal Jr., *The Great Western Land Pirate: John A. Murrell in Legend and History.* Columbia: University of Missouri Press, 1981.

Phelan, James. *History of Tennessee: The Making of a State.* Boston: Houghton, Mifflin and Company, 1888.

Pointer, Zola. *Pointer and Quarles Families.* Baltimore, MD: Gateway Press, 1986.

Quaife, Milo Milton, ed. *The Diary of James K. Polk During His Presidency, 1845 to 1849.* Vol. 1. Chicago: A.C. McClurg and Company, 1910.

Remini, Robert V. *Andrew Jackson and the Course of American Empire 1767-1821.* New York: Harper & Row, 1977.

Remini, Robert V. *Andrew Jackson and the Course of American Freedom 1822-1832.* New York: Harper & Row, 1981.

Remini, Robert V. *Andrew Jackson and the Course of American Democracy 1833-1845.* New York: Harper & Row, 1984.

Remini, Robert V. *Henry Clay: Statesman for the Union.* New York: W.W. Norton and Company, 1991.

Remini, Robert V. *The House: The History of the House of Representatives.* New York: Smithsonian Books, 2006.

Richards, Leonard L. *The Life and Times of Congressman John Quincy Adams.* New York: Oxford University Press, 1986.

Rule, William, George F. Mellen, and J. Woodridge. *Standard History of Knoxville, Tennessee.* Chicago: Lewis Publishing Company, 1900.

Sargent, Nathan. *Public Men and Events from the Commencement of Mr. Monroe's Administration, in 1817, to the Close of Mr. Fillmore's Administration, in 1853.* Philadelphia: J.B. Lippincott & Company, 1875.

Scott, Nancy N., ed. *A Memoir of Hugh Lawson White.* Philadelphia: J.B. Lippincott & Company, 1856.

Sellers, Charles. *James K. Polk: Jacksonian, 1795-1843.* Norwalk, CT: Easton Press, 1987.

Sevier, Cora Bales and Nancy S. Madden. *Sevier Family History.* Washington D.C.: Self-published, 1961.

Shackford, James Atkins. *David Crockett: The Man and the Legend.* Lincoln, NE: University of Nebraska Press, 1986.

Sistler, Byron and Barbara, eds. *Early West Tennessee Marriages.* Nashville, TN: Self-published, 1989.

Slaughter, Garbriel. *Acts Passed at the First Session of the Twenty-Sixth General Assembly for the Commonwealth of Kentucky, Begun and Held in the Town of Frankfurt, on Monday the First Day of December 1817.* Frankfurt, KY: Kendall and Russells, 1818.

Smith, Jonathan K.T. *Adam Rankin Alexander, A Life Sketch.* Jackson, TN: Self-published, 1992.

Smith, Jonathan K.T. *Antebellum Militia, Justices and Some Early Taxpayers, Madison County, Tennessee.* Jackson, TN: Self-published, 1998.

Smith, Jonathan K.T. *Genealogical Abstracts from Antebellum Circuit Court Records, Madison County, Tennessee.* Jackson, TN: Self-published, 1997.

Smith, Jonathan K.T. *Genealogical Information from The Western Methodist 1833-1834.* Jackson, TN: Self-published, 2003.

Smith, Jonathan K.T. *My Riverside Cemetery Tombstone Inscriptions Scrapbook.* Jackson, TN: Self-published, 1992.

Smith, Jonathan K.T. *Reported Council Minutes of the City of Jackson, Tennessee, 1871-1878.* Jackson, TN: Self-published, 1993.

Staples, Arthur G. ed. *The Letters of John Fairfield.* Lewiston, MA: Lewiston Journal Company, 1922.

Sullivan, James, ed. *The Papers of William Johnson.* Albany, NY: University of the State of New York, 1921.

Thomas, Jane H. *Old Days in Nashville, Tennessee.* Nashville: Methodist Episcopal Church South, 1897.

Thompson, Ernest T. *The Fabulous David Crockett: His Life and Times in Gibson County Including Tall Tales and Anecdotes.* Rutherford, TN: David Crockett Memorial Association, 1956.

Van Deusen, Glyndon G. *The Jacksonian Era, 1828-1848.* New York: Harper & Row, 1963.

Wallner, Peter A. *Franklin Pierce: New Hampshire's Favorite Son.* Concord, NH: Plaidswede Publishing, 2004.

Weaver, Herbert and Kermit L. Hall, eds. *Correspondence of James K. Polk.* Vol. 3. Nashville: Vanderbilt University Press, 1975.

Weaver, Herbert and Wayne Cutler, eds. *Correspondence of James K. Polk.* Vol. 4. Nashville: Vanderbilt University Press, 1977.

White, Robert H. ed. *Messages of the Governors of Tennessee 1796-1821.* Vol. 1. Nashville: Tennessee Historical Commission, 1952.

White, Robert H. ed. *Messages of the Governors of Tennessee 1821-1835.* Vol. 2. Nashville: Tennessee Historical Commission, 1952.

White, Robert H. ed. *Messages of the Governors of Tennessee 1835-1845.* Vol. 3. Nashville: Tennessee Historical Commission, 1954.

White, Robert H. ed. *Messages of the Governors of Tennessee 1845-1857.* Vol. 4. Nashville: Tennessee Historical Commission, 1957.

Wilentz, Sean. *The Rise of American Democracy: Jefferson to Lincoln.* New York: W.W. Norton, 2005.

Williams, Emma Inman. *Historic Madison: The Story of Jackson and Madison County, Tennessee from the Prehistoric Moundbuilders to 1917.* Jackson, TN: Jackson Service League, 1972.

Williams, Samuel Cole. *Beginnings of West Tennessee, 1541-1841.* Johnson City, TN: The Watauga Press, 1930.

Wilson, Clyde N., ed. *The Papers of John C. Calhoun.* Vol. 18. Columbia: University of South Carolina Press, 1988.

Wilson, James Grant and John Fiske, eds. *Appleton's Cyclopedia of American Biography.* New York: D. Appleton and Company, 1887.

Womack, Walter. *McMinnville at a Milestone.* McMinnville, TN: Standard Publishing Company, 1960.

Young, James Sterling. *The Washington Community 1800-1828.* New York: Columbia University Press, 1966.

Articles

"Battle Scars." Jackson *Sun*, 18 December 1994.

"Bicentennial Project: Restoration of Old Salem Campground Cemetery." *West Tennessee Historical Society Papers* 30 (1976).

Cisco, Jay Guy. "Madison County." *American Historical Magazine* 7 (October 1902).

"Civil War Site to Be Marked." Jackson *Sun*, 12 December 1994.

"David Crockett, As I Knew Him, by Uncle Billy Ridgeway of Buford, Arkansas." San Antonio (TX) *Express*, 1912.

Flowers, Paul. "Paul Flowers' Greenhouse." Memphis (TN) *Commercial-Appeal*, n.d. Adam Huntsman folder, Tentative Box 4 (Individuals). Seale Johnson Collection (Unprocessed collection). Tennessee Room, JMCPL.

Garrett, W.R. "Northern Boundary of Tennessee." *American Historical Magazine* 6 (1901).

Gates, T.M. "Jesse Russell Sr." Jackson (TN) *Sun*, 7 March 1912.

Gresham, L. Paul. "The Public Career of Hugh Lawson White." *Tennessee Historical Quarterly* 3 (Dec. 1944).

Maiden, Leota Driver. "Colonel John Williams." *East Tennessee Historical Society's Publications* No. 30 (1958).

Mooney, Chase C. "The Political Career of Adam Huntsman." *Tennessee Historical Quarterly* 10:2 (June 1951).

Mooney, Chase C. "The Question of Slavery and the Free Negro in the Tennessee Constitutional Convention of 1834." *Tennessee Historical Quarterly* 12 (1946).

"Vandals Mar Historic Cemetery." Jackson *Sun*, 11 June 1994.

Williams, Emma Inman, ed. "Letters of Adam Huntsman to James K. Polk." *Tennessee Historical Quarterly* 6 (1947).

Williams, Frank B. "Samuel Hervey Laughlin, Polk's Political Handyman." *Tennessee Historical Quarterly* 24 (1965).

Williams, Samuel C. "A Forgotten Campaign." *Tennessee Historical Magazine* (1926).

Primary Sources

Adam Huntsman Papers, TSLA
Andrew Jackson Papers, TSLA
Emma Inman Williams Collection, JMCPL
Samuel H. Laughlin Papers, TSLA
Tennessee Historical Society Miscellaneous Files, TSLA
Vanderpoel Family Papers 1815-1839, New York State Library

Official Records

1800 U.S. Census—Charlotte County, VA
1810 U.S. Census—Charlotte County, VA
1820 U.S. Census—Overton County, TN
1830 U.S. Census—Madison County, TN
1840 U.S. Census—Madison County, TN
1850 U.S. Census—Madison County, TN, Shelby County, TN

Journal of the House of Representatives, at the First Session of the Ninth General Assembly of the State of Tennessee, Begun and Held at Knoxville, on Monday, the Sixteenth Day of September, One Thousand Eight Hundred and Eleven. Knoxville: George Wilson, 1812.

Senate Journal of the First Session of the Eleventh General Assembly of the State of Tennessee. Nashville: M & J Norvel, 1815.

Journal of the Senate, at the First Session of the Twelfth General Assembly of the State of Tennessee, Begun and Held at Knoxville, on Monday, the Fifteenth Day of September, One Thousand Eight Hundred and Seventeen. Knoxville: George Wilson, 1817.

Acts Passed at the First Session of the Twelfth General Assembly. Knoxville, TN: George Wilson, 1817.

Journal of the Senate at the First Session of the Thirteenth General Assembly of the State of Tennessee, Begun and Held at Murfreesborough, on Monday the Twentieth Day of September, One Thousand Eight Hundred and Nineteen. Murfreesborough, TN: G.A. and A.C. Sublett, 1819.

Journal of the Senate, of the State of Tennessee, at the Seventeenth General Assembly, Held at Nashville, from the Seventeenth of September [to the] Fifteenth of December, in the Year Eighteen Hundred and Twenty Seven. Knoxville: Heiskell & Brown and Hall & Fitzgerald, 1827.

Journal of the Senate of the State of Tennessee at the Eighteenth General Assembly Held at Nashville. Knoxville, TN: F.S. Heiskell and A.A. Hall, 1829.

Laughlin, S.H. and J.F. Henderson. *Journal of the Convention of the State of Tennessee Convened for the Purpose of Revising and Amending the Constitution Thereof. Held in Nashville.* (Nashville: W. Haskell Hunt and Company, 1834

Congressional Globe, 24th Congress, 1st and 2nd Sessions.
Journal of the House of Representatives, 24th Congress, 1st and 2nd Sessions.
Niles Weekly Register, 24th Congress.
Register of Debates, 24th Congress, 1st and 2nd Sessions.

Documents

1835 Congressional Election (12th District) Official Tally Sheet. David Crockett Vertical File. Tennessee Room JMCPL.
Adam Huntsman and John B. Cross circular to "Fellow Citizens," 27 November 1819. Early American Imprints (2nd Series). Shaw-Shoemaker Bibliography, 1801-1819. Jean and Alexander Heard Library, Vanderbilt University, Nashville, Tennessee.
"Administration of the Executive Departments." Report No. 194. 24th Congress, 2nd Session. House of Representatives. www.heritagequestonline.com
"Fellow Citizens of East Tennessee." Printed Ephemera Collection: Portfolio 174, Folder 1. Library of Congress, Washington D.C.
"Proceedings of a Meeting of the Citizens of Washington in Favor of Recognizing the Independence of Texas, &c." U.S. Congress, Senate Serial Set Vol. 283, Session Vol. No. 5, 24th Congress, 1st Session. S. Doc. 384. www.heritagequestonline.com
"Return of Jackson Lodge No. 45 from the 1st Monday in October 1824 to 1st Monday in October 1825." Grand Lodge of Tennessee Free and Accepted Masons, Nashville TN.
Statewide General Elections Returns, Overton, White, Jackson counties. Record Group No. 87, Roll 1815-1. TSLA.
Statewide General Elections Returns, Record Group No. 87, Box 13, Folders 24 and 63. 1827-1. TSLA.

Virginia and Tennessee County Records

Charlotte County VA Chancery Court Files
Charlotte County VA Tax List—1782

Charlotte County VA Will Book 2
Knox County Court Minute Book 7
Knox County Deed Book 0-1
Knox County Settlements and Administrations, Vol. 2
Knox County Tax Lists—1810, 1811
Knox County Wills, Inventories, and Settlements, Vol. 0
Madison County Circuit Court Minutes, 1848-1850
Madison County Deed Books 11, 12, 14
Madison County Marriages 1838-1847
Madison County Will Book 7
Overton County Deed Books D, E, F
Rhea County Court of Pleas and Quarter Sessions, Minute Book B
White County Court Minute Books, 1806-1811 and 1815

Newspapers
All newspapers are Tennessee-based unless otherwise noted

Amherst (NH) Farmer's Cabinet
Arkansas Advocate
Arkansas Gazette
Augusta (GA) Chronicle
Bennington Vermont Gazette
Boston (MA) Daily Atlas
Boston (MA) Daily Courier
Boston (MA) Liberator
Boston (MA) Reformer
Carthage Gazette
Cincinnati (OH) Daily Gazette
Columbus Ohio Daily Statesman
Fayetteville Village Messenger
Florence (AL) Gazette
Franklin Western Weekly Review
Greenville (SC) Mountaineer
Hartford Connecticut Courier
Hartford (CT) Patriot and Eagle

Haverhill (MA) Gazette
Indianapolis Indiana Journal
Jackson District Telegraph and State Sentinel
Jackson Gazette
Jackson Southern Statesman
Jackson Sun
Jackson Truth Teller and Sentinel
Jackson West Tennessee Whig
Keene New Hampshire Sentinel
Knoxville Gazette
Knoxville Register
McMinnville Gazette
Memphis Enquirer
Milledgeville (GA) Southern Record
Milwaukee (WI) Sentinel and Gazette
Murfreesborough Central Monitor
Nashville Banner and Daily Advertiser
National Banner and Nashville Whig
Nashville Clarion
Nashville Republican
Nashville Union
Nashville Whig
New York Emancipator and Republican
New York (NY) Transcript
Norfolk (VA) Advertiser
Philadelphia (PA) Inquirer
Philadelphia (PA) Public Ledger
Portland (ME) Eastern Argus
Raleigh (NC) Register and North Carolina Gazette
Randolph Recorder
Rhode Island American and Gazette
Richmond (VA) Enquirer
Salem (MA) Gazette
(Salisbury NC) Carolina Watchman
Sparta Review

Vermont Gazette
Vermont State Paper
(Washington D.C.) United States Telegraph
(Washington D.C.) Daily National Journal
Washington (D.C.) Globe
(Washington D.C.) National Intelligencer
Weekly Memphis Eagle
Wisconsin Territorial Gazette and Burlington Advertiser

Websites

www.bioguide.congress.gov
www.familysearch.org
www.fold3.com (formerly www.footnote.com)
www.genealogybank.com
www.heritagequestonline.com
www.loc.gov
www.lva.virginia.gov/chancery
www.salemcemeterybattlefield.com/index.html
www.tn.gov/tsla/resources/19th_newspapers.htm
www.tngenweb.org
www.usgenarchives.org
www.wpquarles2009.info
www.wvgenweb.org/hardy/tgart3.htm

Index

Page numbers in *italics* refer to illustrations.
Page numbers ending in fn indicate references contained in footnotes.

Acres, James N. 222
Abingdon, VA 6, 48
Adams, John II 78fn
Adams, John Quincy 54, 55, 57, 57fn, 71, 77, 78fn, 79fn, 134fn, 139, 139fn, 140fn, 142fn, 143fn, 144, 145, *146*, 150, 155, 164, 199, 212, 251, 260, 269fn
Adams-Onís Treaty 144
Aesop's Fables 94, 94fn, 261
Agricola 22
Alamo, The 143, 166, 166fn
Alexander, Adam R. xviii, 69, 72, 100
Alexander-Munsell Line 35
Alexandria, TN 46
Allen, Robert 103
Altrusa Club of Jackson TN 210
American Anti-Slavery Society 137, 140fn
American Colonization Society 101, 139
Anderson, Alexander 192
Anderson, Gabriel 234
Anderson, Joseph M. 31
Antislavery petitions
  in Congress 137-139
  in TN constitutional convention 100-106
  in TN state senate 26
Arkansas 147, 148

Armour, William 236
Asheville, NC 146
Augusta Chronicle 16
Augusta County, VA 4

Baltimore Patriot 147, 196
Bank of the State of Tennessee ("Saddle Bags Bank") 36fn, 39, 41, 58, 59, 60, 142
Bank of the State of Tennessee at Knoxville 29, 30
Barton, David 269fn
Barton, Thomas 78
Beaver Creek (Carroll Co., TN) 51
Bedford County, TN 56fn, 94, 128fn
Bedford, Jonas 24fn, 25fn
Bedford Letter 128fn
Bell, John 27, 30, 73, 108, 109, 114, 114fn, 115fn, 124, *127*, 128, 134, 146fn, 153, 159, 174, 175, 177, 194, 197
Benton, Thomas Hart 131, *132*, 136, 159
Birdsal & Brother of Cincinnati 229
Birney, James G. 199
Black Hawk (nickname of AH) 86, 87, 91
Blair, Francis P. 74, 134, 144
Blair, John 269, 269fn
Bledsoe County, TN 27, 30, 246
Blount County, TN 105fn

Blount, William 7, 91
Blount, Willie 12, 91
Bolivar, TN 143fn
Book of Chronicles, West of the Tennessee and East of the Mississippi rivers 82, 79, 80, 88, 188, 267-278
Boston Patriot 138
Bouldin, James W. 251
Bouquet, Henry 4
Bowlegs Town, FL 17
Bradford, Theodorick 56fn
Branham, Martha M. 230
Branham, Robert E. 230
Bradford, Alexander B. 51, 64
Bransford, Thomas L. 182
Brooks, John J. 229
Brown, Aaron V. 54, 55, 184fn, 200, 202, 262fn, 263fn, 264
Brown, Harry H. 22
Brown, Henry H. 51
Brown, Hervey 208
Brown, Milton 208, 228, 229fn, 234, 235
Brown, Mr. 234
Brown, Neil S. 202, 262fn
Brown, William T. 201fn
Brownlow, William G. 263
Brownsville, TN 58fn, 84, 86, 143
Buchanan, James 197fn, 205
Bullock, Micajah 197, 209, 228, 237
Bunch, Samuel 153
Burges, Tristam 74, 75fn, 269fn
Burnett, Peter H. 118
Burr, Aaron 49
Burton, Robert M. 99
Butler, Anthony 163
Butler, Burwell 234, 235, 237, 238
Butler, William E. 53, 128, 163fn
Butler, William O. 265
Butler's Creek (Madison Co. TN) 50, 227
Byrne, J.W. 27

Cahal, Terry H. 94
Caldwell, Angelyn 230
Caldwell, Robert A. 230
Calhoun, John C. 136, 172, 212
Callahan, Peggy Jane 231
Callahan, Roy H. 231
Cambreleng, Churchill C. 197fn

Camp Pinckney 17
Campbell County, TN 246
Campbell, George W. 9
Campbell, James 59fn, 63
Campbell, Thomas J. 30
Candee, Mix & Company 219
Cannon County, TN 182, 182fn
Cannon, Newton 11, 91, 92, 107, 175
Carringer, Christian E. 161
Carroll County, TN 46, 51, 83, 126
Carroll, William 36fn, 58, 61, 73, 107, 110, 120, 126, 183, 206, 247fn
Carter County, TN 91, 103
Carter, William B. 91, 131, 133, 153fn
Cartmell. Robert H. 223
Caruthers, James A. 191
Cass, Lewis 205, 265
Cassedy, Charles 128fn
Catron, John 22
Cedar Fork (Cannon Co., TN) 182fn
Celina, TN 182
Charlotte County Court House, VA 5
Charlotte County, VA 3, 4, 5
Charlotte, TN 50
Chattahoochie River 15fn
Cherokee (Native American tribe) 29, 241, 242
Chester & Huntsman 65, 66
Chester, John K. 65, 65fn, 233
Chester, Robert I. 51, 163fn
Childress, William G. 91
Chilton, Thomas 74, 75fn, 78, 80fn, 269, 270, 276
Chisum, James 25, 43, 244
Choctow (Native American tribe) 168fn
City Lumber Company 230
Claiborne, John F.H. 140fn
Clarksville, TN 33, 197
Clay County, TN 19
Clay, Henry 41, 54, 57, 57fn, 72, 79fn, 80, 136, 172, 174-176, 176fn, 194, 196, 197, 199, 259-261, 269fn, 270, 273, 276
Clayton, John M. 74, 75fn, 80fn
Cocke, John 11, 13, 17, 26
Cocke, William 17fn
Coe, Levin H. 179, 182, 183, 197, 200, 201fn
Coffee, John 160

Colerain, GA 16
Columbia, TN 109
Conner, Henry W. 148, 251
Cook, Roland 80, 272-275
Cooke, John W. 72
Cookeville, TN 41
Coe, Levin H. 179, 182, 183, 197, 200, 201fn
Collier, William H. 230, 232
Collierville Presbyterian Church (TN) 220
Cotton Grove, TN 44, 45, 188, 209, 227, 236
Cotton Grove Road (Madison Co., TN) 229, 231
Court day 22
Craighead, David 197
Crawford, William 155
Creeks (Native American tribe) 13
Crockett Almanacks 112, *113*
Crockett, David xiii, xvi, xvii, xix, 6, 41fn, 54fn, *68*, 69-73, 75-88, 78fn, *81*, 89-91, 108, 109, 111-130, *119*, *122*, 123fn, 125fn, 126fn, 142-143, 143fn, 151, 165, 169, 206, 208, 212, 232, 258
  and the Chronicles 267-276
  on AH 82, 83, 120, 129, 130
  possible duel with AH 122, 123
  response to the Chronicles 277, 278
Crockett, John 6
Crockett, John Wesley 169, 170, 170fn, 175, 175fn, 258, 278
Crockett Tavern 6, 6fn
Croom, William 238
Cross 24fn, 25fn
Cross, John B. 48, 244
Cullender, John 107fn
Cumberland Mountain 25, 33

Daily National Journal (Washington D.C.) 74, 75
Dale, The (Overton Co., TN) 20
Dallas, George M. 205
Danville, KY 19
Davidson County, TN 29, 31, 36, 40, 59fn, 91, 95
Davis, James H. 226

Davis, Patricia Sue 226
Decatur, Stephen 79
DeKalb County, TN 182
Deniard, Christley 215fn
Denmark, TN 57, 86
Dickson, David 160fn
Dickson, Robert 215fn
District Telegraph and State Sentinel (Jackson, TN) 169, 172
Dix, John A. 205
Dodd, Captain 7fn
Donelson, Andrew Jackson 123
Downing, Major Jack 112
Dowson, Alfred R. 131, 131fn
Dowson's Row boardinghouses 131, 131fn, 133, 159, 160fn
Dresden, TN 124
Duane, William J. 88
Dulaney, F.C. 65fn
Dunlap, William C. 133fn, 143fn, 159fn, 160fn, 201fn
Durham, E. 223
Dyer County, TN 51, 83

Eason, John G. 11fn
East Florida 11-14, *14*, 15fn, 18
East Tennessee College 9
Eaton, John H. 53, 73
Endorsement Act of 1819 35
Erwin, James P. 40
Evans, William 25
Everett, Edward 74, 75fn, 269
Ewell, Thomas 191fn

Fairfield, John 133
Farmer, Stephen 215
Fayette County, TN 53, 54fn
Fillmore, Millard 265
First National Bank (Jackson, TN) 230
Fitzgerald, William 72, 76, 80, 82fn, 83-88, 123, 197, 201fn
  and the Chronicles 270-273, 275
Florida, 144
Flournoy, Thomas 16, 17
Fogg, Joseph 210, 228fn, 229, 235, 237, 238
Force, Peter 74

AH on 75
Forked Deer River 51, 246
Forrester, John B. 159
Foster, Ephraim H. 59fn, 103, 175, 176, *180*, 181, 181fn, 183, 194fn, 200
Francis, James 3
Francis, Obedience (Carrington) 3, 5fn, 215
Franklin County, TN 27, 59fn
Franklin, Walter S. 134
Fraternal Order of Police Lodge (Jackson, TN) 229
French Broad 39
Friends of Man, The 140

Gag rule
　in U.S. House of Representatives 138, *139*
Gaines, Edmund P. 106
Gainesville, FL 17
Gales, Joseph 71, 72
Gales and Seaton's Register of Debates in Congress 71
Gammon, Nathan 161
Gardner, John 264
Garland, James 140fn, 197fn
Gass, John 26
Gates, William W. 263
Georgia 15, 17, 157
Gholson, Samuel J. 162
Gibbs, George W. 194, 197
Gibson County, TN 47, 51, 80, 83, 84, 150, 191
Giles County, TN 54
Gillaspie, Richard G. 11fn
Gillespie, Berry 48
Gillespy, James 105fn
Givens, Samuel 254
Goliad, Battle of 166
Goodell, William 140, 140fn
Gore, Ambrose 43fn
Gore, Joseph 43fn
Green, Duff 74
　AH on 75
Greene County, TN 26, 105fn, 179
Greens, John 254
Greer, Alexander 228, 229fn

Grundy, Felix xv, 31, 35, 38, 47, 114, 128, 184fn, *185*, 186, 187, 192, 206
Gwin, James 106, 106fn
　AH on 106fn

Hale, George 11fn
Hall, William 58
Hamer, Thomas L. 133fn, 164
Hamilton, Alexander 4
Hamilton County, TN 27
Hammond, James H. 138
Hannegan, Edward A. 133fn, 160fn, 251
Haralson, Herndon 50
Hardeman County, TN 53, 54fn, 118
Hardin County, TN 69
Harmon's Mills (Henderson Co., TN) 187
Harris, Jeremiah George 183
Harrison, Samuel S. 251
Harrison, William Henry 156, 157, 176, *177*, 178, 180, 186-188, 191, 257, 259
Haskell, Joshua 63, 64, 120, 194
Haskell, William T. 194
Hatchie River 51
Hawes, Ann. *See Quarles, Ann Hawes*
Hawkins County, TN 103
Hays, Samuel Jackson 76
Haywood County, TN 51, 53, 54fn, 84, 87
Henderson County, TN 46
Henderson County Courthouse 64
Henderson, Thomas 90, 91
Henderson, Ruthie (Pritchard) 229, 231, 232
Henderson's Line 33
Hengy, George C. Sr. 226
Henry County, TN 51, 83
Henry, George J. 220
Henry, Jane F. 220
Henry, Patrick 5, 6
Hicks, George 45, 46fn, 227, 227fn, 228fn, 234, 237, 238
Hill, Fannie 230
Hill, Col. M.R. 47
Hill, Robert Lee 229, 230, 231
Hiwassee District 54
Hoar, Samuel 165-167
Hodge, Samuel 274
Hogue, Charlie W. 225

INDEX   297

Hogue, James A. 225
Hogue, John B. 225
Hogue, Louie G. 225
Hogue, Nellie 225
Hogue, Powell E. 225
Holly Springs Church (MS) 220
Holmes, John 74, 75fn, 269
Holston River 39
Horton, J.P. 234, 235
Houston, Sam 58, 73, 106
Hughes, Archelaus M. 169, 170
Hull, William 79fn
Huntingdon, TN 48, 51, 175fn, 178, 194
Huntsman, Adam
  Aaron Burr anecdote 48-49
  admission of Arkansas and Michigan 147, 148
  affair with Elizabeth Witt 10, 11
  and 1844 presidential election 197, 199,
  and use of Aesop's Fables 94, 94fn, 261
  and Andrew Jackson 38, 40, 56, 57, 73, 74, 75, 76, 153, 155, 160, 161, 187 188
  and David Crockett 6, 69, 70, 71, 73, 76-88, 91, 108, 109, 111-126, 129, 130, 142, 143, 169, 170
  and Hugh Lawson White 114, 115, 127, 153, 155-157, 159-161, 174
  and James K. Polk 31, 109, 127, 128, 172, 174, 203, 205
  and John Quincy Adams 54-57, 143-146, 150
  and John Sevier family 20
  and John Williams 9, 15, 16
  and Timothy P. Scurlock 188, 188fn
  anecdotes 47, 121, 122, 124, 125
  as a "prophet" 202, 203
  as Democratic Elector-at-Large 178, 179, 181-183, 187, 188
  asked to run for Congress in 1829 67, 69, 70, 71
  attitude toward the Whigs 183
  Bank of the State of Tennessee 58, 59, 60
  birth 3
  Black Hawk moniker 86, 87, 88
  boarder at Dowson's Row in Washington 131, 133, 159, 160
  Book of Chronicles 79, 80, 82, 267-276, 277
  candidate for solicitor of 5th Judicial Circuit 30
  candidate for 12th Congressional District 115-126
  chastises abolitionist editor 140
  childhood 4-5
  chooses not to run for reelection to Congress 169, 170, 257, 258
  compared to Crockett 117, 118, 142, 143
  congratulates Polk on presidential nomination 196
  congressional routine 136, 137
  criticized 179, 181
  death 206
  death of wife Elizabeth 194
  death of wife Sarah 53
  defends John Q. Adams 54-57
  description xvi, 133, 142, 143, 146, 148, 183
  dislikes criticism of Turney by Nicholson 201
  Dutch ancestry 4, 5, 252
  East Florida expedition 15-18
  education 5
  farm at Cotton Grove 227-231
  fence controversy 156, 160, 161
  first congressional speech 141, 142
  Free Mason 50
  "Going! Going! Gone!" parody 77-79
  Haskell impeachment
  house at Cotton Grove 231, 232
  humor 18, 48, 49, 77-79, 116, 145, 175, 191, 196, 199, 206
  illegitimate child 10, 11, 116
  impeachment of Joshua Haskell 64, 65
  indebtedness 64, 65, 66, 209, 210
  initial support of Zachary Taylor 203, 204, 205
  internal improvements 51, 60, 61
  investigates banks in Washington 140, 141, 142
  Jackson/Madison County commissioner 46
  journey to Washington 130
  judiciary reform 29, 61, 62, 63
  land speculation 24, 51, 64

law practice
  in the Mountain District 10, 20, *21*,
    22, 24
  in the Western District 46, 47, 50
  prejudice toward lawyers 116
leaves Virginia for Tennessee 6
linked to Crockett
loan office bill 35, 36, 38-41
marriage of daughter Ann 188
marriage to Sarah Quarles 41, 42
marriage to Elizabeth Todd 57
marriage to Nancy Waller Mosely 201,
    202
member of the Committee on Private
    Land Claims 134, 149, 150
mentioned as U.S. Senate candidate 200
merchant with John K. Chester 65, 66
obituary 208, 209
on Andrew Jackson 153
on banks 142
on campaign practices 69, 70, 71
on David Crockett 85, 86, 87, 121, 124,
    126, 165
on education 54
on Ephraim H. Foster 181
on Henry Clay 172, 174, 197, 199
on Hugh Lawson White 127, 153, 157,
    255-257
on future of the Whig party
on "Immortal Thirteen" 193
on James K. Polk 199, 205
on John Tyler 191, 192
on Martin Van Buren 155, 157, 159,
    172
on Newton Cannon 107
on nullification 117
on construction of penitentary 61
on Polk's cabinet choices
on Polk's election as governor
on Reuben M. Whitney controversy
    162, 163
on Texas 164-167, 196, 197
on Whigs burning John Tyler in effigy
    191, 192
on William Henry Harrison 177
on Zachary Taylor 204, 205, 264, 265
peg leg 18, 116, 121, 122, 133, 143
political principles 117, 155, 156

possible duel with David Crockett 122,
    123
predicts 1844 election results 199
presidential elector in 1816 27
slavery 26, 30, 100, 101, 137-140, 147,
    148
  personal involvment 102, 103, 139,
    232-239
settles in Madison Co., TN 45, 46
settles in Overton Co., TN 20
solicitor for White Co., TN 22, 24
studies law 7, 9, 10
supports Lewis Cass in 1848
TN constitutional convention 89-108,
    109, 110
  AH's committee assignments 92
  AH's efforts to bring about 90
  AH elected as delegate 90, 91
  AH on the convention 100
  age requirements for senators and
    justices 99, 100
  amendments accepted 98
  amendments rejected 98, 99
  diversions 106
  emancipation 100-106
  judicial reform 98, 99
  oaths for officers 92, 93
  payment of delegates 93
  preliminary actions 91, 92
  property taxation 94-96
  representation 96, 98
  Shelby County election 100
  swindler 106, 107
  visit by Andrew Jackson 107
  visit by Edmund P. Gaines 106
  visit by Sam Houston 106
TN state senate
  1815 25-27
  1817 27-30
  1819 31-41
  1827 53-57
  1829 57-64
teller in TN house of representtatives
    11
Tennessee-Kentucky boundary dispute
    25, 29, 31, 33-35
Texas recognition 163-167

INDEX

Huntsman, Adam F. (child of AH) 57, 206, 209, 216, 218, 220-223 *222*, 239
Huntsman, Adam (father of AH) 3-5, 213, 215fn, 226
Huntsman, Adam Hugh 224
Huntsman, America (child of AH) 57, 188fn, 206, 209, 216, *218*, 219, 239
Huntsman, Ann (child of AH) 46, 205, 206, 216-218, 222, 223, 235
Huntsman, Ann (sister of AH) 4, 215
Huntsman, Anna (Henry) 209fn, *219*, 220
Huntsman, Barbara (grandmother of AH) 4, 213, 214
Huntsman, Catherine 215fn
Huntsman, Edith 224
Huntsman, Elizabeth 213
Huntsman, Elizabeth (Todd) (2nd wife of AH) 57, 151, 194, *195*, 201, 206, 216, 234, 237
Huntsman, Elizabeth (Kenner) 214, 214fn
Huntsman, George T. (child of AH) 57, 188fn, 206, 209, 209fn, 216, *219*, 220, 222, 239
Huntsman, Gertrude 224
Huntsman, Jacob (uncle of AH) 4, 6, 213, 213fn, 214
Huntsman, James (brother of AH) 41, 215
Huntsman, Jeane (Francis) (mother of AH) 3, 5fn, 214
Huntsman, John (uncle of AH) 4, 6, 214, 214fn
Huntsman, Kate (Beatty) 221, 224
Huntsman, Lawrence 213
Huntsman, Mary Ella 224
Huntsman, Mary (Farmer) 215
Huntsman, Mary Katherine (Fletcher) 221, 222, 224
Huntsman, Melinda Jane (child of AH) 10, 11, 53, 53fn, 216
Huntsman, Nancy (Mosely) (3rd wife of AH) 188fn, 201, 202, 210, *211*, 216, 218, 222
Huntsman, Nancy (Pugh) (stepmother of AH) 214

Huntsman, Paradise (child of AH) 57, 206, 209, 216, 218, 220, 221, 239
Huntsman, Sarah (Quarles) (1st wife of AH) 41, 41fn, *42*, 44, *52*, 53, 194, 216
Huntsman, Stephen (nephew of AH) 41, 215, 235, 236
Huntsman, Susan Jane (child of AH) 57, 206, 209, 209fn, 216, 220, *225*, 226, 239
Huntsman, Susan Jane (child of Adam F.) 224
Huntsville, AL 19
Hurt, Robert 229
"Immortal Thirteen" 193, 194
Independence, TN 273
Indian Removal Act 126
Irvin, Elizabeth (McFadden) 232, 233
Irvin, John E. 229, 232, 233, 236

Jackson, Andrew 12, 29, 40, 42, 36, 37, 46, 51, 53, 54, 56, 68, 69, 71-74, 73fn, 79fn, 80, 82, 91, 103, 107-109, 112, 117, 118, 120, 128, 144-*146*, 152, 153, 155, 155fn, *156*, *158*, 160-163, 163fn, 171, 175, 179, 179fn, 183, 184, 184fn, *185*, 186-188, 196, 206, 212, 256, 260
  in the Chronicles 267, 269, 270, 272, 273, 277
Jackson County, TN 19, 22, 24, 30, 31, 41, 42, 182, 243, 244, 246-248
Jackson Auxiliary Colonization Society 101fn
Jackson Gazette 50, 51, 65, 67, 69, 72, 90
Jackson Lodge No. 45 of Free and Accepted Masons 50
Jackson, Rachel 56
Jackson, William 137
Jackson *Southern Statesman* 80, 82, 195
Jackson, TN xiii, 44, 46, 51, 53, 57, 157, 190, 210, 223, 230
  Democratic meeting in 1840 184-187, 184fn, *185*
Jackson Truth Teller 114, 120, 169
Jackson, William 143
Jarnigan, Spencer 177fn, 194fn
Jarrett, David 51

Jarvis, Leonard 251, 252fn
Jefferson County, TN 6, 105fn, 115
Jefferson, Thomas 5, 49, 52, 89, 94, 196, 202, 254
Johnson, Andrew 179, 179fn, 181, 181fn
Johnson, Cave 133fn, 153fn, 160fn, 184fn, 197, 200, 276
Johnson, Joseph 234, 235
Johnson, Richard M. 206
Johnson's Stand 244
Jonesborough, TN 156, 160, 160fn
Jones, James C. 192, 193, 202, 262
Jones, Richard M. 194

Kane, Elias 136fn
Kendall, Amos 74
Kentucky 33, 34, 35
Kinderhook, NY 178
Kincaid, Joseph 94, 107fn
King, Rufus 27
King Charles II 34
Kinnard, George L. 160fn
Knox County, TN xviii, 27
Knoxville, TN xviii, 6, 7, 10, 15, 16, 18, 28, 39, 58, 103, 130, 153, 156, 232, 242

Lacy, Thomas 51
Lafayette Street (Jackson, TN) 46, 48
Lancaster, Samuel 254
Laughlin, Samuel H. 9fn, 24-26, 115fn, 179, 197
Lawrence County, TN 69
Lea, Luke 153fn
Lebanon, TN 153
Ledbetter, William 107fn
Lewis, Dixon H. 164
Lexington, TN 64, 187
Lexington Road (Cotton Grove, TN) 50
Liberia 104
Liberty party 140fn, 199
Liberty Street (Jackson, TN) 48
Life of Martin Van Buren, the Heir-Apparent to the "Government," and the Appointed Successor to General Andrew Jackson, The 118, 120
Lincoln County, TN 53

Lion of the West 112
Livingston, TN 43
Loan Office Bill *See Bank of the State of Tennessee*
Long, Henry 217
Louisiana Terrirtory 48
Loyell, George 251, 252fn
Lucas, George 251, 252fn
Lucky, Samuel 229
Lyon, James L. 233

Madison County, TN xvii, xviii, 46, 51, 53, 54fn, 64, 76, 83, 84, 86, 87, 90, 91, 102, 103, 108, 110, 117, 179, 199, 206, 232, 254, 255
Madison County Court 50
Madison County (TN) Courthouse 53, 184, 228, 238,
Madison, James 4, 15, 46
Malone, caroline W. 229
Malone, James R. 229
Malone, W.G. 229
Manning, Robert I. 251, 252fn
Marathon automobile 230
Marchbanks, William 25
Marion County, TN 27, 94
Martin, Andrew L. 48, 64, 65fn, 172, 174
Martin, Menan M.
Mason, Samson 165, 166
Matlock, Valentine 20, 215fn, 249
Maury, Abram P. Sr. 36, 59
May, William L. 140
Maysville, VA 5, 6
Maze, John
McClanahan, Samuel 184
McClellan, James D. 238
McCorry, H.W. 254
McGaughey, John 105
McIver, Duncan 50fn, 53, 54fn, 57
McIver, Roderick 50, 65, 220, 222, 235-238
McIver, Susan (Todd) 220, 222, 226
McKay, James I. *132*, 133fn, 160fn, 251, 252fn
McKinney, John A. 103
McLean, John 258
McMeans, James R. 108, 109, 115
McMinn, Joseph 27, 31, 35

McMinnville, TN 24
McMinnville Gazette
McNeill, Philip 220, 222
McNeill, Sarah (Todd) 220, 222
Melly, Mary 222
Memphis, TN 150
Meriwether, M.D. 222
Methodist Episcopal Church (Nashville, TN) 106
Micanopy, FL 17
Michigan 147, 148, 148fn
Miller, Pleasant M. 11, 17fn, 38, 172, 254, 258
Miller, William B. 172, 254
Milley (slave of AH) 10
Mills' Point, KY 150
Mississippi River 33, 35, 67
Mitchell, David B. 16
Monger, Lavenia 230\
Monger, Ray 230
Monroe, James 27, 144
Monroe, TN 24, 25fn, 43, 43fn, 45fn, 245, 247
  description of 19-20, 43
Montgomery County, TN 57, 91, 95, 201
Monticello, KY 19
Mooney, Chase C. 210
Moore, Ely 197fn
Morgan County, TN 243, 244, 245
Morgan, Charles L. 224
Morgan, Sam D. 224
Mosely, John S. 201, 201fn
Mosely, Nancy Waller. *See Huntsman, Nancy (Mosely)*
Mountain District 19, 23, 108fn, 130, 182, 183, 232
Murchison, William A. 234
Murfreesborough, TN 31, *32*, 36
Murrell, John A. 148, 148fn

Nally, Dennis 86, 87
Narrative of the Life of David Crockett of the State of Tennessee, A 112
Nashville Bank 29
Nashville Banner 82fn
Nashville Daily Republican Banner 184, 187
Nashville Inn 91, *92*

Nashville *Republican* 99
Nashville, TN 25, 39, 58, 73, 75, 91, 101, 179, 230, 259
Nashville Union 24, 128fn, 183, 189, 201
Nashville Whig 39, 171
Natchez, MS 12
National Banner and Nashville Whig 112
National Intelligencer (Washington D.C.) 71, 125, 126, 168
Nelson, A.M. 11fn
New London, CT 79fn
New Orleans, LA 12, 48
New York State Anti-Slavery Society 140
Newload, Mr. 252
Nicholson, Alfred O.P. 192, 197, 201
North Bend, OH 178
North Carolina 33, 34, 57
Norvell, John R. 228
Norvell, Thomas G. 228

Obed's River 25
O'Brien, John 160, 160fn, 161
Obion River 51, 83
Old Salem Cemetery (Madison Co., TN) 52, 53, *195*, *207*, 210, *211*
Oregon 262
Outlaw, Alexander 17fn
Overton County, TN 19, 20, 22, 24, 27, 31, 41-43, 43fn, 45-48, 51, 53, 182, 188, 243, 244, 246-248, 249
Overton, John 53
Oxendine, Stephen 25

Panic of 1819 30, 31, 90, 171
  response to 35, 36, 38, 39-41
Paris, TN 53, 82,fn, 108, 123, 183
Parrish, Joel 59
Parsons, Peter 17fn
Pavatt, Stephen C. 175fn
Payne's Town, FL 17
Perryville, Battle of (KY) 222
Petty, Garton 215
Peyton, Balie 153, 159, 162, 163
Phillips, William 43
Pierce, Franklin 131, *132*, 140fn
Pinckney, Henry 138, 146
Pittsylvania County, VA 215

Point Petre, GA 16
Polk, James K. xviii, 31, 54, 91fn, 109, 114, *127*, 128, 128fn, 134, 153fn, 168fn, 170, 172, *173*, 174, 177, 179, 181, 184, 187, 189, 191-194, 196, 200, 201, 203, 206, 212, 217, 259, 263
  attends Jackson, TN barbecue 186
  and AH 199
Pollock, Patricia (Grames) 123fn
Powell, Joseph 103, 103fn
Preston, William C. 164
Private Land Claims Committee 138, 149
Putnam County, TN 19

Quarles, Ann (Hawes) 41, 46, 188, 188fn, 217
Quarles, Sarah Wesley. *See Huntsman, Sarah (Quarles)*
Quarles, William Pennington 41, 42, 108fn

Ragland, Elizabeth 225
Ragland, Nathaniel 225
Ragland, Pattie Ann 226
Ragland, Samuel 209, 225, 226
Ragland, Samuella 226
Raleigh Register and North Carolina Gazette 151
Randolph, John of Ronoake 6, 259
Read, John 254
Red Hill (Charlotte Co., VA) 6
Reed, John 140
Reese, James 215
Rhea County, TN 10, 27, 30
Richmond Enquirer 174
Rives, John C. 134
Roane, Archibald 9, 11
Roane County, TN 25
Robertson, James 91, 91fn
Robertson, Julius Caesar Nichols 91fn
Rogers, James 243
Ross's Ferry Road (Madison Co., TN) 47
Rowan, Stockley D. 24fn

"Sacrificial Club" 48

Salem Campground. *See Old Salem Cemetery*
Salem Presbyterian Church (Shelby Co., TN) 220
Sansum, S.D. 53
Santa Anna, Antonio López de 129, 165, 166fn
Schay, Edith (Grames) 123fn
Schenck, Ferdinand S. 251, 252fn
Scruggs, Phineas T. 183
Scurlock, Ann (Huntsman) *See Huntsman, Ann*
Scurlock, Ann (child of Ann) 217
Scurlock, Catherine L. 217
Scurlock, Clarence H. 217
Scurlock, Fanny B. 217
Scurlock, Joseph M. 217
Scurlock, Martha E.A. 217
Scurlock, Timothy P. 179, 188, 188fn, 205, 206fn, 217, 218, 220-222
Second Bank of the United States 65, 74, 117, 162
Seminoles (Native American tribe) 12, 17
Sevier, Adam Huntsman 20
Sevier, Charles Robertson 20
Sevier, John 9, 20, 27
Sevier, Katherine (Sherrill) 20
Shannon's Landing (Madison Co., TN) 51
Shelby County, TN 53, 54fn, 57, 100
Shields, Ebenezer J. 133fn, 159fn, 160fn
Slavery
  AH on
Smith County, TN 22, 103, 249
Smith, Bird 247, 247fn
Smith, Daniel 91
Smith, Jonathan K.T. 236
Smith, Nathan 136fn
Smith, Thomas 274
Smith, William 232
Snider, George 191fn
Sons of Confederate Veterans
  John Ingram Camp 219-220
Southern Engine and Boiler Works 230
Southern Statesman (Jackson, TN) 76, 77, 80, 83fn, 86, 87, 188
Southerner automobile 230
Sparta, TN 10, 22, 108fn, 188fn, 247, 248
Specie Circular 172
Stephens, W.H. 222

Spring Creek (Madison Co., TN) 67, 273
St. Louis Daily Commerical Bulletin 112
St. Luke's Episcopal Church (Jackson, TN)
    218, 222, 228
St. Marys River 16, 17
Standifer, James I. 153fn
Stephenson, Matthew 105fn
Stewart, Andrew 65
Stewart, Bartholomew 65fn
Stewart, James 29
Stewart, John E. 206, 206fn, 229fn
Stoddert, William 50, 50fn, 53, 64
Stone, Thomas 24fn, 25fn
Strong, Caleb 79
Sumner County, TN 27, 29, 91

Talbot, Joseph H. 64, 217
Taney, Roger 168
Taylor, Abner Utley Jr. 230
Taylor, Zachary 203, *204*, 205, 264, 265
Tennessee constitutional convention
    (1834) 91-110
  emancipation
  efforts to convene 26, 89, 90
  judicial reform
  property taxation
  protest against emancipation report
  representation
Tennessee-Kentucky boundary dispute
    31, 33-35
Tennessee Colonization Society 101
Tennessee River 54, 67, 241
Tennessee Supreme Court 22, 75, 153
Terrell, George W. 123
Texas 163, 196, 197, 200, 262
  AH's defense of 164-167
Thomas, Francis *132*, 133, 140, 160,
    197fn
Thompson, Jean L. 230
Thompson, Jesse 230
Thompson, Waddy Jr. 144, 164
Tippecanoe and Tyler Too
Tipton County, TN 53, 54fn, 57
Tisdale, James 54fn
Tittle's Old School House (Cannon Co.,
    TN) 182fn
Todd, Elizabeth. *See Huntsman, Elizabeth
    (Todd)*

Todd, George (father-in-law of AH) 54,
    54fn, 57, 65, 219, 227, 234-238
Totten, Archibald O.W. 20, 47, 182, 191fn
Totten, Benjamin 20, 47, 51
Trenton, TN 86, 150, 197, 278
Troup, George M. 53
Troy, TN 150
Truxton (race horse) 27
Turley, William B. 201
Turney, Hopkins L. 63, 182, 182fn, 201
Tyler, John 176, 191, 192, 196

Union Bank of Tennessee 228
United States Telegraph (Washington
    D.C.) 74, 75, 155
University of Tennessee
U.S. Capitol Building *142*
U.S. House of Representatives 133, 139
  description 133, 134, 149
  late-night sessions 148, 149
U.S. Supreme Court 33, 34, 205

Van Buren, Martin 112, 114, 115, 118,
    123, 129, *152*, 153-155, 155fn,
    156, 157, 159, 168, 171, 175, 178,
    183, 186, 188, 194, 196, 252, 253,
    256, 257, 267, 277
  AH on
Van Den Bosch, Elizabeth 230, 231
Van Den Bosch, John Jr. 230, 231
Vanderpoel, Aaron 261, 161fn
Vaulx, James 65fn, 235
Vauxhall Garden (Nashville TN) 73, 107
Virginia 33, 34, 197
Volunteer Infantry Regiment of East TN
    Mounted Infantry 16

Waldon, William 64
Walker, Joel 54fn
Walker's Line 33, 34
Wallace, David 38, 39, 277fn
Waller, Nancy. *See Huntsman, Nancy
    (Mosely)*
Wallick, David 234
Wallis, George 25
Walton Road 42
Walton, Issac 91, 107fn

War of 1812 11-13
Ward, Anne (Frances) 215
Ward, Edward 25, 27, 40, 100
Ward, William 215
Warren County, NC 201fn
Warren County, TN 22, 24, 27, 30, 59fn, 107fn, 243
Washington County, TN 105fn
Washington County (VA) Courthouse 48
Washington D.C. 130, 137, 138
  attempts to abolish slavery in 138, 139
  recharter banks in 140, 141
Washington Globe 74, 75, 76, 123, 126, 144, 159, 174
Washington, George 4, 5
Washington, Thomas 75, 76
Watson, J. 54fn
Wayne County, TN 69
Weakley County, TN 51, 83, 85, 112, 123
Weakley County Court 124
Weakley, Robert 31, 91
Webster, Daniel 78, 80fn, 136, *156*, 157, 172, 176, 205, 257, 259, 265
  mentioned in the Chronicles 270, 271
Webster, Taylor 251, 252fn
Weekly Memphis Eagle 206
West Florida 11, 12
West Tennessee Whig 206, 228, 238, 263
West Tennessean (Paris, TN) 123
Whig party 157, 168, 169, 170, 172, 203, 204
White County, TN 10, 19, 22, 24, 27, 30, 41, 42, 182, 188, 243, 244, 245, 247, 248
White County (TN) Court 16fn
White, Hugh Lawson 6fn, 7, 8, 9, 17fn, 27, 30, 73, 109, 114, 115, 115fn, 125, 127, 152-155, 155fn, *156*, 157-159, 161, 172, 174, 176, 177fn, 179fn, 192
  on AH 156, 157, 206, 212, 252-257
White, James 7
White family 229fn
White Plains, TN 41, *42*, 217, 235
White, B.I. 17fn
White, Robert H. 61
Whitney, Reuben M. 162, 163
Whittington, Gibson 232, 233, 235
Wildman, Zalmon 136fn

Wilkes County, GA 232
Williams, Bettie 221
Williams, Emma Inman 232
Williams, Fannie 221
Williams, John 7, *8*, 9, 13-17, 41fn, 153, 154, 206, 212
Williams, John (Smith Co., TN) 56fn
Williams, Joseph L. 221
Williams, Melinda (White) 7, 11
Williams, Nathaniel W. (judge) 63, 90, 243
Williams, Nathaniel W. (son-in-law of AH) 63fn, 218, 220, 221, 239
Williams, Robert L. 221
Williams, Sally 221
Williams, Sampson 27, 247, 248
Williams, Thomas L. 17
Williams, Timothy H. 221
Williams, William (grandson of AH) 221
Williams, William 38, 39
Williamsburg, TN 247, 249
Williams's Quarter (Overton Co., TN) 247
Williamson County, TN 27, 36fn, 59, 91, 107, 233
Williamson, Lucy (Cook) 5fn, 215
Williamson, Thomas 54fn
Wilmot Proviso 203
Wilson County, TN 95, 99
Wise, Henry A. 161-163
Witt, Elizabeth 10, 11, 216
Witt, George 10
Witt, Rutilia. *See* Huntsman, Melinda Jane
Witt, Thomas 53, 53fn, 216
Woodbury, Levi 205
Wright, John 7
Wright, John C. 77, 77fn

Yallabusha County, MS 163fn
Yorktown, Battle of 4

About the Author

KEVIN D. MCCANN has written several books on subjects related to the history of Jackson and West Tennessee. A Jackson native, he earned a Bachelor of Science Degree in History from Union University. He is a member of the Tennessee Historical Society and the West Tennessee Historical Society. Among McCann's books are *Hurst's Wurst: Col. Fielding Hurst and the Sixth Tennessee Cavalry*, *Jackson Diamonds: Professional Baseball in Jackson, Tennessee*, *The Kitty League* (co-author), and *The Jackson Generals: Minor League Baseball in Jackson, Tennessee*. He lives with his wife and two children in Dickson, Tennessee.

www.ingramcontent.com/pod-product-compliance
Lightning Source LLC
Chambersburg PA
CBHW070631160426
43194CB00009B/1428